Joyce *May your life be abundantly full of your own*

NeverEnding
GODSTORIES

OUR ADVENTURES OF A LIFETIME

Love you, Cathy Vincent
Apr 2022

CATHY VINCENT

NEVERENDING GODSTORIES—Our Adventures of a Lifetime

Section Illustrator: Pamela Collard (sister of author)
Cover Design: Rob Williams, fiverr.com/cal5086
Interior Design: Courtney Artiste, fiverr.com/pastorcourtney

ISBN 978-0-9600587-0-9

First Edition 2019 / Printed in the United States

Publisher: www.cathyvincent.com

Author's note:

I have given credit to sources as best as I can remember. For over fifty years I have avidly read books and journaled the many words that have touched me. Hopefully, I have not quoted someone's words unaware, for I did not always record the source as I had no intention of ever writing a book from those journals.

This memoir is an accurate recollection of my life based on over 50 years of memories and journal entries. It reflects my perspective of life which God is still upgrading. I have also reconstructed some dialogue to capture the essence of an event. A few names have been changed to protect the privacy of others.

Dedicated to

My Dear Family

Don, the love of my life,

Shawn, Damon and Kristi,

Jenny and Chris, Christy and Orestes

Taylor, Toby, Kelsey, Kasey, Kassidy, Mateo, Raquel

F

A

M

I

L

Y

"Let each generation tell its children of your mighty acts; let them proclaim your power." (Psalm 145:4 NLT)

The best gift I can offer is myself.
Entire futures are at stake in the power of our words.
—DONALD MILLER

TABLE OF CONTENTS

Introduction

My Quest

*The thief's purpose is to steal and kill and destroy. My purpose is
to give them a rich and satisfying life.* —Jesus
(John 10:10 NLT)

My never-ending quest has been to experience a rich and satisfying life. I discovered early on that our Creator holds the secrets to such a walk and is quite eager to reveal them to us as we get to know Him better.

Still nothing had prepared me for encountering His Presence. God turned out to be quite unlike what I had been told, more loving than I deserved, more powerful than I had imagined. Above all, He was more present than all the things visible to my big brown eyes.

As life continually turned me upside down, He kept turning me right side up. I asked Him lots of questions... *What are you really like? Do you care about me? Are you interested in my daily life? Will you help me? Do you still do miracles? How can I connect with you? What is my purpose?*

I was surprised when God answered my questions, often by showing up smack dab in the messy middle of life.

In my 27,000+ days on this earth, I've lived thousands of ordinary days. We all do. But what I want to tell about are all those other extraordinary days when He changed my life through encounters that I like to call GodStories.

In these pages you won't find a model Christian life. Nor will you find a comprehensive picture of all the ways we can connect with God. What you will find is a true adventure of one lifetime walked with Him which I hope will surprise you, entertain you, touch you, and help you to live a fuller version of your own story.

Openly sharing these real and raw encounters with a powerful God isn't easy. It takes courage to share some of the stories with a supernatural flair that seem too good to be true...at first. I totally get it because there was a time in my life that I would have had a hard time believing my stories too, but then they kept happening.

Other stories are difficult to share because they reveal my many shortcomings as a very imperfect human who is still very much God's work in progress as one of His kids whom He loves. Divulging my weaknesses is worth it because it is where His grace and strength shows up most clearly.

Sharing how I've wrestled with truth and my beliefs is also hard because sometimes my views don't line up with the traditions of religion. Neither did the views of Jesus.

Yet, my biggest concern is that I won't reflect God as He truly is because of my limited human viewpoint. I try not to explain Him but to show how He is always with us. These pages aren't filled with flawless theology; they are filled with impactful stories of getting to know our 'here and now' God. Fully understanding God is not a prerequisite to experiencing Him.

When I hear of the thousands of Christians under siege over the world who are daily being persecuted and killed for their faith, I ask God if my story is significant enough to share. The answer is *Yes*. Each one of our stories matter as we tell how God shows up in our specific world in our unique circumstances.

There is so much more to knowing God than what we can fathom. As we each share what we have seen, collectively we get a clearer picture of Him. In hopes that others will relate, I choose to be vulnerable and courageous rather than private and comfortable.

The Father created each of us to have our own GodStories or encounters with Him. You may see similarities in our stories, or your story may look nothing like mine. God relates to each of us individually as He gives us a glimpse of Him and gives us each our own *one of a kind* story to tell.

I have always connected with God through the stories of others and find them contagious as they ignite me with fresh desire to know Him more. God hardwired us to love stories because they affect us differently than good teaching which is also vital. Stories touch our emotions and slip their message directly into our hearts. Some things are just easier caught than taught.

Different parts will touch different people. You can choose to skim through this as a neat storybook and cherry pick stories that look interesting. But if you persevere to read the whole story, you will be impacted much deeper as you read of an entire lifetime soaked with His Presence. It will be well worth it.

I write these words to those hungry for more life regardless of who you are—men or women, young or old, rich or poor, single or married, believer or agnostic. Hopefully some of my words will propel you into new adventures of your own as you ask, "If God does that in your life, what will He do in mine?"

Then you will be the one experiencing Him more fully. You will be the one bringing hope to others facing life's problems as you share how there is more to life than this and then tell them one of your own GodStories. Mysterious as it seems, you give God glory when you tell your story.

I humbly offer you my imperfect adventure of how He and I have done life together through a lot of wild and crazy stuff. Come along and enjoy the ride.

As long as the earth endures, seedtime and harvest, cold and heat, summer and winter, day and night will never cease. (Genesis 8:22 NIV)

Season 1

Springtime Seeds

Planting His Seeds of Faith

In the Midwest we enjoy ever-changing seasons as winter gives way to the promise of spring, and summer morphs into the beauty of autumn, often surprising us with their unpredictability. Likewise, we move through the different seasons in our lives. Learning to embrace this normal rhythm of times that come and go helps us relax as we acknowledge that this, too, shall pass.

3000 years ago King Solomon poetically proclaimed the ebb and flow of common times which human beings still experience today.

> For everything there is a season, a time for every activity under heaven. A time to be born and a time to die. A time to plant and a time to harvest. A time to kill and a time to heal. A time to tear down and a time to build up. A time to cry and a time to laugh. A time to grieve and a time to dance...
> A time to embrace and a time to turn away. A time to search and a time to quit searching. A time to keep and a time to throw away...A time to be quiet and a time to speak. A time to love and a time to hate. A time for war and a time for peace. Yet God has made everything beautiful for its own time. (Ecclesiastes 3:1-8 NLT)

Rarely do we see the full beauty of a season while we are going through it. Only in the winter of my life did I slow down enough to contemplate the reasons for the seasons and see how God was working in me from beginning to end.

My walk with God began early in the springtime of my life as He generously planted seeds of faith in His love and power in me. The faith seeds grew in the fertile soil of trials and troubles where I learned how to ask Him for help, to hear His voice, and to imperfectly follow Him one step at a time, left foot, right foot. He planted within me a hunger to fully know Him and then kept showing up whether the times were mundane, refreshing, or devastating.

God was there up-close teaching me to do life *with* Him, not just *for* Him as we began traveling on our great adventure.

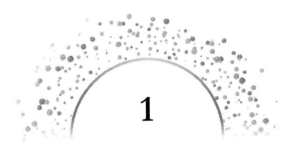

1

Wowed by God

L ife was good. Then I turned nine.

One moment I was a happy little girl playing the piano at the end of the busy day. The next moment my idyllic world began to spin out of control. Suddenly my head was swimming as my brain malfunctioned, and I could no longer think. My surroundings disappeared into a fog while waves of electrical impulses washed through my brain. My mind sank into darkness. My hands fell limp on the piano keys.

I sat in a daze, unaware of time passing, until I faintly heard Mother's voice as if coming from a distant tunnel, "Cathy. Cathy, are you all right?"

"I...I...I don't think so," I stammered as my consciousness returned. Confused, I thought, "Something isn't right. What is wrong with me?"

I did not know what was happening. Neither did my parents. Fear of the unknown loomed as the frightening spells continued. A bevy of doctors did test after test and gave their bleak prognosis to my parents who listened with tears, "Your daughter is having petit mal epileptic seizures. Hopefully, we can control the seizures with medication, but there is no known cure. I am sorry, but she will have to learn to cope with epilepsy for the rest of her life."

My enemy now had a name—epilepsy. Anxiety slowly erased the scene of a carefree childhood. I was no longer confident in what my body might do. I no longer felt that I fit in. I was not like the other kids. I now lived with a new set of rules—don't over-exert yourself, don't get too tired, don't go too far. Be safe, be careful, be cautious.

I felt insecure as I now pondered new more adult questions: When will the next seizure strike? What if it happens at school? Will my friends pull away? What does the future hold? Will anyone love this imperfect me?

Fortunately, the seizures were not public but came at night when I got overly tired or stressed.

Time passed, but the seizures did not. For the next fifteen years my life looked fairly normal from the outside as my seizures happened at home, and we kept them fairly controlled with doctor visits, medicine, rest, and lifestyle.

Night Terrors

At age 25 I experienced the rest of the story. I was married to my high school sweetheart, living out our version of the typical *too busy* American family lifestyle as I cared for a toddler, taught high school English, and stuffed activity into every available crack.

Seizures had escalated to several nights a week despite the anti-seizure meds I took three times a day. Each night I locked the bedroom door to lessen my anxiety over a new fear that now gripped me.

I remember one night lying in bed when an epilepsy attack began at midnight. In my semi-conscious state, I sensed a dark figure lurking at the door. "Who is there?" I yelled as I helplessly tried to move my arms and legs.

"Help. Help me. Please help me!" I cried as the looming presence came closer to my bed. I started screaming louder and louder. Terror gripped me when I imagined what would come next.

Nobody came to my rescue although my husband lay asleep at my side. Stiff and immobile, I concentrated on prying loose one single finger and then another. Little by little, I inched my hand and then my body back into motion. As my mind began to clear, I lay there in a cold sweat, realizing that the attacker was a mere hallucination. So were my screams. Only then could I shake off the fear and slowly calm down so that sleep might come. Nights became exhausting.

Feeling hopeless, I cried out in desperation, "Lord, is this how my life is always going to be? Isn't there more to life than this?"

I wanted an instant answer at microwave speed but would learn that God's answers often came more like in a simmering crockpot. While I waited, I stewed, unaware that all the while, He was quietly at work tenderizing me. Then at just the right time He brought the answer.

Along Came a GodStory

I was nine years old when God moved in quietly to show me His great love. This was the year I invited Jesus into my life. Epilepsy came shortly after, trying to rob me of my newfound love and joy.

I was twenty-five years old when God moved boldly into my life to show me His great power. It all began with a man who shared a GodStory, a personal encounter with Him.

My husband Don and I had lots of questions about knowing God so we joined an adult Sunday school class at our Methodist Church to learn more. We were enjoying the people, but we didn't seem to be getting many answers...until the morning a man named George walked in and sat down in our circle. He looked like any other middle-aged local farmer. I sized him up, "He doesn't look like he'd know much about God or the Bible."

But as he opened his mouth, I changed my judgmental mind. He held my attention as he shared his intriguing story,

"For the past few months I have been curious what God is like, so I began to explore the Bible and check Jesus out. I saw how He supernaturally healed person after person. Then I read *Jesus Christ is the same, yesterday, today, and forever.'* (Hebrews 13:8 NLT) I wondered, 'Does Jesus still supernaturally heal people today?'

Then he asked our class, "What do you all think?"

We chimed in with our opinions. "No, that supernatural stuff only happened back in Bible days...Healing ended with the apostles...Today God only heals through doctors...No, never heard of anyone being healed today."

We were all pretty much in consensus, "Nope."

Brother George continued,

"Well, that's what I thought too. Then I saw this verse: *'These signs will accompany those who believe...they will place their hands on the sick, and they will get well.'* (Mark 1:19-21 NIV) I thought, I am one who believes in Jesus. Is that still true for me?

15

On Tuesday I came down with a nasty sore throat and thought, 'I'm going to experiment.' I put my hand on my throat and said, 'Sore throat, I command you to go in the name of Jesus.' Then I left my hand there for a while as I pictured Jesus touching my throat with His healing power. Slowly I lifted my hand…the sore throat was gone.

And that's my story."

I thought, "Really? Hmmm."

I was skeptical and slightly annoyed that George's reality didn't line up with mine. Yet his story had planted a seed. I couldn't shake it off as my mind wrestled, *"What if this supernatural healing stuff is true? But it couldn't be. If it were, why haven't I heard about healing today? I've been going to church all my life, and nobody talked about that. I don't know of anyone being healed supernaturally. In college I was taught that miracles died with the last apostle. But what if God does still heal?"*

My logical mind said *Nah*, but my hungry heart wasn't so sure. I didn't want to miss out on something that big, and I really was tired of those seizures. I prayed, "I want to know you more, Lord."

God took note! A slight move toward God on our part can put into motion a remarkable response on His part.

Off On a Quest

Over the next few months He kept piquing my interest. Instead of being consumed with my crazy busy life, I was off on a quest to find out more about God. I began at the source and prayed, "God, will you show yourself to me? Show me the truth."

We were surprised when a steady stream of enthusiastic believers began crossing our paths to share similar faith-filled stories along with some far-out ideas:

"God loves you just the way you are…He is here right now and wants to walk with you through each day…He wants to talk with you…You can hear His voice…He wants to fill you with His Spirit to work powerfully through you…He is still doing the supernatural."

Whoa! That didn't sound like the God I knew. I pictured Him as a *holy Father who art in heaven* and not someone that involved in my life on earth. I thought His love depended on how much I strived to please Him.

I thought being a Christian was all about being good and serving Him as best that I could. Now hearing all these stories from others made me question my beliefs. Could my picture be incomplete? Was there more? Was I missing out on something BIG?

I thought, *"Maybe I should read the Bible for myself. People do call it God's Word."* Climbing up a step stool, I retrieved my Bible off the top shelf of the bookcase, dusted it off, and began reading in the New Testament. Over the next few months I discovered more about God which led me to ask Him to fill me up with His Spirit. He did, and I experienced a new awareness of His Spirit's constant presence along with a voracious appetite for the Bible.

As I read in Matthew, the first book of the New Testament, I saw what Brother George had said how Jesus kept going around healing the sick—a man paralyzed from birth began walking, a blind man could suddenly see, a deaf girl could hear again, a woman was cured of a blood flow she'd had for ten years. Why had I barely noticed these stories?

Several accounts told of people being healed of incurable diseases such as leprosy. Then I came across a passage that jumped off the page:

> *News about him spread as far as Syria, and people soon began bringing to him **all** who were sick. Whatever their sickness or disease, or if they were demon possessed or **epileptic** or paralyzed—**he healed them all.** (Matthew 4:24 NLT emphasis added)*

I felt as if God were speaking directly to me as I read the words again—*"He healed them all...the epileptic."*

I cried out to Him, "Really? Is this true? Do you heal? Do you even heal epileptics— like me?" This was a faith seed worth watering.

It was *Show and Tell Time* as God began to show me with His works what He was telling me in His Word.

A Tiny Seed of Faith

A few nights later I went to bed with a miserable cold and sore throat. Unable to quit hacking and coughing, I slipped out of bed so that at least my husband could get some rest. Sitting on our couch, I pondered all the stories we were hearing and the verses I was reading in the Bible. Something was shifting in me as I began realizing that the Bible was true. God was depositing a new measure of faith inside me.

So faith comes from hearing, that is, hearing the Good News about Christ. (Romans 10:17 NLT)

Confident that it is still His desire to heal, I decided to declare this new truth that was dawning out loud. I boldly proclaimed, "Jesus, I do believe you. I believe that you still heal people supernaturally. Thank you for giving me this faith. Jesus, I believe you will heal me too."

I remembered the story of how Brother George had prayed. Taking a deep breath, I laid my hands on my throat and spoke out loud, "Sore throat, I command you to leave in the name of Jesus."

All pain in my throat instantly left, gone without a trace. My eyes opened wide as I exclaimed, "Wow! This is incredible. You really do heal today. Thank you, Lord!"

I went back to bed with a big smile and no sore throat, no sniffles, not even an urge to cough. I quickly fell asleep. At 3 a.m. I awoke with a scratchy tickle in my throat. My body wasn't feeling healed, but my spirit was certain that it was, so I spoke, "I believe Jesus healed me. No, sore throat! You go away in Jesus name, and don't come back."

The tickling sensation left in an instant, and I fell right to sleep. I woke in the morning symptom free – no sore throat, not even an inkling of a cold. I had encountered a living God...here...now...in my own house...in my own body. Stunned, I was also curious. What else about Him did I not know? What other of my impressions of Him were wrong?

"Oh God, teach me more. I want to know you more!" I cried out.

I began sharing my own healing story with everyone around me. In a way, it seemed a small thing to get instantly healed of a sore throat, but it was a big thing to me because it was *my* throat!

The seed of faith in His power to miraculously heal was growing. He must have sprinkled it with His own Miracle-Grow, for it burst into a full-blown miracle within the week.

Free At Last

The following Saturday we had packed way too much *busy* into the day, triggering an attack at midnight. Once again I went through the grueling ordeal of a seizure combined the fear of my imaginary attacker as I lay there unable to move. Afterwards I quietly got out of bed and headed back to the couch.

But this night was different. Smiling, I leaned back on the couch aware of how peaceful I felt. I sensed Jesus was present right there with me as I meditated on how much He loved me. I thanked Him again for healing my sore throat.

Then I began wondering about my seizures and blurted out, "I know that you healed me from a simple sore throat, but what about an incurable disease? Jesus, would you heal me from epilepsy?"

Deep within me, I heard His resounding response *Yes!* Once again faith swelled inside me. It was time for another Brother George prayer. My enemy was going down.

I breathed a deep sigh and spoke out loud with authority, "Epilepsy, I command you to leave in the powerful name of Jesus."

I waited…

Nothing. No sensation, no lights or angelic visit, no supernatural sign. There was no instant visible way to verify a healing. Outside, my body felt no different, but inside I just knew. Stirred by strong faith, I was confident that I was free from this enemy that had gripped me for sixteen years.

I returned to bed and quickly drifted off to sleep, feeling as if I were wrapped in an invisible down comforter of peace. When I awoke the next morning, something had shifted. Inside me was a deep assurance that Jesus had healed me.

But how could I prove it? I thought, *"I'll quit taking my anti-seizure medication, and I should know by morning."* This plan was risky, and it might not have been the most sensible thing to do and not what I recommend to others, but this is how it actually happened. I stopped daily meds cold turkey.

The seizures had ceased. I was ecstatic. Filled with hope for the future, I wondered what other surprises God had in store.

Then a month later, I had a light seizure. *"Now what do I do?"* I thought as I lay there wide-awake. Then I recalled how the symptoms had returned after He had healed my sore throat, and when I commanded the symptoms to leave, they left for good. Could this be a similar test of faith?

I cried out, "Jesus, I believe you have healed me, and I rebuke these symptoms that say otherwise. Symptoms, I command you to go and not return. In Jesus name, Amen."

Another month passed–not one seizure. Then six months went by, and I'm thinking, *"This is real. Jesus healed me."* I felt as if chains had fallen off. No longer was I under the physical strain and torment; the anxiety of epilepsy no longer constantly weighed me down. My mind relaxed, and I began to see things with more clarity. My energy soared, and I gave thanks to God for feeling fully alive.

That year passed and then the next. Still no seizures. Over fifty years later, I still have had no seizures. I am beyond thankful to be set free. Jesus had defeated the enemy and made me whole just as in Bible days. It is true. He is still powerfully involved on earth and still supernaturally healing today.

So if the Son sets you free, you will be free indeed. (John 8:36 NIV)

So did Jesus heal me because I was someone special? *Yes* and *No. Yes,* I am special, but *No,* I am not any more special than each of His kids whom He loves just as dearly. Each of us are special to Him.

I was awakened to a new truth. Jesus isn't up in Heaven waiting for us to arrive. He is right here on earth, eager to enjoy walking intimately with us daily. He does this for our sake and also so that we can tell others. Jesus works through us to release the power of Heaven on earth right now to set others free from the things that weigh them down. I was grateful to find out we have a God who heals, but even more important I found out that we have a God who is present. Now that's good news.

He was opening my eyes to see that salvation not only includes the priceless gift of life into eternity, but also transformation, intimacy, healing, deliverance, and power encounters with Jesus in the here and now.

I wanted to shout out like the blind man whom Jesus healed,

One thing I do know. I was blind but now I see! (John 9:25 NIV)

God was adding to my desire to live my life *for* Him a hunger to live life partnering *with* Him each day to make a difference in lives around me.

How did I arrive at this place? It began long before this story in those years between the ages of 9 and 25. So let me take you back to the beginning.

20

Conversion puts you at the entrance of an entirely new way of living, but there's a lifetime of experiences beyond the entrance that most people don't experience. They never enter into their purpose.

—BILL JOHNSON, *When Heaven Invades Earth*

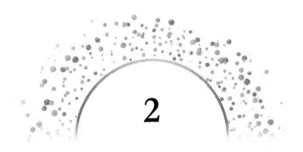

Back to the Beginning

Before this major encounter with God as a young adult, I knew about His love but very little about His power. Yet God was very present even when I was a child as He quietly planted small seeds of faith in me.

My childhood was simple and good. Fun-loving, hard-working parents raised me with my four brothers and sisters on our farm in Pike County, IL. In the spring we headed to the hills, our 300-acre wooded playground where we rode ponies, built forts, created high adventure, and gathered wildflowers, mushrooms, geodes and varied critters.

When my epileptic seizures began, my parents kept me close to make sure I was safe, careful, and rested. Their caution seemed to damper my desire for vigorous outdoor adventures with my free-spirited siblings. Sometimes it was just easier to be inside in my make-believe world with my dolls, playing the piano, or reading a book.

While my family loved the outdoors, I developed a love for the indoors. As a child I enjoyed working as much as playing, staying close to my mother, helping her cook, clean, and do projects while she taught me to help and serve others at an early age.

Our family lived two miles outside of New Canton (population: 403). My siblings and I rode the school bus home forty minutes as it wound through the hills to drop off the other kids. I quickly forgot that long bus ride when I ran into the house where Mother waited with fresh cookies and milk and a listening ear. Is it any wonder that I still have a 4 pm hankering for chocolate chip cookies?

If we complained, Dad would tease, "You're lucky to have a bus to ride. Why I had to walk barefoot to school three miles in the deep snow uphill both ways."

I can't remember a time I didn't believe in God. Talking about Him was as common as picking blackberries in the summer. On Sundays we all piled into our station wagon and headed to church. Our family said bedtime prayers and held hands at every meal, affirming our trust in God when we bowed our heads and prayed out loud together, "God is kind, God is good. Father we thank you for this food. Amen." This childlike prayer expresses the basics of a simple life with Him.

During the week we tried to live out what we prayed by being kind and good to people, honoring God, and being thankful for His provision. While this was a good foundation, I would discover that there is a whole lot more God has in store for us as we come closer to Him.

The Big YES!

Although epilepsy loomed big in my nine-year-old world, an even larger life-changer took place that same year. I said *Yes* to a lifetime with Jesus and began an adventure that would rock my world.

I can still picture walking down the aisle of our little Methodist church with my older sister Becky to make public our decision to follow Him. My heart raced as I repeated this prayer: "Jesus, I believe You are the Son of God. I believe that you died to pardon all my sins so that I can freely connect with my heavenly Father. Forgive me. I receive your forgiveness and ask You to come into my life."

He did. Now I was one who believes in him like I had seen on the signs at ballgames:

> *For God loved the world so much that he gave his one and only Son, so that everyone who believes in him will not perish but have eternal life.* (John 3:16 NLT)

Did I know what all that prayer entailed? Of course not. My young mind didn't understand it all, but my heart was all in. I thought I was signing up for an eternal life insurance policy to be with Jesus in Heaven. Later I discovered that it came with an invitation to enjoy walking with Him here on earth.

But even on that very first day I felt different. I knew that Jesus loved me and that He had moved inside me to live. He was my new love, and

I began a lifelong quest to know Him intimately. I had no idea how to go about that, but I did the best I could with what I knew at the time.

God saw my heart and was pleased with His precious child who had just said *Yes* to the gift of life and was now part of His big family of faith.

Yet to all who did receive him, to those who believed in his name, he gave the right to become children of God. (John 1:12 NIV)

Striving to Be Perfect

Though I knew Him at an early age, I didn't know God very well. I just thought my role was to be a good girl until I died and Jesus came to pick me up. I began to strive to be good in order to earn approval, a habit which later blossomed into full-blown people-pleasing. All through my school years I strived hard to be perfect. My big sis didn't call me *Goody Two Shoes* for nothing.

Years later I found out that my heavenly Father loves me because I am His child, not because of anything I did or didn't do. He accepts me as I am because Jesus's sacrifice had taken care of my sins and imperfections.

So now there is no condemnation for those who belong to Christ Jesus. (Romans 8:1 NLT)

Another misconception I had was that it was my job to make sure everyone else was perfect. Now that was a huge mistake as I would learn the hard way. I wish I'd figured that out a lot sooner.

Soon I was in junior high, and my aspirations of appearing perfect shattered when the event I had feared every single day actually happened. I woke up on the floor in my 8th grade science class after a seizure had prompted the teacher to clear the students from the room. I dreaded walking out into the hallway, but to my surprise, nobody thought it was any big deal.

My peers seemed much more concerned with their own image, caught up in seeking approval from each other. Some were unhappy with their appearance or athletic ability or some other way that felt they didn't fit in or measure up. Such is the life of 'tweens and teens wanting life to be normal and problem-free. But we would learn it is never going to happen on this Earth. It isn't supposed to.

In Love Again

As a teen I felt like I didn't fit in and was totally unaware that almost every teen feels this way at times. Physical feats were challenging, and I was often the last one picked to be on a team. Sports were not my thing, so I turned my efforts to studying and making straight A's. Meanwhile, I strived to be a good Christian but should have focused on what I was *to do,* instead of what I should *not do.*

> *So in everything, do to others what you would have them do to you...* (Matthew 7:12 NIV often called The Golden Rule)

In my senior year of high school my life totally changed when I encountered a cute junior boy named Don who sat behind me in English class and liked to annoy me with his constant teasing. Before long I was intrigued with this venturesome guy who was quite the opposite of me. English became my favorite class. Don had many admirable qualities. He was friendly, funny, curious, strong, athletic, brave, honest, prone to adventure. He was a strong leader, a hard worker, and also quite the big dreamer.

But I was seventeen, and honestly, I just saw tall, dark, and handsome who looked mighty good on the basketball court through my star-struck eyes. Even better, he was actually pursuing non-athletic bookworm *me,* and dispelling my haunting childhood fear, "Will anyone fall in love with this imperfect me?"

I was hearing a new answer, an emphatic *Yes.* We began dating, and I didn't even mind that my guy was a farm boy who wouldn't show up at my house until 9 pm on Saturday nights after he had finished field work and chores. Well, I didn't mind it at first anyway.

Soon I could think of little else. I was falling in love. Surely finding my own true love would give me the fulfilling life I dreamed of. I pictured Don and I, hand in hand, on an adventure with God to make a difference in the world. There was only one thing awry in this vision: Don had many interests in life, and following Jesus was not one of them.

It didn't take long before pursuing my two loves, Jesus and Don, caused inner conflict. Unwilling to give up either one, I juggled my attention between them. In this tug-of-war, it seemed easier to love the one I could see more than the One whom I could not see.

My picture of the unseen strict Father in Heaven expecting me to please Him certainly didn't help God's case. I did not yet know that this

Father who knew everything about me loved me with a love far exceeding Don's. No wonder He was coming in second place in my heart. As I drew closer to Don, I began to drift away from God. My roots in God did not go very deep.

High school went by quickly, and it was time to begin adulting. Don finished his senior year while I headed off to a small Christian college in Missouri, a naïve 18-year-old eager to renew my quest to know more of God. I chose my grandfather's alma mater, planning to follow in his footsteps, for I loved how Granddad Craig personally walked with God on a daily basis. I wanted to know Him that way too.

Eager to learn, I studied hard and still strived hard to make straight A's to please my parents and my God, all of whom I falsely assumed expected perfection from me. I was also pursuing a goal to get prepared to make a difference.

Deep down, I wanted to be a pastor like Granddad who loved people and taught them to know God. But then I found out that a woman couldn't be a pastor in my church world back then. Frustrated, I settled on becoming a religious education director so I could work with women and children.

My Faith Nose Dive

For years I had envisioned how wonderful Christian college life would be, hanging out with new friends hungry for God, and sitting at the feet of godly scholars who would teach me to know Him. It would be like Heaven on Earth. I could hardly wait.

College life was far from what I had pictured. When I arrived, I met quite a variety of people, but I had a hard time finding all those believers on fire for God. This new world was vast with many new opportunities that caught my attention. As an avid learner, exploring all of these options intrigued me. It didn't take long before I was in conflict. Few people I met saw things as I viewed them from my sheltered childhood environment. I began to wonder: Was my worldview even accurate? Did it need adjusting?

Soon I expected to be equipped to sort all these thoughts out because I was enrolled in Religion 101. Surely here I would learn to know God intimately. On the first day of class, I walked into the stately old building and slipped into the classroom early to soak in the sight of eager freshmen filling the well-worn oak seats of the hundred-year-old lecture hall.

My eyes zeroed in on the tall podium in front where the man of God would soon appear. My heart was hopeful; my mind was eager. I opened my notebook and held my pen, ready to record his wisdom, not wanting to miss a word.

The door opened, and a tall seasoned professor in a suit and tie proceeded to the podium. He meticulously reviewed his course overview and then with a long face announced his mission:

"My purpose in this class is to challenge you to examine your childhood beliefs and explore the question, 'Is the Bible really true?'"

My disbelieving eyes opened wide. Did I hear him right? I took a deep breath as inside I screamed, "What do you mean? Not true?" Such a thing had never crossed my mind. I walked out in confusion.

Each day this professor kept chipping away with his logical questioning of the Bible. Little by little, my faith was weakening. Slowly he convinced us that that the stories of the Bible were not actual but figurative and that the miraculous stories could easily be explained by science. Who was I, a naive un-enlightened freshman, to argue? By the end of my freshman year he had me believing that the Bible isn't literally true.

My faith took quite a hit as I began to question what I read. I had been blinded to this truth:

All Scripture is inspired by God and is useful to teach us what is true and to make us realize what is wrong in our lives. It corrects us when we are wrong and teaches us to do what is right. God uses it to prepare and equip his people to do every good work. (I Timothy 3:16-1 NLT)

The professor's plan was to break down the childhood beliefs of freshmen in Religion 101 and help them rebuild their faith in Religion 201, a required sophomore class. But I transferred at the end of the first year with my beliefs in shreds and no next year to rebuild. Years later I found that this professor had been dismissed for his methods, but it was long after my faith was shattered.

Now I was reading my Bible with a questioning mind, analyzing whether it sounded rational and scientifically plausible. If not, I simply tore out that page, not literally, but practically speaking.

I don't believe that God orchestrated this faith dive, but He never wastes any of our experiences. As I examined my beliefs, I realized that they mostly came from my parents. It was time for a faith of my own. I began checking things out on my own as I read the Bible, had lively discussions, and went to the source, my heavenly Father, asking Him to show me what to believe.

Exploring the hand-me-down faith of my parents turned out to be a good thing in the long run. As I wrestled with what I personally believed about God, a new living faith slowly began to emerge, one that I had worked through and owned. This time was an important metamorphosis in my journey as a believer.

We each need our own personal faith. God desired a one-on-one relationship with me. Now I understand the saying, *Father God has no grandchildren*. It is all about relationship—He wants a direct relationship with each one of us.

Becoming comfortable to be real with God, to question Him and examine what I believed also made it easier later on to have an open mind and to consider other new things He wanted to show me the answers to some of my questions would be outside the God box of my church experience as my questions continued to flow... Can we hear God speak? Are supernatural gifts for today? Does God love everyone? And I'm really curious: can a woman be a pastor?

Hallelujah Moments

Ironically, while my freshman year of college had dealt a major blow to my faith, it gave a major boost to my guy's faith. Don's first college visit was to hear me sing with our choir and orchestra performing Handel's *Messiah*. He sat spellbound, fighting back the tears as his ears filled with breathtaking classical music for the very first time. During the majestic *Hallelujah Chorus*, everyone in the chapel rose to their feet. Don saw grown men weeping all around him, and he openly joined their worship as the glorious presence of God swept through the chapel and funneled into his hungry open heart.

At that moment, the Spirit indelibly put His mark on Don's spirit. Is it any wonder that classical music pours out of the speakers in his welding shop today, often surprising customers? Such strains still connect Don's heart to his Creator like when he first felt His Presence.

As a sophomore, I transferred to Western Illinois University (WIU) to pursue a teaching degree...okay, maybe to just be with Don. Our every YES means saying NO to other things. By transferring from a Christian college, I gave up the pursuit of educational credentials for church leadership. Over the years I would almost forget that dream of being a pastor, but God would not.

During our first year at WIU, if we weren't in class, we were together. At Christmastime Don bent his knee and put a ring on my finger, asking, "Will you marry me?"

I said, "Yes! Yes!"

Hallelujah! I knew that now life would be next to perfect living with this man of my dreams! Even my four-year-old sister Pam thought he was Prince Charming as she tearfully tried to convince him if he'd just wait a few years, she would make a better choice.

When I decided to marry Don, I chose to ignore a major command in 2 Corinthians 6:14 *"Do not be unequally yoked with unbelievers."* Deep within, I passionately wanted to follow Jesus, but Don and I didn't have that passion in common. The scripture made sense because not sharing common core beliefs and goals would most likely pull us apart rather than draw us together.

But I loved him deeply, took a chance, and married him anyway. Our marriage might have gone smoother if we had waited on marriage until we had worked through and agreed on life's basics; instead we were following different compasses.

Two choices would impact every day of my life. The first was deciding to follow Jesus. The second was deciding to marry Don. Marriage was a big risk. Would our marriage be fruitful and long lasting? Only time would tell.

A Teen Bride

That June I fittingly pledged my life to Don in the same little Methodist Church where I had pledged my life to Jesus. A new season began for me as a joyful 19-year-old bride stepping into a brand-new life with my handsome 18-year-old husband heading into our lifelong *happily-ever-after.*

Our folks were not quite as confident that we understood exactly what *happily-ever-after* would entail, certain that we were too young and inexperienced to have a clue. Were they ever right! That first year was turbulent. We survived mainly because we grew up in an era when the norm was to follow through on vows of *'til death do us part,* when folks worked hard on fixing something broken because getting something new wasn't an option.

Fortunately, neither of us considered bailing out as an option, or it would have been over quickly. We had vowed to stay together *for better or worse*, and after a short honeymoon, a lot of days looked like we were together *for worse*.

For the next three college summer breaks we packed a few belongings and moved back to the farm where Don helped his dad and brothers. That first summer was a doozey. I began to wonder if I had made a huge mistake. Don was sure that he had.

We lived out in the boondocks where he worked in the fields from sunup to after sundown seven days a week. That left me, his young bride, with little to keep me busy. The house was clean by 9 am, my college correspondence lessons were done, and I was bored all day with few books, no cell phones, internet, or cable tv. There was nothing to do but eagerly await the arrival of my Prince Charming in the evening. He arrived, hot and sweaty, hungry and exhausted, with just enough energy to eat supper and go to bed. Not much conversation and not much of a start!

That first year was tough because I was looking to Don for my fulfilment, not God. I thought my happily-ever-after package included a hubby who would be my best friend and fill my social, emotional, psychological, and physical needs. Wasn't it his job to keep me safe, comfortable, entertained, and happy? And the expectations he had of his bride? We won't even go there. We both had a lot to learn, such as how the honeymoon bliss tends to fade and along with it our expectations that having a spouse will now solve all our problems and make us incredibly happy.

In reality, marriage brought a few new problems, but the surprise was how it unexpectedly highlighted the junk that each of us brought into the union. Our issues, like with most couples, could be summed up in one word– selfishness! Living in close proximity 24/7 with another human meant no longer being free to do whatever we pleased.

Still crippled by distorted perceptions of God from my freshman year of college, I wasn't in the habit of taking things to Him for help. I wasn't yet aware that He cared about my daily stuff and wanted to help.

I remember in our second month of married bliss how I just wanted to get away. I wanted to vent my frustrations. I was bored living with this young farmer who worked non-stop. So I just left. That evening when Don came home, there was no supper on the table, no car in the drive, and no wife in sight. Something was badly wrong. Don feared that I had walked out on him. He drove his truck around, searching for me for several hours.

Finally he found me at the house of my best friend—I had gone home to my mother. I planned on being back before he got home, but I had lost track of time, and honestly, I really didn't care that much. I was busy whining, "What about me?" not even considering "What about Don?" That night he realized that he might need to pay attention to his bride, not just his farming.

But it wouldn't be the last time we clashed, as we each focused on "What's in it for me?" We often headed in different directions, getting nowhere fast. After a few years of duking it out, we realized 'til death do us part didn't mean until one of us killed the other. We discovered saying "*I do*" meant "*I do* want to learn to love others, and since you will be the closest person to me for the rest of my life, *I do* want to begin with learning to love you." This has been God's idea for marriage from the beginning.

This first season of our life was a mixture of easy and hard times. Though our early years were rocky, we also enjoyed our more carefree college days, especially the three years in Champaign, IL, while Don finished college at the University of Illinois (U of I). Living in our cozy little castle (10' x 60' mobile home), we cruised around on our motorcycle (50-cc motor scooter) and enjoyed simple pleasures such as Friday night burger, fries, and shake at Steak and Shake and a fifty-cent movie at the theater. We often didn't make it to church on Sundays because back then, God was only one of many interests and certainly not the focal point of our world.

Slowly Don and I would learn to care, but it was evident that we would never actually pass the *I Do* class. Signing that marriage license also meant signing up for a lifetime of never-ending daily lessons on loving. Meanwhile, we were both still wondering, "*Will we make it for a lifetime?*"

And Now We Were Three

While Don finished college, I taught high school English and took some graduate classes. At age 22 I had become quite anxious and having more frequent epileptic seizures with bouts of depression that lasted for weeks. When I got pregnant, my doctor prescribed daily tranquilizers. Today I cringe that I took them, but back then I innocently followed my doctor's orders, unaware of the drug dangers for our child in the womb. Thank God he protected our baby.

Shawn Lee, our firstborn, arrived healthy and quite robust. Words cannot describe how special it was to cradle our newborn in my arms for the first time. As soon as they brought him to us, we unwrapped our little miracle and counted...ten fingers and ten toes. Yes, he was perfect.

I was now beginning a lifelong calling of being a mother. Our baby boy brought so much joy. Yet this new 24-7 job began with a struggle as I slipped into post-partum depression for a few months and exhaustion from dealing with major health issues. I would nap whenever my little guy did. I was embarrassed to admit to anyone that I struggled to stay upbeat with this precious new baby.

As I did with all my problems back then, I kept my struggle to myself which only made things worse. Had that happened today, I would find someone to talk with to get some help.

Slowly this weakness did send me back to God for help to do what I could not on my own. I began to cry out to Him several times a day, "Help, Lord. Deliver me from this funk." He heard my cry, and help was on the way. He began changing me slowly while Don made a major leap, once again because of a man who boldly shared his GodStories.

The Granddaddy of Them All

Fishermen eagerly try to land the big fish sometimes referred to as the granddaddy of them all. After Don graduated, we moved back home, and we hooked a live one who lived a mile up the road, a real granddaddy of them all. Granddad Craig, big in stature and influence, talked about God as easily as he mumbled, "Please pass me some more biscuits and gravy." When Granddad talked, we listened. Having just retired from serving as a Methodist pastor for 52 years, Granddad spent lots of time with us.

As I observed his daily interactions with God, I began to wonder if my old college professor might have led me astray. Granddad didn't push us or try to persuade us into having faith. He just shared GodStories like when God called him as a young farmer with four small boys to go to college and become a pastor. He hadn't gone to high school but the college accepted him, and he graduated while providing for his family. I wanted to know God intimately like my Granddad.

Don's hunger was also growing. This was when I realized Don wasn't rejecting Jesus. He'd gone to church as a kid but didn't really know enough about what Jesus was like to want to give his life to Him.

Back then I didn't know how to put my faith into words very well and had not yet lived many stories of my own, but Granddad had a never-ending supply. Don was curious, and Granddad patiently helped him explore what God is like. He had a knack of asking Don thought-provoking questions, a skill that Don picked up and still constantly uses.

Granddad showed us God's love in a practical way. He planted seeds helping us raise a huge garden with unique crops like kohlrabi, brussels sprouts and okra, still Don's favorites. Grandad also planted seeds of faith in us as he shared GodStories from lean times during the Great Depression like when he volunteered in a Kansas City soup kitchen.

Night after night when Don came home from work, Granddad gave him a helping hand with his chores of raising hogs. The two men worked and laughed together, becoming the best of friends and barely noticing their fifty-year age difference.

Don didn't only learn through stories and questions. He also learned from Granddad through experiences like when they worked together on a hot Saturday morning to repair an outdoor pump in a pit.

As Don lifted the cover, he jumped back, "Copperheads!"

Granddad replied, "No problem," as he picked up a hoe. Whack. Whack. Now there were two headless snakes dead in the pit. Granddad stopped to simply thank his God.

That fall when Don turned 22, the seeds had grown into beautiful produce, and Granddad helped us with a bountiful harvest. Other seeds Granddad had planted had matured too, those he planted as he worked with us, laughing and crying, doing life together, and investing countless hours answering Don's questions.

Granddad asked Don one more question, "Are you ready to follow Jesus?"

Don answered, "Yes, I am."

Granddad led him in a simple prayer of faith, and Don began his eternal life with Jesus. Once again Granddad helped rescue Don from both the serpent and the pit.

Now Don and I began to walk hand in hand on our journey to know God well.

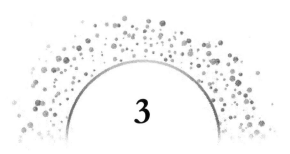

The Transformer

We launched a new chapter in our story when we made our seventh move in five years of married college life, glad to settle down in Winchester, IL (pop: 1700) for the next thirteen years. This season was one of great transformation as we encountered a new town, new jobs, new church, new friends, new babies, and a new powerful encounter with God that would change everything in my life.

I was a 24-year-old with a growing hunger for God and one simple prayer, "Show me more of You, Lord." He loves to answer that one.

Rivers of Living Water

This time God sent His answer special delivery via a stranger who handed me a simple pamphlet entitled *Have You Made the Wonderful Discovery of the Spirit Filled Life?*

As I read it, I was thinking, *"Well, no, I don't think I have. I know the Father and I know Jesus, but I don't really know much about the Holy Spirit."*

The tract went something like this,

> Are you ready to surrender your whole life to Jesus? You can ask Him to fill you with His presence, the Holy Spirit, to equip you with power for dynamic daily living.

Intrigued, I read on,

> When we ask Jesus into our lives, He comes as the Holy Spirit to take up permanent residence in us, but there is more power available when we ask Him to fill us up with His Spirit. Jesus promised this with the last words He spoke before He left Planet Earth,

And now I will send the Holy Spirit, just as my Father promised. But stay here in the city until the Holy Spirit comes and fills you with power from heaven. (Luke 24:49 NLT)

Anyone who believes in me may come and drink! For the Scriptures declare, "Rivers of living water will flow from his heart. By this he meant the Spirit who those who believed in him were later to receive." (John 7:38,39 NIV)

I wondered, "Flowing rivers of living water...the Spirit...maybe this is what I have been missing. Since I was a little girl, I've been striving to please God by my own efforts. What if I just need more of His Spirit empowering me on the inside to make a difference on the outside?"

The pamphlet went on to say how it is simple to be filled with the Spirit:

If you are thirsty for more of God, ask Him to fill you with His Spirit, and believe that if you ask, He will do it.

It made sense. I was all in. So I prayed, "Jesus, I need more of you. Now I invite you to come and be Lord of my life, the boss. I am thirsty for your rivers of living water. Fill me with Your Holy Spirit, your presence and power. Thank you, Lord. I believe you are filling me up in Jesus name." It was a simple prayer anyone can pray anywhere.

Then I breathed in deep breaths as I pictured drinking in His Spirit. "Spirit of God, I believe you are filling me up."

I waited for the living water wondering if anything really happened. I felt a little trickle of peace and confidence but no river. But I believed His promise:

So if you sinful people know how to give good gifts to your children, how much more will your heavenly Father give the Holy Spirit to those who ask him. (Luke 11:13 NLT)

Things are often not as they seem, for an unseen river was rising inside of me. By the next morning it was flowing.

I woke with a big grin on my face, joyful and energized. Deep inside I experienced a strangely warm and toasty feeling. Outside I surged with a fresh confidence that the Father loved me, His little girl, with all my imperfections. I lay there praising Him for His presence, wondering what new things the day would bring. I knew somehow I was different, more vibrant and fully alive.

I mused, "So this must be the Holy Spirit Jesus promised, His river of living water inside of me." I'd never felt God so close.

The Little Old Lady   *His Fruit of Love*

God's Presence felt like a strong surge of power within me. Would this bubbling river overflow and spill out all around me? Isn't that what rivers do? I headed to town to get some groceries with that big grin still on my face as I was lost in thoughts of how much God loves me. On an ordinary day I would run in, get my groceries, and zoom home. But this was no ordinary day.

As I walked into the IGA store, some little old lady (probably the same age as I am today) was coming out the door. She was a total stranger but I felt warmly drawn to her. Somehow I really cared about her. I slowed down and took time to see her wrinkled face worn by the sun, her light blue dress, and the limp in her step. A fresh tenderness welled up inside of me, and I wanted to take that little old lady, wrap my arms around her, and give her a bear hug. I didn't, but I wanted to.

Something new was stirring. I was so struck by what was happening inside that I didn't even speak to her. *"How strange. Could this be His Spirit…Of course it is! His Presence inside of me is loving someone through me. Holy Spirit is a living river bubbling out of me with love."* It all made sense.

> *But anyone who does not love does not know God, for **God is love**.*
> (I John 4:8 NIV emphasis added)

It follows that being filled with the Presence of His Spirit would also fill me with His love for others. Eureka! I no longer had to strive to do it on my own. My job wasn't to be perfect. My job was to learn how to allow His Spirit to love others through me.

Being filled with the Holy Spirit was a simple experience, the first of many as I frequently asked God to fill me again. A famous evangelist, D. L. Moody, was asked why he had to be filled with the Spirit so often.

He said simply, "Because I leak."[1]

There was so much more I didn't know about the Holy Spirit, but over time He would teach me just like Jesus said He would,

> *But when the Father sends the Advocate as my representative— that is, the Holy Spirit—he will teach you everything and will remind you of everything I have told you.* (John 14:26 NLT)

As usual that Sunday we went to church, and I felt so full of joy. However, I felt uncomfortable sharing with others about the Spirit for some had made it clear that they weren't interested in hearing. So I just talked a lot to God during those days. Still clueless in many ways, one thing I was certain about was that my life would never be the same. For now I was hosting His transforming Spirit.

I was learning to know God more intimately by relating to all three persons of the Trinity, knowing the Father's love, enjoying Jesus the Son, and working with the Holy Spirit within and around me. While this three-in-one concept is too unfathomable to fully comprehend, the Trinity has helped me better see God better. Paul prayed this blessing of all three over believers:

> *May the grace of the Lord Jesus Christ, and the love of God, and the fellowship of the Holy Spirit be with you all.*
> (2 Corinthians 13:14 NIV)

At times I would pray to one of them and then the other, afraid I was addressing the wrong one. Then I realized they didn't mind which name I used. They were not jealous of each other at all but had been one together since before creation. (Genesis 1:1, John 1:1) Their united desire was to fill me with their love and power to transform and energize me. Sometimes I just addressed my three-in-one God as *the Lord* for that is what He was becoming to me.

"Are You Fun to Live With?" *His Fruit of Joy*

God's Spirit was quickly and powerfully answering my prayer for *more* as He quietly and gently began to change me, growing the fruit of His Spirit within me as I had just encountered by sensing His *love*.

> *But the Holy Spirit produces this kind of fruit in our lives: love, joy, peace, patience, kindness, goodness, faithfulness, gentleness, and self-control...* (Galatians 5:22,23 NLT)

I noticed the other fruit growing as His Spirit enabled me to do what I had formerly struggled to do my own. Next came abundant *joy* as the Spirit began to spill over into those around me, especially my hubby.

While reading a book[2] I was struck with a chapter title which posed a haunting question: *Are You Fun to Live With?* I realized that the Spirit of God was enabling to answer *Yes* most of the time as I found new joy in my busy days.

God still asks me this question which serves as a barometer of how connected we are. Of course, He usually brings it up when my answer is *No* and I need to ask for a Holy Spirit refill. There is joy in His presence.

You make known to me the path of life; you will fill me with joy in your presence, with eternal pleasures at your right hand.
(Psalm 16:11 NIV)

In our early years together sometimes Don was especially stubborn and I was very self-centered; then I would be the stubborn one and he would be self-centered. I would often over-ride Don's preferences whenever they conflicted with my comfort. But I noticed that as the Spirit took up more room inside he shifted my attitude and my behavior. Even Don noticed.

As a young woman in the 1960s, I followed a painful beauty ritual of sleeping all night with long hair in curlers that yielded marvelous curls. It would have been enough that Don had to wake up to the sight of me in curlers, but it made matters worse when I dropped one or two on the bathroom floor most mornings and didn't bother to pick them up. I was just too lazy. Then I would get offended when he pointed out how inconsiderate I was.

I'd quip, "It's no big deal."

He'd return, "Yeah, for you!" And back and forth we'd go. This was no poufy foam curler either. In that era, curlers had stiff prickly bristles poking out that could bring pain to any foot. Of course, that foot always seemed to be Don's. And, to him, it was a big deal.

Then overnight, things changed. When a curler fell to the floor, without even thinking, I picked it up so that he wouldn't step on it. This might sound common courtesy to you, but for me, it was God.

Another area of contention was how to handle a tube of toothpaste. Don neatly rolled up the end as he squeezed toothpaste out while I was a "squeeze it from the middle" gal. Now I became a "holy roller," squeezing it from the end, again to honor my husband. I even began replacing the toilet tissue roll instead of leaving him an empty roll with three measly sheets.

Trash was definitely the biggie. Since the day we had said *I do,* we both had been loudly saying *I don't!* when it came to taking out the trash. In Don's family, his mom did garbage duty, so he thought that was the wife's job. In my family, my dad did that dirty task; so obviously, it was hubby's job. We both learned a lot about doing married life by mirroring how our parents had done it, especially when it worked for our personal advantage.

After several years of constant trash talk, I quietly began doing the job without a word. Don was amazed. The Holy Spirit was at work. It is often the small things that erode a relationship. I was learning that it can also be the small things which build it stronger.

A Technicolor God   *His Fruit of Goodness*

I grew up in a black-and-white world where we viewed life in black-and-white photographs and on black-and-white television as we learned black-and-white values of a black-and-white God.

Now His Spirit was transforming my life into living color. From the moment I saw the radiant little old lady in her light blue dress, I was off on a mission to bring out the God-colors in this troubled world as I experienced a Technicolor God whose goodness was coming alive in me.

You're here to be light, bringing out the God-colors in the world. Keep open house; be generous with your lives. By opening up to others, you'll prompt people to open up with God, this generous Father in heaven. (Matthew 5:14-16 The Message)

My Father created this earth and declared, *"It is good"* as He filled it with endless hues of color: fish, animals, birds, the sky, landscapes, flowers, even people. I embarked on a brand-new adventure of experiencing His rich variety in life. Had we not experienced the Transformer, Don and I would have missed out on a colorful wild ride together. We may have even missed out on *together*.

I so enjoy how God's goodness touches each of us so uniquely. He touches us in the exact way He knows we will respond like when He sent the stranger to give me the tract that led to my praying to be filled with the Spirit, and a few weeks later sent Brother George to share his story that led to my being healed of epilepsy. It may even explain my unique love of going to the grocery store, for it was there when I encountered His Spirit's river of love effortlessly flow out of me.

Teach me to do Your will, for You are my God; Your Spirit is good. (Psalm 143:10)

Headed to Heaven   *His Fruit of Faithfulness*

I was also surprised how the Holy Spirit took care of a plaguing doubt that I had struggled with for years, "Am I really a Christian? Saved? Born-again?" Some days I felt I was doing fine and was confident that I would make it into Heaven. Other days I fretted and didn't feel like I was behaving well enough to ever make it in the gate. Intellectually I knew that believing in Jesus was all I needed, but my heart wasn't feeling it. I was still struggling with performing to earn His approval.

When I was filled with the Spirit of God, a new assurance came, and my heart was suddenly flooded with a certainty of what my head had believed for years. Now I *knew*, not just *hoped* that I had eternal life, confident that eternal life didn't depend on what I did or didn't do. It was settled; I had a solid faith that trusted in what Jesus had done for me. This belief has never wavered even once. Never again did I question whether I would spend eternity with Him. What a relief.

> *And this is the testimony: God has given us eternal life, and this life is in his Son. Whoever has the Son has life; whoever does not have God's Son does not have life. I have written this to you who believe in the name of the Son of God, so that you may **know** you have eternal life.* (I John 5:11-13 NLT Emphasis added)

My Big Mouth   *His Fruit of Gentleness and Kindness*

My mouth and what came out of it was no small thing. It was undergoing the biggest transformation. Don and I had fallen into predicable roles when we argued. Sometimes I barked at him meaner than a junkyard dog while Don balked with me, stubborn as a mule. Our animal behaviors didn't help us relate. As the Spirit worked within me, Don noticed that his fiery young bride, who had always been quick to clarify the correct way to think about absolutely everything, was now quieter and taking time to actually think before blurting out whatever popped into her head.

I no longer felt it was necessary to be right in every argument. That one change alone was dramatic evidence of God's amazing transformation. I have observed that this attitude of assumed rightness is one of the top causes of fighting with couples. Not having to be right or have the last word began to diffuse anger. Sometimes we couldn't agree so we agreed to disagree and move on.

Whether to allow the Spirit to be in control of my words or not would a constant choice all my days and wield great power.

> *The tongue can bring death or life; those who love to talk will reap the consequences.* (Proverbs 18:21 NLT)

I'm still working on allowing the fruit of self-control to develop as I also deal with what goes *in* my mouth, but that is another story. Imperfect means I'm in progress, and I hate to say that there would be more days when things such as the trash would pop up again as an issue and I would have to choose again whether to be self-centered or loving. But every time God transforms us when we cry out to Him for His help.

We all, who with unveiled faces contemplate the Lord's glory, are being transformed into his image with ever-increasing glory, which comes from the Lord, who is the Spirit. (2 Corinthians 3:18 NIV)

The Spirit of God uses the Word of God to make the child of God more like the Son of God.

—RICK WARREN

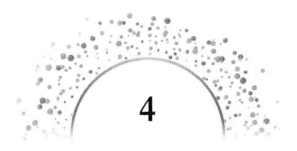

4

Life or Death?

During this same season of experiencing the Holy Spirit, Jesus healed me from epilepsy. So much was happening as my passion for God grew as I carved out quiet time with Him each morning and continued to talk with Him throughout my day.

Life flourished as I taught elementary music two days a week and corralled our one-year-old tornado. Soon we were expecting our second child. Busier but seizure free, I was no longer depressed, nor did I need tranquilizers. Praise God!

Our second son Damon turned out to be a content little boy of joy. We were blessed with an incredibly loving nanny, Norma Jean, who watched our boys while I taught school. She adored watching our free-spirited toddler Shawn play as "her baby Damon," contentedly sat on her lap all day soaking up the love of Jesus. I credit her with helping mold Damon's gentle heart of compassion. Norma Jean quietly fulfilled her simple yet powerful mission that left a lasting imprint in our son and on our family.

Gasping for Air   *His Fruit of Patience*

As our little future engineers grew up, they came up with innovative ideas every day. My mother looked forward to my phone calls with stories of their latest antics. One day when they were 2 and 4, she laughed, "Trust me. You just won't remember these funny stories years from now. Why don't you start a new habit of journaling each day?"

So I did. It was God's ideal timing, for only a month later my first journal records the priceless detail of how we navigated one of our biggest life crises.

God was developing another fruit of the Spirit, patience when our third little child was expected any day. Our first two had been born three and four weeks early, so naturally, we expected our third to arrive early also. Three pregnancies so close together put a major strain on my body and emotions. My due date came and went. The days dragged on into weeks. Three weeks later, I tossed and turned all night praying in faith that this would be the night of deliverance. The next morning I woke up exhausted and still very pregnant. I journaled, *"I am trying to master Philippians 4:11, 'I have learned in whatever state I am to be content,' but I am a really slow learner."* Eventually I learned to wait with uncomfortable patience…another long week.

Our third son, Cory Lee, entered this world at 4:13 am, Tuesday, July 14, 1970. We got to know each other on Tuesday and Wednesday. On Thursday, I was lying in my hospital bed, one happy momma, as I gazed at him, laughing, "You are a carbon copy of your brother Damon." Then I repeated my new baby ritual, nestling him close and smothering him with momma kisses as I counted – ten fingers, ten toes. "Yep, you are perfect."

Yet as I watched him, I noticed something didn't seem quite right. Cory's breathing was erratic, and he often gasped for air. Finally, I nervously buzzed the nurse. "I don't think he is breathing right. Something's wrong. Would you check him out?"

I panicked as the nurse tried to calm me, "I see what you mean. Don't worry. It's probably nothing seriously wrong, but we will have the doctor take a look." Then she took my baby away.

Shortly after, the doctor came in. I could tell by his face that something was wrong, very wrong, "Your baby is having respiratory issues. We are giving him oxygen and are getting ready to transport him to a neonatal specialist in Hannibal, MO. Can you get your husband here right away?"

I immediately called Don on the bedside phone and told him that Cory could be dying and to come quickly. Don dropped everything and rushed to the hospital, arriving just as the ambulance was pulling away. He jumped in, and they whisked Cory away. Don tightly held our son's tiny hand on the forty-minute trip.

At the hospital in Hannibal, the pediatric specialist examined our baby thoroughly. Then he looked at Don and delivered the words we dreaded hearing,

"I am very sorry. He is not going to make it. Your son has a heart valve defect. There is nothing we can do. In a few hours he will simply run out of oxygen, and his life will be over." Don held his little hand tightly as he wept softly, watching Cory struggle to breathe.

Meanwhile back in the hospital, I wrote in my new journal the thoughts racing through my mind:

> I was really upset when they told me Cory's life was in danger. I couldn't hold back the tears when I called Don to come right away. I'm still having trouble. Things keep going over in my mind such as...Why was my delivery so late? Maybe God wanted to teach me to be patient and trust him...
>
> I think about the poem our pastor read on Sunday about how God lends us a child but doesn't tell us just how long, but we are to love him for however long we have him...I want my baby boy to live...I feel Your peace now as I focus on You instead of what might happen. Help me, Lord."

The next six hours drug on with no word on how he was doing in this pre-cell phone era. Then the bedside phone rang, and I hesitantly lifted it to my ear. Don was crying,

"Honey, I am sorry. Little Cory didn't make it. He just ran out of oxygen. He went peacefully, and I was still holding his hand as he gasped his last breath."

Overtaken by Grief

Then we cried together. I hung up the phone and began sobbing deeply, grieving that I would not cuddle my baby in my arms again. A half hour passed before I slowly, but determinedly, took my focus off our loss and lifted my head and heart to God. With blurry eyes, I penned this prayer in my journal:

> Dear Father – I hope you understand all the sorrow I'm pouring out. It's not that I'm bitter or even wondering why you took him back so soon. It's just that I'm going to miss him. There are many tears that have to fall. Oh Father, I guess you must have shed lots of tears when your son died too, didn't you? You know the suffering we're going through, losing part of ourselves.

The next day I was the one gasping for air. Waves of sobbing with deep grief alternated with waves of peace. This ebb and flow of grief and peace continued all day as my focus shifted between the agonies of death which I could see to the presence of God whom I couldn't see. Once again I journaled my thoughts,

Oh, Lord, I'm full of sorrow this morning and I don't have the strength to face this on my own. How can I love a baby so much when he was here so briefly? It makes me wonder how much you have in store for us in heaven when you give us such incredible gifts like babies here on earth.

Though I feel overwhelmed, I also sense a surprising strength rising up. Could it be from those ordinary days spending quiet time with You, getting to know you? I know when I spend time with you, something happens. When I study my Bible, when I pray in faith, something happens, even when I feel like my prayers are bouncing off the ceiling.

I had no idea what was happening in those hidden times with You, Lord, but as I go through these tough times, I realize how You were building my strength and faith."

Life in a Cemetery   *His Fruit of Peace*

Death was not the end of this story. On Saturday we gathered with family and friends at a small cemetery where clouds filled the skies and blocked the sun from our place of sorrow. Billowing clouds seemed a fitting canopy for the tiny white box lying on the ground next to the open grave. I could hardly bear to look at the too-small casket that held the lifeless body of our little son. Had it only been three days since I cuddled him tight and dreamed of his future?

As grief swallowed me up once again, I bawled with uncontrollable sobs. The pain was unbearable, and I could not hold back the wailing that came from deep within. I could not fathom it all. "How can this be? How can we go on living?"

Then our pastor and dear friend stood facing us in front of the little casket and prayed, "Lord, we invite You Presence, Your Spirit, into this place." As he opened his Bible and read the comforting words of Jesus, the Lord came.

Peace I leave with you; my peace I give you. I do not give to you as the world gives. Do not let your hearts be troubled and do not be afraid. (John 14:1 NIV)

Suddenly the atmosphere was charged with electrifying energy as the Son of God, alive and well, spoke through His Word directly into my heart, *"Peace I give **you.**"*

My heavenly Father broke through the thin barrier between Heaven and Earth and touched me, a broken-hearted mother, in my time of deepest grief. He gave me peace in a place of sorrow and brought life in a place of death.

Then I sensed the Father reach down with His strong kind hand into my deepest inner place. He took hold of every last shred of grief and fear and gently lifted them out of my heavy heart. I felt light as the weight lifted. My wailing subsided. I experienced a strange calm.

Next, God gently placed His hand on me and sent a liquid peace radiating through my entire body like a warm soothing love bath. This peace must be a foretaste of the incredible bliss Heaven holds. Yet I least expected to encounter it here in the middle of a cemetery as we mourned the death of our baby boy.

My brain could not understand what was happening. How could it? Peace is a matter of the heart. It was in my heart that I was hearing the voice of God. In my deepest sorrow, the God of the impossible had come and done the impossible. He healed my grieving heart.

An Upside-Down World

"Peace I give you, not as the world gives..." The peace that world gives is when the circumstances shift so that everything around us is just right, but the peace Jesus gives doesn't require everything to be right. On the contrary, I experienced His solid peace landing right in the middle of great darkness.

On Sunday I wrote in my journal:

> How real God is to me now for I know that no matter how deep our sorrow, God can heal us and give us a supernatural lasting peace! Thinking of Cory saddens me, but the overbearing grief and sorrow is gone, no longer ripping apart my heart and mind. His peace is far more real than the pain of sorrow. It has been a day and a half since God's hand touched me, and his peace is still with me constantly.

That peace lasted more than a day. It lasted for a lifetime. The grief never returned. To me, this is as miraculous as being healed of epilepsy.

Only God knows the full impact of Cory's short life. I have shared his story countless times over the years and seen Jesus touch those who hear. Only one month later, I shared his story publicly for the first time at a Lay Witness Mission. A lady came up to me after the church service and reached out to hold my hands as she shared that she had lost a son too and that God had brought her peace as she heard Cory's story. She gave her life to Jesus that morning.

Even the timing of Cory's life spoke to us. Born at **4:13** a.m. he brought hope through his brief life story illustrating God's word in I Thessalonians **4:13**:

> *Brothers and sisters, we do not want you to be uninformed about those who sleep in death, so that you do not grieve like the rest of mankind, who have no hope.*

As I share this encounter with God, I am painfully aware that countless people who suffer with unspeakable pain and death and don't experience God's intervention in this way. Sometimes they live with grief and heartbreak all of their days. Some things we walk through aren't fixed here on this earth.

Although mine was not the normal experience surrounding death, this time His peace did come, right in the middle of the loss. Though I would also face other times when deep pain lasted way too long, Cory's story highlights how the impossible is possible with God. Jesus looked at them intently and said,

> *"Humanly speaking, it is impossible. But not with God. Everything is possible with God."* (Mark 10:27 NLT)

Why Did Cory Die?

I don't know why our son died. How could we ever fully understand how the Lord God Almighty orchestrates life on earth? Often He doesn't explain Himself. Is He obligated to reveal everything to us humans He created?

> *"My thoughts are nothing like your thoughts," says the LORD. "And my ways are far beyond anything you could imagine."* (Isaiah 55:8 NLT)

Perhaps we wouldn't understand if He did explain, or maybe we don't need to know. However, He does wants us to know Him well enough to trust Him and be confident that He is good even when we don't understand all that happens.

I also have seen how God enjoyed my pausing to reflect on His ways and that He often revealed more of His mystery as I got closer to Him. He reminded me this fallen world is not the place where His perfect will is done. Heaven is that place, and we do not live there…yet. On earth we face sickness and death and pain which are not present in heaven.

He will wipe away every tear from their eyes, and death shall be no more, neither shall there be mourning, nor crying, nor pain anymore, for the former things have passed away. (Revelation 21:4 NIV)

Over the years I have learned that God is not responsible for many things that people attribute to Him. Our struggles are often due to the unseen battle going on between two kingdoms. Jesus explains,

The thief's purpose is to steal and kill and destroy. My purpose is to give abundant life. (John 10:10 NIV)

Our enemy Satan or the devil *comes to rob, kill and destroy* in the kingdom of this world while Jesus came to usher in the abundant life found in the Kingdom of God. In the Lord's Prayer, Jesus instructs us to pray: *May Your Kingdom come and Your will be done on earth as it is in Heaven.*[3] As we pray in faith, we can partner with Him to make a difference in this world and help win the battles.

But the Son of God came to destroy the works of the devil. (I John 3:8 NLT)

As in all battles, life will get ugly at times as we have setbacks along with the victories, but the ultimate victory belongs to the Lord.

Instead of making us robots, God created us in His image giving us the precious gift of free choice. In tough times we can choose to press into His presence or pull away from Him.

As I chose to draw close to God, He strengthened my trust and faith and gave me peace. Sometimes we ask, "Why, Lord?" and He says, "Just trust me. I'll tell you later." I was learning to focus on another question, "What now, Lord?"

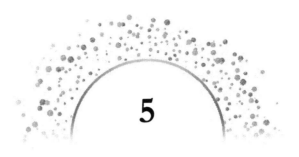

5

Mommy Power

Soon it was 1971, a milestone year as Apollo 14 landed on the moon and Walt Disney World opened in Orlando. Our family anticipated our own spectacular event, the arrival of another baby. Surprisingly, I felt peaceful when I remembered Cory dying and had little concerns or fear that our next baby might also have a birth defect that would cause early death.

Evidently my subconscious wasn't as confident. At each prenatal visit the doctor would assure me that the baby was fine, but I would barely make it to the car before I burst out in uncontrollable sobs. Internally I was still in healing mode.

No, Not Again!

That August our delightful daughter made her debut four weeks early, only thirteen months after Cory. Our little Jenny Marie was beautiful in every way. When the day arrived to take our baby girl home from the hospital, I laid out her new outfit neatly on the bed, impatient for the nurse to hurry up and bring her to us so that we could head home. I looked up and saw the doctor, not the nurse, standing in the doorway, and he was not smiling. He began, "I'm afraid I have some bad news…"

My heart began beating wildly, "Oh no. Not again. Are we going to lose this precious baby too?" I began feeling the fear rise as I fought back tears asking, "Now what? What is wrong?"

He shook his head, "You are free to go home, but I'm afraid we need to keep your daughter. She has jaundice which is common with babies born early. We'll need to treat her for several days."

I fought back panic. Living in a pre-Google age, we had not heard of this condition and had no quick way to research it. We hugged our baby as we walked out of the hospital without her. I got in the car saying, "Okay, Cathy, deep breaths. God, I trust you. Help us, Lord."

Then the scenes began flooding back: the nurse whisking our son away, the ambulance speeding off with lights flashing, the phone ringing, and Don's teary words that Cory was gone, and the tiny white casket in the cemetery. I remembered how I had held him, not realizing it would be the last time.

Was this the last time I would hold Jenny too? Would I see her alive again? Would she be all right?

Once again I had to purposely choose to focus on God to find peace in uncertain days. I read His promises in the Bible, and I prayed for faith to trust Him and to keep from fretting. Worrying would not help anyway. Jesus said:

> *Can any one of you by worrying add a single hour to your life?* (Matthew 6:27 NIV)

As a mom, I was learning my children are best in God's hand, and I would continually need to trust Him and hand them over to Him for the rest of my days.

After ten days in the hospital we brought Jenny home, healthy and vibrant. This time, our trial ended well. We praise God for this passionate daughter who still brings such sunshine into our lives.

Shhh, Be Still

One year and eight days later, our second precious daughter, Christy Jean, was born. She arrived right on schedule. She still does. Everything went as planned. Our tiniest princess was peaceful from the beginning.

> *Children are a gift from the Lord; they are a reward from him. Children born to a young man are like arrows in a warrior's hands. How joyful is the man whose quiver is full of them.* (Psalm 127:3-5 NLT)

Now a young 28-year-old warrior, Don had with a quiver full of arrows with four lively little ones age six and under. Now our task was to help those arrows hit the target of loving God and others well.

The days often demanded more strength than I had. I needed more mommy power to keep up. I knew from experience that God would equip and strengthen me as I studied my Bible and talked with Him. But I seemed to have no spare time, mothering from early morning to late night.

Carving out a regular daily quiet time now seemed impossible. God chuckles when we declare something impossible.

> *Humanly speaking, it is impossible. But with God everything is possible.* (Matthew 19:26 NLT)

Then I came across instructions on what to do about the problem.

> *Don't worry about anything; instead, pray about everything. Tell God what you need and thank him for all he has done. Then you will experience God's peace, which exceeds anything we can understand.* (Philippians. 4:6-7 NLT)

I determined instead of fretting to ask for help, "Lord, the busier I get, the more I need to connect with You. Show me how to make a way. I am desperate."

Our calm baby girl was content with only one slight hiccup. She had this habit of quickly finishing her bottle and then opening her tiny mouth and shooting half of the milk back out in a 3' radius. But if I took 20 minutes to patiently pat her back, she would let loose a robust burp, and all would end well.

Coaxing out that reluctant burp was not so fun at 2 am. But night after night I would feed her and gently pound on her back until I heard that long awaited bubble emitting deep from within. I would be so thankful to *then* lay her down and fall back into bed for a few hours rest before dawn and the other three were up and running.

I have to say that I resented the long 2 am hour feeding and that stubborn critical burp. Forgive me, but I quite often would rather be getting a little sleep.

Then one night I opened my Bible as I burped my sleeping baby, and it came to me, "Oh my goodness, God has provided what I asked for, an ideal Quiet Time. This is it."

For months I happily draped Christy over my shoulder and patted away while I read my Bible propped on my lap. I got to know God well in those wee hours as I talked with Him about how I was feeling and listened for His direction. He gave me strength to run the race set before me, and most days it was quite the race. He had turned my frustration into joy.

I was inspired by a praying momma from another century who carved out special time with God. Susanna Wesley would go to a corner and pull her apron over her head to pray for her ten children. Her children knew never to dare disturb their mother. I wanted to make a difference too. Those prayers were powerful as her son John Wesley founded the Methodist Church, and another son Charles wrote over 6000 hymns including "Hark the Herald Angels Sing."

Quiet Time is still a daily habit essential for me to stay in tune with Father God. Each morning I wake up beneath words stenciled on the wall above our bed with this reminder:

Be still and know that I am God. (Psalm 46:10)

Today time with God is still a must. The voices of our children are gone, but other voices invade my mind clamoring for attention: social media, the news, the internet, unending tasks, all the busyness. My morning Quiet Time grounds me with God's voice before the rpms of my racing mind engage with other voices. It is a time when I can often clearly hear His whisper.

The Intruder Strikes Again

Life continued to test our trust in God. When Christy was ten months old, our family was driving across the Illinois River Bridge one evening. All was quiet, a rarity, so Don looked through the rear-view mirror to check on the kids who were all sleeping soundly. On second glance he saw that Christy looked pale as a zombie with her eyes locked open, mouth drooping, and body collapsed to the side of the car seat. Panicked, Don turned on the dome light, "Cathy, check and see if Christy is okay."

Turning around, I looked into her glazed eyes. "No, she is not okay," I shouted. I jumped up on my knees and leaned over the seat, trying to engage her.

"Christy, Christy," I yelled.

No response. I lifted her head. It flopped back. I gently shook her. No response again. Her entire body was limp and unresponsive. I put my hand on her chest to see if she was breathing. She was, so I concluded that she was just sound asleep. I reluctantly turned back around in my seat.

Then Don looked again in the rear-view mirror again and said, "Cathy, she's still not right."

I checked her again, but this time I felt no breath. Now we were in full panic as I screamed, "Oh no, pull off the road. I think she's dead."

Don raced across the bridge and tore off onto the shoulder. We jumped out of the car to get to her. She remained lifeless, with staring eyes wide open.

Don cried out, "Oh God, please don't let her be dead." After a few minutes that seemed like an eternity Christy blinked her eyes and began to move. By now all the kids were wide-awake, frightened and crying. Then our little girl slowly looked around at the five of us first confused and then breaking out in a big grin. She was back to normal. Eventually, so were our heart rates.

On the drive home Don and I were trying to figure out what had just happened when I remembered a similar incident from a few weeks back. When I laid Christy down for her nap, bottle in hand, she turned limp, with that same glazed stare, mouth wide open, and her body lifeless. I lifted her from the crib and pounded on her back. I thought she had choked on her bottle, so I stuck my finger down her throat to help her breathe again. She gagged and slowly came around.

Now as I put the two incidents together, it dawned on me what was happening. It was that old familiar enemy of epilepsy coming this time to attack our baby girl.

Sleep escaped me that night. Our tiny Christy was so innocent and helpless. I didn't want our daughter to have to fight epilepsy for years as I had. Desperate, I cried out, "Oh God, help us. What is going to happen to her?" I kept replaying the bridge incident in my mind as I searched for answers while panicking from the fear that was trying to take over. Exhausted I fell asleep at 3 a.m.

Words Leapt Off the Page

The next morning I awoke anxiously praying, "Help, Lord. What is going to happen to her?" I randomly open the Bible on the bedside table. My eyes fell on the words of Jesus (highlighted in red in my Bible) as I read this story:

Then a man named Jairus, a leader of the local synagogue, came and fell at Jesus' feet, pleading with him to come home with him. His only daughter, who was about twelve years old, was dying...A messenger arrived..."Your daughter is dead. There's no use troubling the Teacher now."

But when Jesus heard what had happened, he said to Jairus, "Don't be afraid. Just have faith, and she will be healed."

When they arrived at the house...the house was filled with people weeping and wailing, but he said, "Stop the weeping! She isn't dead; she's only asleep."

But the crowd laughed at him because they all knew she had died. Then Jesus took her by the hand and said in a loud voice, "My child, get up!" And at that moment her life returned, and she immediately stood up! (Luke 8:41-55 NLT emphasis added)

The words of Jesus, *"Don't be afraid. Just have faith, and she will be healed,"* seemed to explode with power as if Jesus were speaking directly to me. When as I read, *"Stop worrying. She is not dead; she is only asleep,"* the tears began to flow as I remembered how we had thought Christy was dead when her mind was only asleep. These situations seemed so similar. Jesus was speaking the words afresh to me centuries later.

Once again as I heard God's Word, He deposited faith into me, a confidence that our baby girl would be healed. I responded, "Lord, I have faith. I believe." The tangible peace of God penetrated my being. It was not a faith that I somehow worked up but faith that God had given to me as I had read His Word.

For it is by grace you have been saved, through faith—and this is not from yourselves, it is the gift of God—not by works, so that no one can boast. For we are God's handiwork, created in Christ Jesus to do good works, which God prepared in advance for us to do. (Ephesians 2:8-9)

That morning I wrote in my journal,

I do anticipate some possible problems before she is healed, but I know that we just need to trust Jesus, and she'll be all right.

The following morning I took Christy to her pediatrician who concurred that we were dealing with epilepsy. He handed me a prescription for phenobarbital. I took it home and laid it on the counter for a while instead of filling it as we waited to see what God was up to.

That prescription slip still lies in a keepsake box, never filled, for Jesus completed healed our baby girl that night. It never returned.

Over forty years later, epilepsy is still gone. God had combined His Word and Spirit to powerfully alter our lives once again.

Bible Roulette

The Bible was not given to increase our knowledge. It was given to change our lives. —DWIGHT MOODY

Some might object to my randomly opening my Bible to read a passage and expecting God to speak specifically to me. Over time I did learn other important ways to approach God's Word like studying a text in context to learn its original intent. I also learned much from skilled teachers and pastors. Reading through the entire Bible annually using *The One Year Bible* and its study guide also made a great impact.

While I realize that the Bible isn't to be used like a Magic 8-Ball to get instant answers, God still often highlights a few words in a passage to powerfully impact me. It most often comes when I'm doing my daily reading or when a scripture comes to mind.

It's great to know that God isn't limited in the ways that He speaks. He loves our childlike hunger to hear from Him. I'm glad we don't have to do everything the right way to experience Him.

The Bible is alive, it speaks to me; it has feet, it runs after me; it has hands, it lays hold of me. —MARTIN LUTHER

Throughout my lifetime, the Spirit residing in me makes the Word come alive as God speaks to me through His Word. I hope that you won't skip over the scriptures in these pages but that you savor them and allow them to run after you and take hold of you.

The Bible continues to be my guidebook, so life-changing that I read each day. While it isn't always easy to understand, there is so much I *do* understand that makes a difference.

"It's not the things I don't understand that trouble me in the Bible, but the things that I do understand." —MARK TWAIN

My High Calling: To Be a Mother

With four young kids you could find me on a typical day doing endless chores with a baby perched on my hip, a toddler hanging on my leg as I watched two little boys chase each other around the house. My single goal for this season was to sleep in until 9 a.m. just one morning.

There were days it was easier to let the kids take charge and call the shots. Mothering seemed to take every ounce of energy I could muster, especially when they were little tots and needed us for literally everything. I had felt quite confident out in the work world, but I felt ill-equipped in this new 24-hour a day unpaid job. As soon as I conquered one challenge, another seemed to arise in the land of never enough—never enough energy, enough rest, enough finances, enough time.

We didn't want to get stuck in the hectic yet popular children rule mode where children run the house. We wanted to be the parents, guiding and equipping our kids to be strong in the basics: respecting others, honoring authority, working together, being kind, caring for each other, saying please and thank you. This was a big job.

I was shocked one day as I heard *thank you* consistently coming out of little Damon's mouth. Could it be that all those seemingly futile reminders cumulatively added up until it clicked. I was encouraged not to give up training.

Sometimes days seemed to drag by, but little did we realize how the years would fly by and our children would be grown and leaving us with an empty nest. In the meantime, we discovered that being in a family is a great place to learn from each other. I'm glad I made the effort to jot down stories of how our kids taught us these lessons. The years tend to erase these priceless gems from our memories.

A favorite is when Damon, age 5, tagged along on a shopping trip with my niece. We were busy with girl talk and had to keep telling our little boy to hurry up as he shuffled along three feet behind us. I finally stopped, "Damon, why are you walking behind us?"

He explained, "The Bible says, 'The first will be last, and the last will be first.' I want to be first."

I slowed my walk and smiled at our precious son. That evening I tucked the story away in my journal along with an observation of how this was a great picture of how our heavenly Father loves it when His kids try to walk out His commands the best we know how. These growing up memories that I managed to write down are now priceless, recorded for their children and their children's children.

In God's eyes being a parent is one of the highest callings in life as we learn to create an environment where our children are loved, nourished, taught, and encouraged. One of my favorite plaques reads, "If Momma ain't happy, ain't nobody happy." Slowly I learned that we moms often set the tone for our family. I wasn't aware at the time how important the role of a good mother was.

In the working world around me, few held the role of mom in high esteem. This is part of God's great reversal as He most values roles that the world devalues. The important work of being a parent is repeated day after day, and over time brings God great glory.

At the end of a typical busy day with supper to make, dishes piled in the sink, and all the kids to get into bed (and then to keep them there), I often wasn't feeling the glory. Yet in our weakness, He is strong and loves to equip us parents when we stop and ask for help.

Molding the lives of our children growing up has been my most fulfilling purpose, my hardest task, and my greatest joy.

Keeping the Fire Burning

Keeping our sparks of love alive for my hubby during this child-rearing season also required intentional focus. We longed for more intimacy with each other. On that day eons away when our children would go off to live their own lives, we both wanted to be sitting at the table looking at our best friend and not staring at a stranger. So we asked God for ways to stay close to each other.

Over the years, we tried many different ways to connect; most of them usually lasted only a short season. We purposely carved out some alone time to converse without the kids each evening. Weekly we went on date nights. We made it a point to kiss each other once a day whether or not we felt like it (pecks under three seconds don't count.) We prayed together, took a short evening walk, even scheduled a night to be intimate in case it didn't happen spontaneously. Most importantly we made it a habit to communicate and asked each other questions and listened to each other and shared what we were feeling. We weren't aiming for a perfect marriage. We were shooting for an unstoppable close relationship.

Friends I've Never Met

Being a nourishing wife and mother was a job I wanted to do with God, so I had to stay close to Him, and I constantly prayed, "More God, help me experience more of You." He answered when I spent time alone praying and meditating on the Bible. But I wanted to be more than a Christian who knows the Bible from cover to cover. I wanted to personally know the God of the Bible and walk with Him as I went about my day.

A great source on how to practically walk with God came from friends I've never met. Many of my mentors were dead before I was born. These dear friends helped me grow in faith as I read their powerful words in their gift of the books they have written.

Books by authors passionate for God have given me many fresh insights into His mysteries, especially when touched by their stories. I began the habit of reading inspiring books when my kids were young and have continued this steady stream of encouragement throughout a lifetime.

For example, I read the book, *1000 Gifts,* by Ann Voskamp a few years ago and was impacted by her story of gratitude changing our attitude. I read her beautiful story recounting how God had showed her instead of focusing on the personal tragedies that He wanted her to be thankful for the simple gifts of life, so she began jotting down things like

> jam piled high on toast…old men looking for words just perfect…moonlight on pillows…forgiveness of a sista.

1000 gifts later, she shared her book.

Her book inspired me to begin my own gratitude journal of simple things I saw around me each morning for the next year. My entries, though not elegant as hers, were thanksgiving offerings of His gifts:

> our Farmer's Market bursting with life… the sound of rain on the sunroof…bad days that give good information …my man's consistent morning time with God …free popcorn at the Farm Store…my godly mother…growing old with my love.

This journal entitled *3000 Thank You's* is one of my favorite notebooks. I still continue this gratitude habit by writing down at least three things each day. "Lord, give me relentless gratitude each day regardless of what good or bad might come my way."

Rudyard Kipling said, *"Words are the most powerful drug needed by mankind."* Indeed, the words of others, especially those of impactful authors, have often been medicine that God has used to heal my spirit.

Such writers who have unknowingly mentored me at different times include Bill Johnson, Rick Warren, Joyce Meyer, Brené Brown, Donald Miller, Beth Moore, Dan Allender and Graham Cooke. My list of favorites goes on and on.

Thank you, Lord, for the influence of friends I have never met whose great books and stories have helped me know You more intimately.

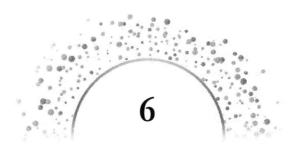

His Faithful Love...

King David repeats the refrain *"His faithful love endures forever"* in all twenty-six verses in Psalm 136 as he shares time when God showed us to help His people. Over 3000 years later I echo his refrain seven more times because the same God is still powerfully showing up for us, His people of our generation.

Taking Care of Business

We got used to bringing life issues to God, big or small as our secular and spiritual worlds melded together and were no longer separate. As a 27-year-old, Don was working hard at his 8-5 job to provide for us, but he longed to create his own business. We prayed together for the right opportunity, and after a few months he found an ideal agri-business for sale.

Now we faced another problem— no money to buy it. The seller was firm on his price as he explained, "It's a real bargain, non-negotiable." Though we felt it was overpriced, we were willing buyers if we could get the money.

First, we began by asking God for the dollars. Then we went to the Small Business Administration (SBA) and applied for a loan. Then we waited for our $40,000 loan to be processed while we trusted God to make a way for us.

After checking daily for an answer for two long months, it finally arrived. Loan denied. So now what? We kept praying for God to intervene while we expected Him to somehow be moving behind the scenes on our behalf. When the seller heard that our loan had been denied, he came down in his price by removing items like a box that we didn't need and dropped the unreasonable sum he wanted for the "good will" of existing customers (aka blue sky.) His phone call cut the non-negotiable asking price in half.

During the two months of our waiting on God to provide, we saved $20,000. Where else could we have made twenty-grand in two months?

We recognized who was behind this. At bedtime we knelt before Him together, "Lord, you are incredible. Thank you for this savings. I love the way You were quietly at work on our behalf."

We ended our prayer with "One more thing, would you please show us the money?" More "hurry up and wait" lay ahead. Short of robbing a bank we tried everything we could think of to get that money. The SBA loan looked like our only possible source. Then one night a dear friend, a widow from our church, called Don on the phone, "I feel that God wants me to offer to loan you the cash value from my life insurance policy to launch your business. I don't know what kind of business it is. Honestly, I don't even care. I have faith that you are hearing God, and that is enough for me."

Don hung up the phone, humbly praising the Lord for the generosity of this saint. God was clearly showing us that He has many unseen resources; he was making sure we recognized that He was our true source, our real provider. The next day, the SBA approved our loan.

Now to him who is able to do immeasurably more than all we ask or imagine, according to his power that is at work within us, to him be glory in the church and in Christ Jesus throughout all generations, for ever and ever! Amen. (Ephesians 3:20,21 NIV)

We bought the business, and Don operated Vincent Feeding Systems installing grain bins and Mix-mill systems for the next nine years, providing for our family and also for the families of 21 employees at its peak. Along with the business came countless challenges stretching our faith causing us to do some heavy leaning on God. He continued to always come through.

...His faithful love endures forever. (Psalm 136:1 NLT)

7200-Volt Jolt

One of these business challenges was a matter of life and death. One autumn day Don and his men were setting up an exhibit for the Farm Progress Show, the nation's largest outdoor annual farm event. As the men lifted equipment with a boom crane near a primary electrical line,

Don alerted everyone to be extremely careful around this deadly power line, so all eyes were fixed on the tip of the crane and the line. No-one paid attention to a tiny ¼" tieback cable until it arced and welded onto the electric line, hissing, popping, and flashing.

Don's right hand was resting on the metal trailer frame as 7200 volts of electricity zapped it, melting the rubber off the tires. The electricity jolted through Don's body and slammed him to the ground. As he hit the dirt, his body was frozen stiff and tingling. He painfully rolled over away from the sizzling electrical field. Miraculously he was not killed instantly and was only slightly harmed. The only remaining evidence an hour later were the blackened burn marks on his right hand where the electricity entered his body and the burn marks on the bottom of his left foot where it left.

Surviving 7200 Volts is a story that few men live to tell. Don had recently been a bit bored with church, but that next Sunday he leaned over and whispered, "I am so thankful to be in church today. It sure does feel good being alive." A close brush with death generates gratitude.

...His faithful love endures forever. (Psalm 136:2 NLT)

My Hubby Steps Up

Sometimes God changes us in an instant through a powerful encounter with Him, but more often He changes us over time through a process. In the messy middle our job is to believe Him and keep working as He strengthens our faith and trust. How we wait counts in His eyes.

While Don was wrapped up in getting his new business off the ground, I was getting more wrapped up in pursuing God. I was often frustrated to have to lead the family spiritually, but I tried not to nag my husband nor meddle. I had learned the hard way how futile that was, doing more harm than good. I determined to do the loving and let God do the convicting. I prayed, "Oh God, show Him more of you. Light his fire. You've said that nothing is impossible for You so I'm going to trust you to work in Don. Help me keep loving and honoring him as I wait and trust you to do Your thing."

God had answered such prayers in the past by sending along people with GodStories like Granddad Craig and Brother George. This time He sent a one-armed blacksmith from Dyersburg, TN, to lead a Lay Witness Mission (LWM) weekend at our small Methodist church. A popular movement in the 1970s, these were fun weekends where we gathered for food, fellowship, and fun discussion and were led by a visiting team of

65

10-15 believers. The team were often strangers to each other who had driven long distances at their own expense to share their stories. Hearing these ordinary lay people share how they connected with Jesus in their everyday lives was a brand-new experience for us with great impact.

The blacksmith stayed the weekend at our house, and Don immediately bonded with this ordinary laborer, a bit rough around the edges but loaded with real-life GodStories such as how Jesus helped him make truck beds. Intrigued, Don told me, "This is not the Jesus I know. I want to know *this* Jesus."

On Saturday night Don joined many others as he bent his knees in surrender to serve the God of the blacksmith. Don handed the reins of his life over to Jesus whom he knew as savior and was now proclaiming as Lord. Don stepped up to lead our family.

Eager to share our own GodStories, we traveled with LWM teams the next few years, spurring a time of great growth in us. God continued to give us never-ending stories. One Sunday morning Don shared about the new birth using an illustration of our baby Jenny being born the night before during the LWM.

At the time we thought that we were serving others sacrificially by going on twenty-seven LWMs. Now we see that ones who made the greater sacrifice were our willing parents and siblings who cared for our four small children in our absence. Grandma even had to carry around our baby on a pillow when she broke out with chickenpox while we were gone. Each believer has opportunities to serve the Lord in different ways, and God especially delights in those who serve in those more hidden way show His love.

"Work willingly at whatever you do, as though you were working for the Lord rather than for people." (Colossians 3:23 NLT)

This life-transforming movement was an ongoing part of the rich legacy we received from the little church where Don and I both found Jesus and learned to be servant leaders.

No longer able to keep our stories to ourselves, we gathered with others in a lively small group on Wednesdays at our place. Together we worshipped, prayed, shared stories, and helped each other walk out what Jesus taught. Small groups became our lifeline and a lifelong habit.

Since this time, we have been privileged to experience being part of several local churches. Every single one has made rich unique deposits within us. God loves His big family meeting in local churches, each making their unique contributions.

...His faithful love endures forever. (Psalm 136:**3** NLT)

A House Hunt

Father God taught us a lot about how He works as we kept asking Him for help in solving our everyday problems. Our 100-year-old little brick rental house began to bulge at the seams when we began running the new business from the house and small detached outbuilding we used to house shop equipment. The boys' tiny bedroom became the office, and all four kids slept in the same room which made bedtime quite an ordeal. In the mornings our men planned at the kitchen table next to our baby in her porta-crib.

Soon the equipment outflowed the shop. It was time to head to wide-open spaces. We began asking God for a new location along with money to buy it, "Help, Lord. Show us what you have for us."

We searched and found the ideal spot to build a split-level house on a lush wooded hillside. We asked Don's dad to come see this place and back our loan. He came and wisely vetoed the idea as he pointed out the downsides that we, being young and inexperienced, hadn't seen. Strike one! Then we prayed and picked out another location. We were sure this was God. This time Don's dad said *Yes,* but the bank said *No.* Strike two!

Then we found some acreage in a great location to build a large shop but with a house that was way too small. This time everyone said *Yes,* and we bought it and began building an addition along with a new shop. A home run!

So did we miss hearing God on the other two locations? Not at all. When we found the first option, we assumed this was the answer to our prayer, but it was only the first step. Overcoming the obstacle led us to the next place and then the next until we reached the destination He had planned for us. Again God answered using a process, not a one-time event, as He revealed His plan one step at a time.

...His faithful love endures forever. (Psalm 136:**4** NLT)

Run Over by a Truck

We had far too many close calls with danger, but thankfully God continued to protect us. One weekend we were spending a relaxing afternoon picnicking in the park with friends. We decided to play some tennis, so I made a quick trip home to get rackets. I pulled up our sloped driveway, put our 4x4 pickup truck in park and jumped out, leaving 6-year-old Damon and 3-year-old Jenny inside. I hollered over my shoulder, "I'll just be a minute," as I left the truck running with the door ajar. It was not my smartest minute.

As soon as I was in the house, Damon followed me with Jenny close behind. Scooting out of the pickup, Jenny bumped the shift lever out of park. The truck began to roll backwards, Jenny fell out the door, and the front wheel rolled over her tiny leg as the truck continued down the slope across a busy state highway. Damon was wailing. Jenny was screaming. Through the window I watched with horror as our truck rolled into the ditch and then I nearly fainted when I saw our daughter lying in the driveway.

"No, no! Please, God, No." I pleaded as I flew out the door and scooped her into my arms. All of a sudden I felt God's gift of faith rise up in me to fight. I cried out, "Be healed in Jesus name."

I laid hands on her legs with my authority as a believer to invoke Jesus' healing power. Just as Paul commanded the lame man, *"In the name of Jesus Christ of Nazareth rise up and walk"* (Acts 3:6 NIV) with God's boldness I proclaimed, "I command any broken bones to be re-fused in Jesus' mighty name. As I held her and prayed, she became calm and quit crying. I took her inside and sat her on the kitchen counter to examine her, picking out pebbles pressed into the skin of her leg. Then with Jenny in my arms and Damon in hand, I crossed the highway, recovered our truck which somehow was unscathed, and drove her to the Emergency Room.

By the time we had made the twenty-minute trip, she was laughing and running. The ER doctor examined her and shook his head, "This is incredible! No broken bones, not even any broken skin. Frankly, I wouldn't have believed your story if I weren't looking at the tire marks running across her leg."

God had released His power as I used the authority He has given to each believer. I felt we had partnered together for her escape from harm, and I thanked Him repeatedly, overwhelmed with gratitude. We were reminded what is really important in life, and it isn't playing tennis.

...His faithful love endures forever. (Psalm 136:**5** NLT)

A Basement Plunge

Later that year we were building the new house addition and had a freshly poured concrete basement and rough-framed a bath and bedroom. I had to make a trip to exchange a left-handed bathtub I'd bought for a right-handed one. There's a difference? The open tub plumbing hole in the floor became a big problem.

The sitter who was watching our four kids heard terrifying screams. She and the kids scrambled around the house trying to find our two-year-year. The panicked sitter thought surely those cries couldn't be coming from the unfinished basement, but when she found a flashlight and peered down the dark opening, there she was. Our curious little Christy had wandered into the bathroom and tumbled through the tub hole onto the concrete basement floor.

Now the question was how to rescue her since there were no stairs to the dark basement yet, just a boarded off stairway landing with an 8' drop. Her siblings gathered at the top of the landing. As she whimpered, they reassured her she would be okay while our sitter ran to our shop next door to get some men with a 10' ladder to rescue her. Christy was quite happy to be carried out of the darkness; so were her rescuers when they examined her from head to toe and found she didn't even have a scratch on her.

When Don and I got home, we surveyed the basement to see how she could have survived this fall uninjured. Tufts of her Pamper clung to the metal tie rods still projecting out of the wall. More tufts hung on the nails sticking out of the wooden pallet that broke her fall. The nails, the tie rods, the concrete—any one of those could have meant death. But God's hand was there to catch her.

That night as I rocked my baby girl to sleep, this passage had a dual meaning,

> For He has rescued us from the dominion of darkness and brought us into the kingdom of the Son He loves. (Colossians 1:13 NIV)

I smiled as I saw how He rescued her from darkness and pulled her out into His light, alive, unharmed. I paused again to offer Him thanks. He is a good, good Father.

> ...His faithful love endures forever. (Psalm 136:6 NLT)

But Now I Can See

These incidents continued as our kids grew up, increasing our confidence in God's power. When Jenny was 9, we took her to the eye doctor after she failed her school vision exam. The tests diagnosed her with a major muscle imbalance with a measurement of 5.0 on a scale where normal was 0.5. As her vision worsened, she sometimes experienced blurring and occasional double vision.

We took her to an eye specialist who prescribed a three-month treatment, three days a week of hour-long machine sessions at his office plus an hour of home therapy the other four days. Treatments required fifty-mile round trips and cost $1500, money that we didn't have. He told us that this was our only option and even then it might not work.

So we did the only sensible thing. We called for our church pastor and elders, and they anointed Jenny with oil and prayed.

Is anyone among you sick? Let them call the elders of the church to pray over them and anoint them with oil in the name of the Lord; and the prayer offered in faith will restore the one who is sick, and the Lord will raise him up... (James 5:14, 15 NIV)

We were experiencing how prayer, although not always, often brings supernatural healing, sometimes instantly but more often over a period of time. Confident that continuing to praying makes a difference, we confessed our faith saying, "We believe that she is going to be fine because God is at work inside her with His healing power."

At first Jenny's sight was only a little better, but it slowly kept improving. After three months her test scores had dropped from five to two, and I explained to the specialist it was because the Lord was healing her.

He laughed, "I don't know about that. I'm more scientific minded. I will agree that definitely something has happened. She certainly doesn't need machine therapy. I'll give you exercises to do at home. Now let's get her fitted for eyeglasses. You know she tested nearsighted with 20-30 vision in one eye and 20-40 in the other.

Hesitating, he added, "On second thought, I'd better check her vision again."

After re-running the tests, he shook his head. "20-20 in both eyes. She doesn't need glasses. I think you could skip those home exercises too."

Over 35 years have passed, and Jenny has had no further eye issues and still has worn no glasses as she reached her 50's.

...His faithful love endures forever. (Psalm 136:**7** NLT)

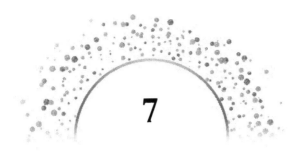

The Power of His Presence

Most people enjoyed hearing our ongoing GodStories about His protection and power during this season. They also enjoyed seeing and hearing about how He was growing the *fruit of the Spirit*: "love, joy, peace, patience, kindness, goodness, faithfulness, gentleness and self-control."

Fewer people were interested in hearing stories about His supernatural *gifts of the Spirit*. I totally get that because I wasn't that interested in the gifts of the Spirit either… *until* I was filled with His Spirit and didn't want to miss out on any gifts He offered.

Godly men and women can and do lovingly serve God and do great things over a lifetime without using these supernatural gifts of the Spirit. Yet these gifts are available to more fully equip us to serve. Jesus valued supernatural ministry and when found out that special gifts were available to impact my world, I was all in.

Fruit and Gifts

Ever open to adventure, I wasn't okay with knowing there was more to experience and not go for it. I boldly asked God to give me all the supernatural gifts I read about: words of wisdom, words of knowledge, faith, healing, miracles, prophecy, discerning of spirits, speaking in tongues, and interpretation of tongues. (I Corinthians 12: 5-11 NIV)

Okay, I wanted them all *except* for the gift of tongues. I wasn't exactly sure what that gift was but it sounded weird to me and rather gross. As a kid in church when we sang the hymn which began, *"O for a thousand tongues to sing my great Redeemer's praise,"* I'd picture a guy who had 1000 tongues all over him all praising God. When I found out the word tongues meant languages, 1000 languages to sing God's praise didn't sound half bad.

When I shared with a new friend how God had filled me with His Spirit, he asked, "Did you receive the gift of tongues?"

"No. What do you mean? I don't know anything about that. Why do you ask?"

He explained, "I was curious because it is often the first supernatural gift people receive when they are first filled with the Spirit. Paul refers to this gift as *"speaking in the tongues of men and angels"* in I Corinthians 13. I've found it to be a very effective prayer language that God's Spirit prays through me." That was news to me.

I read where some churches teach that speaking in tongues is the only evidence of being filled with the Spirit, but that hadn't been my experience. When God filled me with His Spirit, I didn't know anything about tongues. All I knew was that I wanted to hug that little old lady at the store. His love was enough. I wondered if perhaps this prayer language was there dormant inside me, just waiting for me to use it.

Just Do It!

Curious I read more about this gift. One afternoon I was lying on our boys' bunkbed and had just finished reading *Two Sides of a Coin* by Charles and Frances Hunter. I was convinced this gift was powerful and real and a *must* for me. So I just asked, following the three simple steps outlined to release this gift: 1) Pray and ask God to fill you with His Holy Spirit. 2) Focus on God and worshipping Him, not on your voice and the sounds. 3) Begin praising God out loud, speaking out words or syllables which bubble up, but not in English.

Awkwardly, I asked God to fill me afresh with His Spirit. I focused on His greatness and began praising Him with a few sounds that came out. As I pictured His Spirit as a river of living water rising up in me, I began to worship with a few syllables: "Nokia salamente." Then I was distracted as I turned my focus to how odd that phrase was. I repeated the words three or four times before deciding, "Nah, that is just me."

I shrugged my shoulders and said, "Oh well, I tried," then rolled over, pulled up the covers, and took a nice long nap. Back to busy, I soon forgot all about the brief bunk bed utterances.

Two months later Don and I attended a powerful Christian concert. During the last worship song, the leader said, "Close your eyes, life up your hands as a sign of surrender to God. Let's all praise Him as we sing out loud together."

As I closed my eyes and lifted my hands, without thinking, out tumbled the words, "Nokia salamente." Out of mouth Spirit words flowed, powerful words, the tongues of men and angels. *"Oh God, my experience had been real. You did give me the gift of tongues."* What a confirmation. More and more words came as I began worshipping uninhibited, no longer caring what people around me thought as I experienced God's Presence in a fresh way. Now I understood why Paul who wrote a fourth of the New Testament so valued this gift. He writes,

> *...For if I pray in a tongue, my spirit prays, but my mind is unfruitful. So what shall I do? I will pray with my spirit, but I will also pray with my understanding; I will sing with my spirit, but I will also sing with my understanding.... I thank God that I speak in tongues more than any of you....* (I Corinthians. 14:15,18 NIV)

I realized that just as I had a choice of asking God to fill me with His Spirit, the gift of tongues was also optional. I wondered if when the Spirit first filled me I had also received the gift of tongues, but the gift had lain dormant inside me until I believed and chose to give breath to those utterances. It has certainly been an empowering gift in tough times when I am at a loss for words to pray.

A New Boldness

> *But you will receive power when the Holy Spirit comes upon you. And you will be my witnesses, telling people about me everywhere–in Jerusalem, throughout Judea, in Samaria, and to the ends of the earth.* (Acts 1:8 NLT)

Soon Don was also filled with the Spirit and radically changed. As Jesus predicted, when the Holy Spirit came with power, we began telling everyone about God everywhere we went. Don's witness began in our hometown at our kitchen table the very next morning. He had always been very private about his faith but no longer. Boldly he shared all the details of how He had encountered God's presence with his six guys as they leaned in and chimed in with a few stories of their own. Questions flew all morning long, fueled by the Spirit and several pots of steaming coffee. The Spirit of God was changing things up at work.

He was also changing up things with our friends and family. As the months passed we continued sharing about the Holy Spirit with anyone who wanted to hear and quite a few who did not. Many in our extended family were radically transformed by the Holy Spirit. My Mother especially caught on fire with passion for God and stayed that way, radically changing lives at age 93. God doesn't fill us with His Spirit just for our own benefit but also to overflow and change the lives of those around us.

I started making it a habit speaking out words of encouragement to those around me; as I did, I would hear another idea and speak it out. Soon I was realizing that God was speaking prophetic encouragements through me in a very natural way.

The Thunder Rolled

The Spirit continued making us bolder, and Don and I both prayed in tongues daily when alone, but neither of us were bold enough to pray with each other in our prayer language. Then one Sunday afternoon we drove to an amazing home gathering over an hour away to hang out with a group of new friends. They gathered to worship and pray and openly share gifts together. We were beginning to surround ourselves with people more gifted than we were so we could learn.

Heading home, we were both quiet, soaking in His Presence still with us. God was getting ready to etch this day in our memories.

A spring storm rolled in as we arrived home. We fell into bed, peacefully exhausted, enjoying a panoramic view of a raging thunderstorm through our sliding glass door. Sheets of rain pounded the glass, and flashes of lightning illuminated the dark room as the thunder rumbled. We lay there as we pictured His glory in this electrifying display, still awestruck by His display of power and love that afternoon.

Clearing my throat, I mentioned, "My throat is really hurting."

My faith-filled hubby said, "Honey, you don't need to put up with that. I'll pray for you."

"Okay," I replied.

Don prayed, "God, heal Cathy's throat." A few minutes passed.

"How is it?" he asked.

I replied, "It's still there."

Silence. The rain pelted.

He said, "Well, I'll pray in the name of Jesus… In Jesus name, be healed. Now how is it?

"It's still there."

Again, silence. The lightning flashed.

He said, "I know what's missing. God tells us lay hands on the sick and they will recover. Let me lay hands on you and pray."

He laid hands on my throat and prayed again... "Now how is it?"

I sighed and said, "Honey, forget it and go to sleep. I'm okay." But we couldn't sleep. We both lay there, eyes wide open.

Eventually Don asked, "Is God telling you to use your prayer language?"

"Yes"

"Well, that is what I am hearing too. Let's do it, okay? At the count of three. Ready? One...two...three." And the thunder rolled.

As we began praying in tongues together, we heard each other praying with the same language, speaking identical words at the same time as His Spirit flowed through us. Boldly we began to worship God together, switching back-and-forth from speaking words of praise to joyfully singing in the Spirit, singing identical phrases in blended harmony just like the night we heard the angels sing. The music we made together was melodic, flowing out without any effort.

God's presence became stronger and more glorious as waves of love washed over us. It felt as if God opened the ceiling and poured liquid love into the room. We swam in it. We laughed and cried and wrapped our arms around each other, rolling around, praying and singing uninhibitedly as we experienced the pleasure of God. This visitation lasted a long time until we were exhausted and fell peacefully asleep in each other's arms as He held us.

Did the sore throat go away? I have no idea. In God's presence it didn't really matter. I'm guessing Heaven will be like this. In His presence those things that we thought we just had to know won't be important at all.

Don described the night this way, "That encounter with God was better than any s-- I've ever had." Don insisted on leaving that comment in, adding, "No earthly pleasure has ever come close." I agree. God had shown up and overwhelmed us with His liquid love and passionate power. This was our most memorable night on earth, the night we experienced the intimate love of the living Presence of God together.

HS – GPS

Back in the pre-technology era of the 1970's, we actually used folded paper state maps to get around. To find a hotel, we dialed on our home phone (yes, dialed) a familiar hotel chain such as a Super 8 or a Holiday Inn for the richer folks. Sometimes we just picked a motel advertised on a roadside billboard.

With a young family and a fledgling business, we didn't take any family vacations. You can imagine my excitement when Don asked me to go with him on a freight trip to Omaha, NE. We dropped our four little ones off at Grandma's, hooked up the gooseneck trailer, and headed out to pick up a trailer full of equipment and return the next day. We were a little nervous to be headed to a big city but also excited. A fabulous vacation for two!

On Sunday afternoon we made the l-o-n-g drive across the flatlands of Kansas with hopes of arriving by dusk. Neither of us had traveled much and had only stayed in a hotel a handful of times. With no clue where to stay, we asked for help, "Lord, would you find us a really special hotel, one that we can afford, a gift uniquely from you? Show us how to find it. We trust you. Thank you."

The city looked huge as we approached, and we wondered how we would find our special hotel. Then Don and I began using the HS-GPS, the Holy Spirit guidance system. We sensed God impressing on us what turns to make, so we exited the interstate following our HS-GPS and meandered through the city streets until we were in front of a towering luxurious hotel called the Embassy Suites. Don proclaimed, "This is it." We hadn't heard of the name, but it certainly looked special! Parking our truck and trailer in the back of the lot, we took our overnight duffle bag and headed inside.

Wow! We entered a spacious courtyard, surrounded by six stories of rooms with balconies overlooking an atrium in the middle. We marveled at the two glass elevators moving up and down. A lush tropical garden filled the atrium with live trees and bold flowers, calming water fountains, and several lounging areas decked out in a bright Spanish décor. Music from a colorful Mariachi band filled the night air. I stood there gawking while my bold man of God secured us a room. As we whisked to the 5th floor in the glass elevator, I hesitantly asked, "How much is the room?"

He looked surprised. "I don't know. I didn't ask."

I swallowed the lump in my throat as I tried to muster up faith that this was the "special hotel" we had asked for; I wondered if God had caught the phrase "that we can afford." Inside I was thinking, "*What are we doing? This is way too luxurious, too expensive for us.*"

As he turned the key, the door swung open to a plush two-room suite with two huge queen beds (which I'd never seen), a mini kitchen, and a living room with two huge tv's. Wide-eyed, I exclaimed, "Oh no, this is a suite! We can't afford a suite. Honey, we need to find out what this room costs."

I called the front desk, "Excuse me. I see that this is a suite. We only wanted a room."

The desk clerk replied, "All of our rooms are suites."

"Embassy Suites, I get it." I gulped. "Oh, I see. How much is this suite for the night?"

I gulped again. "I see. Thank you" as I slowly hung up the phone as Don asked, "And?"

I replied, "$19.99. You are right, honey. This is a gift. Praise you, God. You are incredible!"

Even for the 1970s, that was an unbelievably low rate. I thought that there must be some mistake and tried to relax and trust my ears. Later we found out that Embassy Suites was running this "Sunday night special" rate to promote its new hotel chain.

As young inexperienced travelers (aka country bumpkins) we still missed out on some of the amazing amenities. That night as we made our way to McDonald's, we walked by the Managers Reception where we saw a crowd of V.I.P.'s laughing and enjoying complimentary cocktails and snacks.

The next morning on the way back to McDonald's, we walked by the room with another crowd enjoying cooked-to-order omelets and fresh baked waffles at the breakfast buffet. Oh, the smell of that bacon, my favorite food, but we knew this would be too expensive for our budget.

On our next freight trip six months later, we joined the V.I.P.'s at the Manager's Reception and the sumptuous breakfast when we discovered both were complimentary, included in our Sunday night rate.

I mused, "How often have we missed the upgrades you have for us, Lord? Sometimes I don't realize they are included and already paid for.

Other times I'm too busy to see or they seem too good to be true. God is continually making upgrades available for His kids, more than we can imagine. I began praying, "Lord, help us leave no upgrades unclaimed."

For years we made annual freight trips to Omaha, always staying on Sunday nights at this hotel to take advantage of His upgrade. We celebrated our 50th wedding anniversary a few years back, staying at the Embassy Suites in Charlotte, NC, to commemorate how God had so powerfully provided upgrades in our 50 years together. After sharing with the desk clerk our GPS story of why the Embassy Suites was special to us, He gave us a free upgrade to a suite on the top floor overlooking the city. We returned from dinner to find a complimentary box of chocolates and a bottle of chilled champagne, and we enjoyed another night of His loving upgrades.

R-I-S-K

This experience helped us get bolder in asking God to show us what He wanted us to do. He was fond of showing up when we were bold enough to ask Him and then step out to test if we were truly hearing Him. John Wimber, founder of the Vineyard Church movement often said, "Faith is spelled r-i-s-k," and as we took courageous baby steps of faith, He sometimes responded quite miraculously.

One afternoon I was driving through a nearby village of Bluffs, thinking, "Yay. Almost home" when I began an inner dialogue with Spirit's voice inside me. I felt impressed to stop at a little grocery store to pick up groceries and add an extra bag. I filled it with milk, bread, and a few other specific items as directed. Getting back into my car, I sighed, "What now, Lord?"

"Start driving." I leaned on His HS-GPS again as I drove through the town, turning as I felt prompted until I heard His voice inside say, "Stop here" in front of a run-down house. "Deliver my provision."

I thought I was hearing God, but I did wonder. There was only one way to find out. R-i-s-k! I took a deep breath, scooped up the groceries, and knocked on the door. An elderly woman answered, and I smiled as I offered the sack to her, "I know this sounds strange, but I have some groceries here, and I felt that God asked me to bring them to you."

She began jumping up and down, as she exclaimed, "Thank you, Jesus. Thank you, Jesus. We have run out of groceries. And the milk…we drank the last of the milk this morning. I have been praying and asking God to send us something to eat."

"Well, the Lord loves you and He hears your cries. Enjoy His provision," I replied as I skipped back to my car. With thankful tears, I said, "Wow, God. You care so much for your people. Thank you. Nothing feels better than partnering with you."

And without faith it is impossible to please God, because anyone who comes to him must believe that he exists and that he rewards those who earnestly seek him. (Hebrews 11:6 NIV)

The Night the Angels Sang

God loved to answer as Don and I prayed "More, God, show us more of You" During this era now referred to as the Charismatic Renewal we often traveled to where we could flame the fire of our passion for Him such as the monthly Full Gospel meetings where believers from all denominations gathered to hear the Word and see and experience the miraculous. We traveled to hear charismatic leaders of the era: Kathryn Kuhlman, Kenneth Copeland, T. L. Osborne, Derek Prince, and Kenneth Hagen. As we saw miracles, God deposited more seeds of faith in us to grow.

One memorable night we were late and hurrying down a long corridor of a hotel in a nearby city to attend one such meeting. As we approached the ballroom, beautiful other-worldly worship filled the air.

Don stopped, "Listen...Do you hear that? I hear angels singing."

We swung open the ballroom doors where 800 people, hands raised in worship, were singing in the Spirit. Rich layered harmonies blended together, filling the room with glorious music that sounded more like 10,000 voices. We joined in. Our eyes could not see what our ears were hearing and our hearts were affirming. We sensed the harmonic blending of angelic voices along with men and women in a glorious crescendo soaring heavenward.

Don and I often refer to it as the memorable night when we heard the angels sing.

Then I looked and heard the voice of many angels, numbering thousands upon thousands, and ten thousand times ten thousand. They encircled the throne and the living creatures and the elders. (Revelations 5:11 NIV)

More Than a Freight Trip

For several years we looked forward to those kidless, carefree, semi-annual freight trips to Omaha. On one such trip, God gave me another gift in my toolbelt to help others. Crossing the Kansas prairies, Don began nodding off at the wheel around 10 pm. Hesitantly he asked me, "Uhhh, honey, do you think you could drive?"

"Let me think about it a moment...Nope."

He persisted, "This trailer pulls really easy. Just drive straight down the interstate, and the trailer will follow. I know you can do it."

While I couldn't picture me dragging a gooseneck trailer behind me on the interstate, I could picture Don falling asleep and the truck in a ditch. So he pulled over, and I nervously took the driver's seat. After all, Don would be there to help me.

I pulled back on the interstate, and he was snoring in three minutes. I was wide-awake, both hands gripping the steering wheel thinking, "I can't believe I am doing this. I have to get my mind off what I am doing before I freak out," so I turned my focus to the ultimate stress reliever, God. After asking for peace and protection, I began to thank Him for who He was and all He was showing us. I told Him how hungry I was for more of Him, more of His love, His fruit, His gifts.

I started softly singing a worship song and began to relax. Don continued snoring, so I sang a little louder. Before long I began to feel a strange warmness all over me, that liquid love that I recognized as the tangible presence of God. I realized that I was no longer singing in English but singing in tongues, pouring out my love to Jesus. I kept driving, singing, and praying in an unknown language for over an hour. The air felt indescribably thick with His Presence.

Then I was startled as vivid moving pictures started playing in my mind. I saw pictures of many of the people I had been praying for such as one of my teen friends dancing and holding a hot potato tossing it from one hand to the other. I felt the Spirit was saying that she would be badly burned by her boyfriend unless she dropped him like a hot potato. Unfortunately she didn't and got badly burned.

For a half hour I saw pictures along with interpretations of what they meant. Don stirred, "What's going on?"

I said, "Just feeling God's presence. Go on back to sleep."

Soon, too soon, we were in Omaha at the Embassy Suites. The next morning, I jotted down everything that I could remember in my journal and still have that page containing forty-three names and pictures I saw. Eventually, I did share most with those people after arriving home, and many were touched with a fresh awareness of God. Other pictures I felt weren't for sharing but to guide me how to pray.

For the rest of the weekend God gave me pictures for complete strangers whom he highlighting from other people around me. I remember the first picture I shared with a tall lanky man dressed in a suit leaning against the wall in the hotel atrium. I was thinking, *"I'll never know if this gift is real if I don't risk. And what if this is from God? If I don't share, I am depriving him of a message straight from God's heart."*

So I approached the man and said, "Excuse me, sir. I know this is strange, but I have a picture that I think may be from God. Could I share it with you?"

He replied, "Absolutely. I am a Christian and am waiting for a Bible study to start."

Whew. He's a believer! I continued, "I saw you dressed in blue jeans and boots with a western belt and a huge buckle. The buckle had four gems- two large red gems and two small ones, one green. However, one of the large red gems had fallen out, and I watched as God held the missing gem in His hand and gently put it back into place."

"Does this make any sense?" I asked.

He began shaking as he explained, "Yes. My wife recently left me. I'm having a hard time caring for our small son and daughter, and I really miss her. I have been crying out to God to bring her back. I feel like He is telling me that He will restore her and that our family will be one again. That encourages me to hold on and trust Him that she'll return."

As I looked into his face I knew that God was loving Him through my words. I felt humbled as I saw how sharing such a simple word from God instantly connected a man with His God.

This began a string of sharing such loving pictures with strangers all weekend. I wasn't sure what was going on but later realized that God was answering my request as gifts of the Spirit bubbled up—prophecy, words of knowledge, and words of wisdom as God helped me see others afresh with His loving eyes. What a rewarding gift of sharing compassionate words from God's heart to people and call out what amazing things He sees in them. No wonder Paul tells us,

> *Let love be your highest goal! But you should also desire the special abilities the Spirit gives–especially the ability to prophesy.*
> (I Corinthians 14:1)

Great Fellowship

The next year we joined a lively church, the Winchester Fellowship led by Brother George. In this local church our passion deepened for both the Bible and the God of the Bible.

During the week we worked and played hard together, even pooling our resources as volunteers to build and run a new Christian school. Don helped construct a gymnasium, and I taught for two years along with seven other teachers.

On Sundays we gathered with around 150 believers who loved to express outrageous worship, something that was quite foreign to us. At first we weren't quite ready to join in this odd yet intriguing adoration of God. Soon we were offering Him praise with lifted hands, clapping and dancing with joy right along with the rest of them.

The church grew rapidly as we shared with those around us about Jesus and His abundant life. Many became believers and were baptized and filled with the Spirit often all in the same day, reminding me of what happened after Peter addressed the crowd on Pentecost:

> *When the people heard this, they were cut to the heart and said to Peter and the other apostles, "Brothers, what shall we do?"*
>
> *Peter replied, "Repent and be baptized, every one of you, in the name of Jesus Christ for the forgiveness of your sins. And you will receive the gift of the Holy Spirit"...Those who accepted his message were baptized, and about three thousand were added to their number that day.* (Acts 2:38-40 NIV)

We spent four amazing years together, and then this incredible season abruptly came to an end. An unresolvable rift developed, coinciding with another major event that would literally move us 45 miles away. Sadly, we were not alone but part of a mass exodus of key leaders who scattered and spread their passion for Jesus, becoming pastors, foreign missionaries, and key leaders elsewhere.

This would not be the last time we saw such a shifting in a local church, but it puzzled us. How could such a vibrant church collapse so quickly? Was the church falling apart because of what people did or didn't do? Perhaps. Or maybe God had equipped us and was sending us out like when the early church was scattered and spread the gospel to other parts of the world. (See Acts 8)

Maybe it was both God and man, a combination I've found to be common. As time passed, the cause didn't really matter. Life is ever changing. The key question for us became not "Why?" but "What next?"

Saying Goodbye

In 1980, Post-It Notes hit the stores, and the term *Internet* was first coined, opening up a whole new world. The volcano which erupted on Mount St Helens that year had little effect upon our family, but our own little world was hit with other eruptions of volcanic proportions.

Don lost his strong patriarch father to a sudden stroke, and we were faced with a decision whether we should close our business and move back to the farm he had inherited across the state. Our business was teetering as interest rates soared to 19%, eating up our profits. Agribusiness was hit hard, and our hog farmer customers bailed out.

We decided to sell out and move back home to our roots and begin farming. We auctioned our house, our shop building, trucks, and equipment and prayed fervently for a good sale so that we could come out even and avoid a major financial hit. That didn't happen. Instead we ended up with a hefty debt load of $195,000 which was quite a blow.

We questioned how God could ever pull us out of this deep hole in our lifetime. Our financial future looked futile. So did the rest of our future. We would leave behind so much we had grown to love: this beloved town, our home, my teaching, our business, employees and customers, our close friends, small group, church, our abundant life. In this place we had lived our dream of walking closely with the Lord. The future would be a time of testing without all this support. Would the dream end?

We tried to be optimistic and upbeat for our kids who were 9, 10, 13, and 15 as we talked about all the new possibilities ahead. But Don and I faced drastic change, debt, and death as we made decisions that would significantly alter our lives.

We cried out, "Oh God, we know you haven't caused our pain, but it is still very real. Use it to mold us and make us like you. Give us fresh hope and confidence, Lord. You have promised to be our strength and source. Help us to trust you in the middle of this move when we find it hard to see your path. Thank you for always being here. We are following, trusting wherever you take us."

When I am afraid, I will put my trust in you. (Psalm 56:3 NLT)

While Don's business and economic loss weighed heavy on him, what weighed even heavier on me was the thought of being separated from our close tribe of friends. As we left town with our few physical belongings, we also carried with us many rich intangible treasures: a passion for God, a strong awareness of the partnership of the Spirit and the Word, and some incredible GodStories. Don and I were thankful that we were going forward together with each other and our family.

In the fertile springtime of our life, God had sowed so many seeds of faith in His love and power in us. Now it would be up to us to have soft hearts for them to grow in the times that still lay ahead.

I wondered as we left our solid support system of thirteen years, "Will our faith stay solid? Will we overcome any troubles ahead? Will we thrive?"

Jesus answered, "Yes, because I'll be going with you." Though the future looked tough, deep within we knew that He would be enough.

Teach these new disciples to obey all the commands I have given you. And be sure of this: I am with you always, even to the end of the age. (Matthew 28:20 NLT)

"Every day God invites us on the same kind of adventure. It's not a trip where He sends us a rigid itinerary, He simply invites us. God asks what it is He's made us to love, what it is that captures our attention, what feeds that deep indescribable need of our souls to experience the richness of the world He made. And then, leaning over us, He whispers, "Let's go do that together."

— Bob Goff

Summer Sun

Sunny with Clouds

Moses went through three distinct seasons in his life. For forty years he lived in a palace treated as a son by an Egyptian Pharaoh. The next forty years he spent hidden in the desert tending sheep. His final forty years he fulfilled his calling to lead God's people to freedom to the promised land. Each season was unique and important in its own way.

In our lives, embracing each season and discovering its reason has been part of the joy of living. Whenever we sought Him, He revealed more of His character and His ways. He also gave us wisdom as He showed us what He'd been up to in our lives and helped us see the past through His perspective.

Our summer season of life began in an ideal location in the sun to hang out and have fun as our children grew into adults. This season brought a boatload of activity, hard work, and a heavy dose of life's typical mix of good and evil, victory and failure, faith and doubt. His word rang true: *"Yet God has made everything beautiful for its own time. "* (Ecclesiastes 3:11 NIV)

In the springtime of our life God boldly demonstrated His power. In the summertime, His Presence looked much different. While He still peppered this time with some extraordinary stories, God shifted our focus to learning how to love others in a very practical way. He hid the miraculous in among the commonplace for us to find and enjoy.

Late in the summer season some heavy storm clouds moved in as we began to drift. We took detours looking for more pleasure in our lives. Sometimes we humans choose to learn the hard way. As calamity hit again, it took us a while to get our bearings and embrace the truth that the path to a rich and satisfying life always leads back to Jesus, its one and only author.

...My purpose is to give them a rich and satisfying life. —Jesus (John 10:10 NLT)

8

Fun in the Sun

Moving back to our roots in Pike County when I was 37 marked the change of springtime into our summer. While we anticipated a hot dry spell, we set our sights on trusting God and slowing down to enjoy the pace of country living. Well, that was the plan.

> The mind of man plans his way, But the LORD directs his steps.
> (Proverbs 16:9 NASV)

We Got 'Er Done

When Don left the house in the mornings, he was whistling again. He reveled in being back farming with his brothers. Farming was not just a job but a lifestyle that spilled over into every corner of our family's existence. Our sons loved helping their dad in the fields with the down-to-earth rhythm of sowing and reaping. Raising hogs was more of a chore but held valuable lessons too.

The boys worked long hours and gleaned invaluable hands-on experience operating and fixing farm machinery, overhauling engines, and learning to repair things sometimes with simple tools like duct tape, bailing wire, and prayer. Our younger daughters worked hard also with chores, canning and tanning, adding building projects and summer jobs as they grew older. There was plenty of work to do. Together we all "got 'er done" and had fun doing it.

Work became a fulfilling fun part of normal life for each of us. God gave me a challenging new job of creating a new junior/senior high unit for a Christian school in Hannibal, MO. I've always preferred start-ups, organizing and creating systems far more than maintaining them. If I were a runner which I'm most definitely not, I'd be a sprinter, not a marathoner. Getting this school up and running stretched me. I had little prior experience, a good thing which led me to rely heavily on hearing the Lord's instruction and freed me to implement innovative ideas. It also gave me confidence to boldly take on several jobs later in life with little concern about lack of credentials.

For two years, I taught and thrived, and on most days cheerfully enjoyed the fifty-mile round trip drive to school, towing along our four kids. I loved those invigorating years shaping the lives of my students many of whom still connect with me on Facebook.

God is working in you, giving you the desire and the power to do what pleases him. (Philippians 2:13 NLT)

You've Got to be Kidding

We cruised along enjoying life for a couple of years when life changed abruptly again. Don's brother Paul died from a massive heart attack at age 47. While processing this loss, we were given notice that we needed to vacate our rental house in three months. Finding a house close to our farm seemed impossible.

But Don had a plan. He never was short on dreams, and this was a big one. When he and our boys were feverishly working on a building project during their winter school break, I assumed they were building a machinery shed. About a month into the project, we were finishing lunch when I asked, "Where are you building?"

Don kept eating, staring at his plate. Finally he broke the silence with, "Inside the river levee." (This levee was a 14' tall clay and sand barrier running parallel along the mighty Mississippi.)

Don took another bite.

I frowned, "A machine shed inside the river levee? What will happen when it floods?"

He replied, "Actually we're not building a shed. We're building our new house."

My eyes widened, and my nostrils flared as I blurted out, "You've got to be kidding me!"

"Nope, we finished setting the poles today." Then he pulled out his detailed drawings to show me how neat it was going to be to live in a cabin. Don was excited. Our kids were ecstatic. And me? Not so much. Shocked, I just sat there, speechless. My heart was racing. As I silently continued glaring, the guys quickly finished lunch and excused themselves as they rushed out the door.

I began to spew out my thoughts, "A river cabin? We are going to live in a river cabin?" I saw flashbacks of scenes when I was a little girl on weekend getaways in our primitive family river cabin with no electricity, bathroom, or running water. Being a peacekeeper who desired peace at all costs, I wasn't in a habit of yelling at my husband, so I ranted and raved to my Father...in Heaven, "Why me, Lord? Live in a cabin? Why didn't Don talk it over with me first? I guess my opinion doesn't matter."

I knew God was listening as I spilled it all out. When I wound down a few hours later, I finally got still enough to listen to his gentle reminder that this venture was not all about me. I could picture Don's face lighting up when he showed me his building plans. Somewhere deep inside him, this undomesticated adventure was important in his search for more. He was experiencing a God-given yearning to explore the unconventional, to even risk danger. My man is especially drawn to this kind of challenge. Our kids were right there with their dad, eagerly looking forward to this call to live in the wild. I alone had trouble catching the vision.

I wrestled with God for the rest of the day as I asked for help, tears streaming down my cheeks, "Can I do this?"

I told myself, "Breathe... Deep breaths, Cathy" then continued, "Lord, I suppose it would be a fun place for our teens to finish growing up. But you know I'm not that crazy about wild adventures...or hard physical labor...or the outdoors. You know how I enjoy comfort. This does not look comfortable."

Granted, it would have been much better if Don and I had agreed on this move before he began to build, but we would deal with that issue later. The question at hand was whether I was willing to follow my man and his dream. I felt God was asking me to trust, "Trust me. Trust Don. Come alongside him and embrace this dream together." I wanted to be a Proverbs 31 woman:

> *Her husband can trust her, and she will greatly enrich his life.*
> (Proverb 31:11 NLT)

So at the end of the day, I surrendered, "Lord, thank you for hearing me out. Thank you that I can trust you to help me learn to lay down what I want. I can do this with your help. Besides, what choice do I have? The poles are already set." As I finished venting and gave up control, peace came. Hopefully, I would be able to tap into joy along the way.

> *Don't worry about anything; instead, pray about everything. Tell God what you need and thank him for all he has done. Then you will experience God's peace, which exceeds anything we can understand. His peace will guard your hearts and minds as you live in Christ Jesus.* (Philippians 4:6-7 NLT)

The following week Don took me to the cabin to show me his progress. The stairway wasn't built yet, so I stood at the bottom of the handmade 14' wooden ladder leading to the deck platform, shaking my head as I whimpered, "I don't think I can do this."

Don reached out his hand to me to steady my climb and said softly, "Cathy, you can do it. I'll help you."

At the top, he walked me through the framed rooms, excitedly detailing his plan. The large grin on his face was in sharp contrast to the grimace on mine as I tried to imagine how it would be to actually raise a family here.

At dusk we sat on the edge of the deck, dangling our feet off the ledge while the sun went down. Once again Don, grinning from ear to ear, reached for my hand to hold as he excitedly talked about his plans for our future. I sensed God's favor on this move and pictured my heavenly Father reaching out his hand to me whispering, "Cathy, you can do it. I will help you."

Letting out a long sigh, my words to Don tumbled out hesitantly, "I can do this."

Then a pack of coyotes began howling on the island straight across the river, and I added, "Or not."

Mississippi River Livers

> *So God created mankind in his own image, in the image of God he created them; male and female he created them.* (Genesis 1:27 NIV)

I love how Our Creator made us in His image and placed in each of us different gifts of His creativity for us to discover. My Don, a creative builder, erected this amazing two-story A-frame cabin with the help of our two teenage sons and Carpenter Bob from church. Sitting atop 14' poles, it overlooked the river that stretched 1/8-mile-wide at the cabin site.

Every few years flood waters filled the chute from our cabin to the levee, leaving it stranded in two to six feet deep water for weeks. We normally parked our vehicles underneath the cabin, but in flood season we took boats to the levee 100 yards away to reach our lineup of vehicles. Then we zoomed up the dusty gravel road ten miles into the nearest town of Hull (population ~500). A shopping trip required driving 25 miles to Hannibal or 45 miles to Quincy. In Pike County we called it *living in the sticks*.

Our rustic cabin was quaint and comfy with a tin roof, walls of barn siding, a toasty potbelly wood-burning stove, and Builder Don's custom-designed elevator for hauling firewood etc. onto the deck. Our new home also had many creature comforts: four bedrooms, two baths, central air/heat, a huge outdoor deck and walkway surrounding the cabin.

That March move-in day is etched in my memory. Spring rains and melted snow swelled the river, and we hurried to get moved in before the water covered the road and left our cabin only accessible by boat. Twenty-five family and church friends spent the day moving us in. They made countless trips up the two flights of steps to unload our possessions from large grain trucks and to hoist our piano onto the deck with a tractor with a front-end loader. We constantly kept an eye on the rising water and prayed that we'd get moved in before the elevated road disappeared.

Late in the afternoon Don drove our two-ton truck through muddy waters covering both the running boards and the road underneath. The remaining moving crew departed by Jon boat through water four feet deep and rising.

Day One of our living on the river drew to a close with our cabin an island surrounded by water. I believe that made us official "river livers." We gathered our little family tribe and thanked God for the adventure ahead.

During the first spring, the flood season was unusually looonnnggg. Don and the kids considered the boating in and out every morning and evening part of the high adventure. Three months passed before the floodwaters receded and the mud roads firmed up enough to drive in. I'll have to admit that my brain was churning, "Who is this man I married? A modern-day Robinson Crusoe? What have I gotten myself into? I wonder if Noah's wife fully supported Noah's dream during that whole episode?"

Living in Paradise

Don and the kids considered river living something close to living in paradise, soaking in the sun for the next seven years. Summers brought skiing, tubing, floating, boating, sand volleyball, basketball games, cookouts, parties, trips to the sandbar, and hanging out with friends. This momma enjoyed entertaining, cooking, boating, and having fun with the family and developing new interests and skills. I felt most fulfilled as I served and made a difference in the lives of those around me.

> *God wired the universe so that happiness does not come from status, salary, sex, or success. Happiness comes from service. God designed us to be happiest when we are giving our life away.*
> —RICK WARREN

Looking back, I smile as I realize what a valuable role I had in this priceless season as mom and wife at the heart of our family. Our little tribe of six was my main focus as I worked to help make a nourishing environment where our kids could mature into healthy adults. Together we all created an amazing river place for our friends and family to gather for good food, great fellowship, and a boatload of fun. It was the "happening" place to be.

If Don and our kids were describing this sweet season, tales would abound of hunting, fishing, farming, boating, and friends. I share a little different story, more like being a fish out of water. Both versions are true but told through our unique perspectives. God's version would be entirely different than any of ours.

He is still revealing all that was really happening those seven years in the sun. He doesn't hide the mysteries of life to keep them from us but rather so that He can reveal them to us and bring us pleasure. One hidden surprise in our river days was how much enjoyment we found in just relaxing as we laughed and lived life with a big tribe of friends.

Our unique location also presented a few challenges. When the first hard freeze hit during high waters, it dawned on us that to get the kids to the school bus we would have to chop through the ice in front of the boat. To avoid getting marooned, Don and the kids built a primitive Indiana Jones suspension bridge through the trees to get to the levee.

We were glad when Shawn turned sixteen and helped haul everyone to endless activities. It got easier when they all could drive, although that meant maintaining a fleet of four boats, four cars and a pickup. Flat tires were common along the ten-mile stretch of gravel road. Pre-cell phone survival meant that this momma and her kiddos learned how to change their own flat tires and how to lift up simple prayers like *Help, Lord.*

The Great Outdoors

River living was heavenly for our little tribe of outdoorsmen. Heavenly for five out of six is not so bad. You couldn't call me an outdoorsman because this momma's definition of "outdoors" was "what you have to go through to get from one indoors to another." I was often physically challenged, especially during the flood season when the cabin stood in water. Tears always flowed on the first day when the spring floods came, and Don mysteriously disappeared the entire day farming, confident that this too shall pass. He knew that in a day or two God would have me peaceful and ready to press on.

Sometimes I had good reason to cry such as the evening when I arrived at the cabin in flood season in the middle of a torrential thunderstorm. I popped over the levee hoping to get some help with my carload of groceries, but the only help in sight was a Jon boat tied up to the shore. I shouted for help, but without a phone, no-one heard me, so I loaded the eight sacks into the boat and headed to the cabin. I totally fell apart. So did the paper bags, spilling groceries all over the boat. I climbed the stairs and opened the door, drenched as a drowned rat. All the family rallied around, eager to make it all better.

When my head hit the pillow that night, I had recovered, reaffirming, "Yes, I can do this with your help, Lord." This was a season to *'learn to be content whatever the circumstances."* (Philippians 4:11) We were the lone family living year-round inside the river banks for miles and miles. I think I was the only one in the family that really understood *why* we were the only ones.

Though these years are packed with sunny memories, I also recall how challenging it was for me. Sometimes I felt like a contestant on "Survivor." As a farm wife living in a river cabin caring for a family of six and teaching school full-time, there was always work to be done. This rustic location highlighted my weaknesses which led me to the strength and grace of God. I spent a lot of time with Him, thanking Him for His amazing goodness, pouring out my feelings and needs, reading His Word, and trying to actually live out what it said. Little by little, He began to change me.

As I gained trust, I grew to embrace adventure and to enjoy the exhilaration of risking and taking chances. This was the season that I determined to go with gusto for a life fully lived. River living would prove to be an intense seven-year hands-on course in "His Strength in Our Weakness" as our ever-present God provided basic needs and more when we cried out for help.

My grace is all you need. My power works best in weakness. So now I am glad to boast about my weaknesses, so that the power of Christ can work through me. (2 Corinthians 12:9 NLT)

Lessons from a Boat

Jesus enjoyed boat people like Peter, James, and John. He taught them a lot from boats, revealing the hidden fish in the lake, rescuing them in trouble, bringing calm in the storm, and giving Peter the boldness to step out in faith as he walked on water.

Jesus taught us a few things from boats too. We kept four well-used vessels to navigate our watery world: a Jon boat and canoe for shuttling us across the flood waters, a pontoon for leisurely group rides and sunset dinners, and a speed boat that zipped up and down the river full of kids, usually with a skier in tow.

Revealing the Hidden

As Don and I took a short weekend trip, Shawn and Damon convinced us to let them stay home alone since they were now responsible teenagers. They spent most of the weekend in the boats and eventually engaged in a little horseplay as boys will do. Full speed ahead, they tried to drench each other with a hefty spray of water as they saw how close they could get without hitting the other's boat.

Then the unthinkable happened. Their boats collided, and the two horrified boys watched as the 10 HP motor detached from the Jon boat and sank into the muddy river. Fun turned to toil as the boys drug the 15' deep river bottom for hours, but the motor was nowhere to be found.

When we returned home and they told us their story, they got a few choice words from us, but then we all prayed together, "Thank you, Lord, it is only a motor at the bottom of the river, not one of our sons. Lord, we really need that motor. Help us find it." We searched again but no motor was appeared.

Three years later, our family was relaxing on the deck when some fishermen in a boat began diving for clams in the front of the cabin. On a whim we offered them $50 to dive for thirty minutes in search of the motor. The divers said, "Sure."

As our sons pointed out the approximate location of the sunken treasure, I shook my head, me of little faith, and chuckled, "No way!" Twenty-five minutes later a diver came up out of the water with the motor dangling from his rope. It had been hidden in tangled tree branches on the bottom of the river. Our boys immediately took the motor to the shop, oiled it to avoid rusting as it hit the air, then tinkered until it was purring. Over thirty years later that engine is still running. Long after we had given up, God had answered as He revealed that which was hidden.

Rescuing in Trouble

Countless boat rescue stories have been omitted such as when Shawn tipped over the canoe and his calculus book floated down the river. Then there was the time when 8-year-old Christy lost her oars on her first solo boat trip to the cabin after school. She arrived unharmed. (And no, Christy, you didn't almost die!)

My most vivid boat rescue memory involved my hobby of making wedding cakes for family and friends. To transport cakes in the trunk of my car to the wedding hall in mint condition had always been a tall order, but now I first had to boat the cake across 6' deep floodwaters to my waiting car, a Herculean feat for me.

I had spent ten hours creating an elaborate three-tiered wedding cake. When it was time to transport it, I was not surprised to find that no-one was around to help. So I slowly carried each of the decorated tiers down two flights of stairs and into the Jon boat.

I let out a sigh of relief when that beautiful 14" bottom cake tier weighing eight pounds was sitting secure on the front deck. Being very careful not to rock the boat, I inched my way back to the driver's seat and turned the key, thankful when the motor began purring.

My eyes locked on the cake as I shifted into reverse. Within seconds I heard a loud thud as my neck suddenly jerked backwards. I didn't even need to turn around to know that I had backed smack dab into a huge tree sticking out of the water.

I gasped as the 14" cake tier began to slide off the deck in slow motion and teeter precariously as it hung over the edge. I pictured the bride and groom at the wedding reception, knife in hand, with no cake.

"Oh God, please help me." I tiptoeing to the front of the boat and slid the cake securely back onto the deck.

"Whew! Thank you, Lord. Saved again."

The next night at the reception, still in awe, I could hardly take my eyes off this most memorable wedding cake that God had saved for the celebration.

The righteous cry and the Lord delivers them out of all their troubles. (Psalm 34:17)

River Liver Hospitality

People enjoyed coming down to the river to relax on weekends. Friends felt free to drop by our cabin anytime as did our big extended family who had summer cabins nearby. I never was asked to feed 5000, but a weekend meal for the six of us could quickly turn into feast for twenty. I enjoyed cooking and got used to spontaneously feeding a large crew. God was training us how to have servant hearts, to offer hospitality, and spend our time loving people. He was showing us how wasting time with people isn't really wasting time.

Offer hospitality to one another without grumbling. Each of you should use whatever gift you have received to serve others, as faithful stewards of God's grace in its various forms. (1 Peter 4:9,10 NIV)

While I enjoyed both working and napping, I wasn't much of a player like the rest of my family. I found it hard to relax and enjoy life as a human being, preferring to be a busy human doing. Most people need no lessons on learning to play, but I did. The river was a veritable playground and an ideal place to learn. The kids enjoyed summers so much that we only took two family vacations because they were having too much "stay-cation" fun to want to go anywhere else.

Don's favorite t-shirt read "River Liver", a status we all enjoyed, especially on Sunday evenings when the weekend campers packed their gear, pulled out their boats, and headed home to get ready for the work week. We just climbed the stairs and walked into the cabin. Home Sweet Home.

Our Christmas Message

Wintertime made visiting our remote cabin difficult, so few vehicles would venture down our mile-long lane, especially when the snow fell. Our first river Christmas season we were so eager to celebrate by lighting up the cabin. The visitors arriving by car would be few, so we got the bright idea to proclaim the Christmas message to the boat crews who spent weeks at a time working on the barges pushing heavy cargo up and down the river. Together our family created an elaborate lit 4'x6' banner and hung it facing the river: "Wise Men Still Seek Him." It was a Hallmark moment.

Two days later the river froze over, and all barge traffic ceased until the spring thaw. The sign was one of those "risk and fail" ideas that seemed like such a good idea at the time. Maybe all the Christmas hoopla wasn't that important. That year our family declared that *Jesus is the reason for the season,* not with a sign but with reaching out and loving those around us. But isn't that the only way to effectively communicate His message?

9

Adrift

Sunny days were plentiful during our first few years of river living for six happy campers busily working and playing. After completing the two-year school start-up, I began teaching high school English and Chorus at West Pike, where Don and I had gone to high school, just ten miles away. Our family was "all-in" as our kids began public school, quite a change from their six foundational years in Christian schools. The kids were constantly running up and down on the gravel road to a new bevy of activities. We soon got "too-busy," unaware that "too-busy" would soon get us.

Storm clouds were gathering on the horizon, but we paid little attention. The storm first hit the place where our hearts were deeply vested, the church. For four years we had led and served in two churches, helping them implement small groups, leading worship, showing up whenever the doors were open. When leadership issues came up that we couldn't resolve, we chose to move on.

Wounds from a bad church experience and unresolved church issues often go deep causing some to give up on the organized church. We teetered ourselves. Alienating ourselves from other believers proved costly. We took our concerns to God and asked Him to give us a tender heart of forgiveness and wisdom on where and how to connect with His people. In the process, he taught us not to idolize leaders nor to expect perfection. We all fall short, and I do mean *we*. Yet God delights in His church, His imperfect people, who gather in different locations to worship and serve Him in different ways. He wanted us to delight in them too.

Starting A Church

The week after we had stopped attending our regular church, a friend called to ask where we were going to worship the following Sunday. I replied, "Probably with our own kids in the living room."

"Could our family join you?

"I suppose so." The word spread, and by the next Sunday our living room was full of people who showed up to worship God with us. In a couple of weeks, there were twenty of us meeting on Sundays, and a new church had sprung up. We had no intentions of starting a church. We knew nothing about running one and had access to few resources about how to lead a church.

Though shaky about leading, we kept on meeting, and new people kept joining us. Before we knew it, we were a local church, lively and full of life. Within a year, around ninety people gathered for Sunday morning worship and small groups during the week. We enjoyed doing life together as we learned to love God and each other. It was a lot of work with very few evenings that weren't full of connecting with people.

Pastoring a church was not as easy as it looked. Being in charge turned out to be much harder than having great suggestions as a leader. Now we understood why pastors shouldn't be put on a pedestal. It's too easy to fall off. I hardly noticed how much Don was struggling with this new role because I was thriving. Once again, we were experiencing the same life but living a different story.

Don was called to be a pastor, not a preacher. While Don enjoyed gathering and connecting with people, he did not relish leading endless meetings and making countless crucial decisions. His hardest task was spending long hours preparing a weekly sermon. We had gifted leaders like my brother, a gifted teacher, who could have lifted his load. I could have helped also had we not believed that women should not pastor or preach. In this era, having a team co-lead a church to collectively use our different gifts wasn't that familiar to us. Now we see things clearer, but we had 20/20 vision only in hindsight.

Don had a lot on his mind in addition to running a new church. In a few years' span, he had closed his business, sold our home and property, amassed a $195,000 debt load, lost his father and brother, and built the cabin home. Now he was running a farm, fathering four busy teens, and pastoring a church. No wonder he was stressed. I tried to ignore his growing fatigue as I hoped he would snap out of it. I mean, weren't we really enjoying doing church?

I Quit!

After a year of juggling too much, Don had little hope of catching up. One morning he sat with his head heavy in his hands, "Cathy, I just can't do it any longer." That Sunday he announced to our congregation that he was stepping down as pastor. The church quickly dissolved, and our people joined other communities of believers.

No one was more shocked than I was. Crushed, I had no idea what had just happened. I loved what we were doing. I felt we had failed people big time and struggled to get my bearings. I cried out to God for answers to questions as I wondered, "Was pastoring this church only *my* dream? Was Don just joining me like when I joined him in *his* dream of building the cabin?"

God seemed silent. We began walking with a limp and not nearly as wholeheartedly or as confidently as before. We had thought we knew so much. We were so focused on teaching just the right message when maybe we had should have just relaxed and figured out how to just live out the message together.

> *Teacher, which is the greatest commandment in the Law?" Jesus replied: 'Love the Lord your God with all your heart and with all your soul and with all your mind.' This is the first and greatest commandment. And the second is like it: 'Love your neighbor as yourself.* (Matthew 22:36-39 NIV)

On weekends we began visiting different area churches, most of which were 45 minutes away. Then we began skipping church some Sundays and going out on the river. It was tempting to withdraw and hide our hurt, shame, and sense of failure, but we were making a big mistake. The times when we are hurting and feeling like a failure is when we need others the most. That is why God urges us to stay connected.

> *Let us think of ways to motivate one another to acts of love and good works. And let us not neglect our meeting together, as some people do, but encourage one another, especially now that the day of his return is drawing near.* (Hebrews 10:24-25 NLT)

Free choice is a costly gift from God to humans, free choice to live our lives with or without His help, with or without His people. We can choose our actions, but we can't choose our consequences. We would pay a big price when we chose to go it alone without the support of the church. Little did we know what a spiritual drought was coming as we began to lose our first love.

Slammed

While I battled the jolt of our church break-up, Don was battling to keep our farm. The economy continued plummeting. We were in the middle of the Farm Crisis of the 1980s, but without instant internet news and analysis, we weren't that aware of being caught up in it. Farmers typically depended on ongoing loans for machinery and operating expenses until harvest. Many faced ruin as farm debt load doubled. When annual interest soared to 19%, we knew that we were in trouble.

Do the math. On our $195,000 business debt load we paid interest of $37,000 each year. There was not enough money left to pay expenses. And live on. As much as my hard-working husband loved farming, we could not turn a profit. We simply had gotten into farming at the wrong time.

In the third year of farming, we sold our farm to pay off the debt. Thank God, Don found a good job at Pet, Inc. as a maintenance supervisor where he enjoyed solving problems and keeping machinery operating.

Selling the farm was just one more blow to Don's fragile state. As he approached forty, he struggled through an intense wrestling time of exploring his inner thoughts and emotions. I remember the night that Don shared, "All my life I have tried to do what other people wanted me to do. First, I tried to please my parents, and then I tried to please your parents. I'm always trying to please you and am constantly thinking about how my actions affect you and the kids. When is it my time? When do I get to do what I want to do?"

My "*happily ever after*" melted with that question. What had happened to my husband who loved every person and his dog? Who was this discouraged, unhappy man I was living with? I loved him and didn't want him to live in quiet desperation and come to the end of his life regretting that he had never fully lived. I wondered if we would make it through this together.

His Mid-Life Crisis

When I confided in a friend about our shaky relationship, she said, "Don's coming up on age 40 and just might be going through a midlife crisis.

I responded, "A what?" Then I devoured all I could find on the subject which was not much in this pre-Google era. I read about this stressful period of evaluation often triggered by a realization of major loss of some sort. Well, Don definitely had some of that going on.

I learned that this "midlife unraveling" (as Brené Brown calls to it) is most likely to hit us as we near the age of forty when our body and mind start hinting that we may not still be on the upward climb. We begin comparing where we are in life to where we expected to be by now. Those who seem to "have it made" often feel discontent asking, "What is life all about? Has my life mattered? What is my purpose? What do I do with the rest of my life?" Those caught in this struggle often try to reclaim lost youth by adding something new—a new sports car, new companion, new lifestyle, or new adventures in their attempt to escape the present or search for an identity that fits. This can go on for years.

Don was facing such discontent. Although he did enjoy his job, he did not enjoy working long weeks or working for someone else after being his own boss for so many years. On weekends he just wanted to take a break and began drifting away from church. Tired and disillusioned, he shared, "I still love God but I'm not so sure about His people." We were headed for trouble.

Then Don began checking out what else was available, what the world had to offer. He began stopping by a bar in Hannibal on his way home for a few drinks with his buddies. One night he said, "I feel more camaraderie with friends at the bar than with people from church. These guys are real and vulnerable."

I had to ask myself, "Is that true? This shouldn't be."

Yet as Don pulled away, God came close to woo him. On an overnight visit with my brother and his wife near Kansas City, Don reluctantly agreed to go along to their little church on Sunday morning. He planted himself on the back row and sat there with his arms folded in protest. After the sermon their guest speaker did something my brother said he had never seen before in that church. The speaker walked to the back row, pointed to Don, and proclaimed, "You are running from God, aren't you? He wants you to know that He loves you and that He will never leave you or forsake you."

Nailed! While we were in a season when such supernatural encounters seemed rare for us, that word of knowledge came straight from Heaven and deposited a powerful seed of hope to grow inside. God left no room for doubt: Don couldn't hide from Him, for God was not giving up on him. Thank you, Lord, that You are faithful, even when we are not.

Her Mid-Life Crisis

I was so undone trying to respond to *his* midlife crisis that I was oblivious that there were actually two crises going on, *his* and *hers*. Quite frankly, I was a hot mess.

> *So, if you think you are standing firm, be careful that you don't fall!"* (I Corinthians 10:12 NIV)

My world was crumbling. I missed our boys away at college, Winchester life, our church, our friends, my students, and my life-giving ministry roles. I had no idea what to think of the past nor any idea what to expect from my future. I felt like a failure and wasn't courageous enough to talk openly and honestly with anyone. I didn't trust others enough to be that vulnerable. So I stayed busy and stayed shallow in my interactions while stuffing my feelings down further inside.

I was constantly with people but felt alone. If you'd asked me "So how are you doing?" I would reflect the question, "Fine, so how are *you* doing?" I had become one of those church people Don described who kept up a good appearance but failed to be real and vulnerable, even with myself. Now I feared losing Don, my closest friend and love of my life, as he began exploring another world without me. We drifted farther apart, and I didn't know what to do.

One evening after work Don walked in with a six-pack of beer. Incredulous, I stood there and told him in no uncertain terms, "We're not having any beer in *my* house!" as I grabbed the six-pack out of his hands, marched out the door, and threw his six-pack over the cabin deck rail.

Really?

Yep, I did.

Controlling? Religious? Self-righteous? Guilty on all counts.

Didn't I have the right to be concerned about our four teens who had never seen alcohol inside our home? Of course I did, but my rage was motivated by my crumbling ability to keep up a righteous image. I was thinking, "What would people think? Why, as a 40-year-old, alcohol had only touched these lips four times, and I was d… proud of it.

Alcohol is a dangerous idol that many worship. Not me!" My motto hadn't changed much from my teen years: "I don't drink, don't smoke or chew, and I don't hang with guys who do."

It was much easier to see the vice of alcoholism than it was to see my vice of self-righteousness, a more acceptable sin in the church. I had fallen into the trap of trying to *appear* to be a model Christian. There was that people-pleasing perfectionism again.

I was also ashamed to talk to God because I felt when we dissolved the church that I'd failed Him too. I wanted to be close to God but didn't know how when I felt so inadequate. I did some soul-searching: What if I am not really authentic in my love for God and others? Where does the church fit in? What about those outside the church? Can I be real and vulnerable and still serve Jesus? What should the rest of my life be like?

For years, church related activities had consumed 80 – 90% of our waking hours, but they were gone. Don declared that he was done with the church! He had been my love since I was 17. I wanted to stay beside him to save our marriage. I faced a critical choice: Should I pursue being a model Christian without my husband. Should I come alongside him? Could I do that and serve God too?

I made the choice to hold on to God with one hand and Don with the other. I had my hands full. I began joining Don for Happy Hour hoping to find happiness with him, and an hour was about as long as *happy* lasted. But over time I began to relax and start to connect with the people around me as I let go of my judgements and high expectations of others. I found myself enjoying all sorts of interesting people and eager to hear their heartfelt stories each wanted to share.

Underneath the outer crustiness of folks and the walls they had built to protect themselves were hearts like mine that wanted to connect, belong, and find joy and purpose. The compassion in me from God was real and I saw it in my care for others, regardless of their beliefs, not only at the bar but at school, at work, even at home. We added a whole new circle of friends with lives far different than ours.

With my upbringing I expected lightning to strike me as I began to drink socially, but it didn't. I was learning that Christianity is much more than striving to "be a good girl." At the time I felt as though I had chosen Life Plan B and was surprised that God had not abandoned me. Instead He was transforming me from a person striving to do good works and be perfect to being someone relaxing to enjoy my life with Him and to really care for others.

My *Miss Goody Two Shoes* no longer fit. Knowing God loved me right where I was helped me love others right where they were. Instead of doing the right thing in order to earn His love, I was beginning to do things as a result of knowing that I was loved.

> *Don't just pretend to love others. Really love them. Hate what is wrong. Hold tightly to what is good. Love each other with genuine affection and take delight in honoring each other.* (Romans 12:9,10 NLT)

Did I Miss God?

Was this a detour? Maybe. I don't know what would have happened if I'd chosen to stay on my former path. Yet strange as it seems, I do know that He used this worldly time for good as He began setting me free from my pride and religious attempts to be perfect. He is good and uses our weaknesses to draw us to Him. I'm sure that the devil intended to rob, kill and destroy us, but God turned things around to give us abundant life in Him.

> *You intended to harm me, but God intended it for good to accomplish what is now being done, the saving of many lives.* (Genesis 50:20 NIV)

Fortunately I hadn't read that midlife crises often last six to ten years. I've no doubt that this season would have passed quickly if we had been connected with a solid group of believers to help us process these issues with God's help. Who knows how much more effective those years could have been?

Nevertheless, the Lord stuck with us as we waded through this time adrift. We praise Him that this difficult season did not end up in infidelity or divorce which could have easily happened in this loose environment. Instead He gave us new interest and passion for people who didn't know Him yet and showed us how to love our neighbor, anyone in our world around us at the time.

Is This The End?

> *You're blessed when you feel you've lost what is most dear to you. Only then can you be embraced by the One most dear to you.* (Matthew 5:4 The Message)

Another crisis hit when Don turned 46 as once more the thief came to "rob, kill, and destroy." After work Don stopped by a gym in Hannibal to shoot some hoops. Dribbling down the court, he began to feel sharp pains in his chest. He reasoned, "I'm getting too old to play ball with these young guys," so he sat out for a while to get his wind back. However, the pain intensified, and he thought, "I need to go home," so he took off his tennis shoes and headed out the door.

When the crisp winter wind hit him, his chest tightened, so he went to a nearby grocery store to get some aspirin. The pain intensified. As he turned his car toward home, he remembered that our family was in Quincy as he wondered, "What if this is actually a heart attack? If I make the 25-minute drive home, no-one will be around if I get worse. I could die. I'm going to drive straight to the hospital and check it out."

He walked in and told the ER nurse, "I think I'm having a heart attack."

She smiled, probably thinking, "Right. You drove yourself to the hospital having a heart attack." She hooked him up to the EKG, she exclaimed, "Oh my, you definitely are having a heart attack!" After a $1500 clot-busting injection that opened the restriction, the excruciating pain subsided.

When we arrived home, Don's truck was not parked in its usual spot. Where was he? Anxiously I checked the answering machine on our home phone (pre-cell phones) and heard the message from the ER: Your husband has had a heart attack. We have admitted him. He is stable at the present, but you need to come to the hospital right away.

As I rushed to the hospital, I wondered, "Is this it?" I cried out to God, "Thank you that he went to the hospital. Oh please let him live."

I stayed the night by his side praying. In the morning he was sitting up in bed outlining the day's work for his mechanics. He said, "I don't think I actually had a heart attack. I feel fine." The doctor showed him films to convince him otherwise and sent him by ambulance to Columbia, MO.

After more tests, the cardiologists explained, "You need open heart surgery. However, since you are an otherwise healthy 46-year-old, we recommend waiting. When the time comes, we will harvest the vein in your leg from groin to ankle to use for the bypasses. At best, grafted veins usually stay open about ten years." (Stints were unheard of back then.) We agreed to try medication to buy us some time.

We praised God that this didn't turn out to be the end of his life. But it was the end of an era.

Living Happily Incompatible

Both the mid-life crises and facing death with a heart attack were wakeup calls, but we kept pushing the snooze button and ignoring God's call to wake up just a little longer.

We decided to work on our marriage to make whatever days we had left living together enjoyable ones. I wanted to be a wife that brought out the good in my man and to be someone he could trust.

> *Who can find a virtuous and capable wife? She is more precious than rubies. Her husband can trust her, and she will greatly enrich his life. She brings him good, not harm, all the days of her life.* (Proverbs 31:10-12 NLT)

Over the years God had taught us some priceless lessons, but we constantly needed refresher courses as the wear and tear of living kept bringing to light our incompatibilities. We could have been the poster couple for the book, *Men are Like Waffles and Women are like Spaghetti: Understanding and Delighting in Your Differences.*

It was certainly a challenge to understand and delight in our differences. I loved the indoors while Don loved the outdoors. I preferred sedentary activities like reading and cooking; he enjoyed physical activity and sports.

My mind enjoyed racing full speed, constantly analyzing what was going on while Don enjoyed his breaks watching football and going to the "nothing box" in his male brain where he wasn't thinking of much of anything. Every so often we enjoy laughing through the short YouTube video *A Tale of Two Brains* by Mark Gungor that helped us laugh at our hard-wired differences. Check it out.

On joint projects when I opted for "Let's get 'er done…fast" he preferred "Let's get 'er done right." We gave up painting or wallpapering together. Don says that there are usually at least ten ways to do anything, and five of them work well. But we each preferred our own way of doing everything. While God had gifted me with a "book smart" high IQ, He had graced Don with very practical skills and wisdom to navigate life. I enjoyed multi-tasking, flitting from one thing to another; my hubby was single minded, tenacious, tackling one thing at a time until it was finished quite well.

Looking back I realize that I was coping with some mild attention deficit disorder (ADD) in a time before that was a familiar label. Back then *add* was just the opposite of *subtract*. Now I realize my lack of focus and tendency to get distracted and multitask had far reaching effects in many areas like my constant attempts to organize, overthink, and overanalyze to find the best way to do things. Such awareness could have helped us smooth out a lot of issues over our years together. In addition, we were both sidetracked with an ADVenture disorder as we tried out new things.

Don and I constantly had to work on both understanding and delighting in our differences. We discovered that the key to being close was to connect emotionally, not only to talk about what was happening but to share with each other how we felt about things.

Even today we continue to work on connecting, often by ending the day being positive and thankful by a simple habit of sharing three things:

Here's what went well today...

I appreciate this about you...

I want...

One night my response to *I want...* was "more hugs," and his was "to go to sleep." Sometimes this is a 3-minute exercise; on other days it leads us into a longer intimate conversation. It always draws us closer.

Carving out time for this little exercise helps us connect emotionally. We also enjoy sharing this with our family, friends, whoever. Complaining comes easy; developing an attitude of gratitude is more difficult but so worth it. Often the little things make the biggest impact in life.

Change in the Wind

Times had been tough, and we were bruised and had begun drifting off, exploring on our own, as we set aside some of our God-given tools that had brought us true satisfaction in the past: being part of a vibrant community, daily reading His Word, praying, journaling, and reading powerful books. We were slowly slipping away from our quest of drawing closer to Him.

Fully recovered from the heart attack, Don grew restless and ready for a new adventure. After being a school teacher for ten years and office manager at my brothers' company, US Cooler, while juggling kids and river living, I, too, was ready for a fresh start. Our days of having four lively preschoolers changed to having four busy college students off on their own. As empty-nesters we decided to move on. Don accepted a job as maintenance supervisor with Kraft Food Ingredients, and we relocated to Champaign, IL, our home from our college days in the 1960s.

Tucking away his favorite "river liver" t-shirt, I savored the end of this special season of river living; the cabin now became a prized family vacation spot for the coming decades.

Standing on the deck, I thought about what an amazing place this had been to raise our kids, even with all its challenges. I smiled as I remembered the first time I stood on that deck listening to the howling coyotes in the distance.

In all those years, I had not seen a single coyote. So I wondered, *"Why do I fear what's ahead? Most of what I fear doesn't ever happen."*

With hands lifted to the sky, I offered my final prayer as a river liver, "Thank you, Father, for this wonderful season. 'When I am afraid, I put my trust in you.'" (Psalm 56:3 NIV)

I'm ready…I'm set…Let's go.

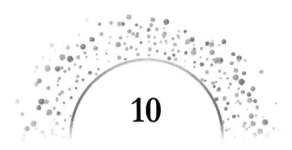

10

Is Life Rich and Satisfying?

As I turned 47, our adventure searching for abundant life continued in the bustling city of Champaign, IL and its surrounding communities which swelled to over 230,000 with the university. Vastly different from living in the country, this city life mesmerized us with its charms.

A Taste of Champaign

The first summer thanks to a generous job relocation package, we enjoyed living in a nice townhouse with a pool. We dined in new restaurants each night with our daughters home on break. We were living *high on the hog*. Together we savored the city's Midwest charm with all the U of I sports and cultural events, the symphony, festivals, music, concerts, parks, and endless shops within a few miles. Now earning far more money than we had ever dreamed of, we experienced many luxuries we knew nothing about.

Years ago when we first caught on fire for Jesus, Granddad Craig told us that the real test of our faith wouldn't come in the tough times but in the prosperous times when our need for Him wasn't as obvious. He was right.

In this prosperous time we lost our focus on Jesus as we continued our midlife unraveling. With so much to explore, we were distracted from keeping first things first. God was still part of our life, but certainly not the center.

Life became a blur of activity as we were easily attracted to competing sideshows experiencing fleeting happiness which only mimicked real joy. No matter how much fun we had, it never was quite enough, and we'd soon on the lookout for the next thrill.

The seed that fell among thorns stands for those who hear, but as they go on their way they are choked by life's worries, riches and pleasures, and they do not mature. (Luke 8:14 NIV)

The parable of the sower warns us about letting God's Word get choked out by everything around us. This pretty much sums up our life in this season. We fell into a trap as we chose to let the things of this world crowd out God.

Yet looking back, I marvel at how God was so faithful, so very present letting us know how much He loved us because we were His kids. And the sideshows? He didn't waste any of our experiences but used them to teach us valuable lessons, weaving them as colorful threads into the multi-colored fabric of our overall story.

Near Death...Again!

We humans are all terminal from birth, but we usually ignore it until an event jolts us into remembering that life is fleeting and can be literally gone in a heartbeat. Our jolt came one afternoon when Don came in from mowing the yard and plopped into a chair complaining, "I feel totally wiped out." He breathed deeply as he struggled to get air. Then he added, "Oh man, my chest really is hurting."

My mind raced, "Oh no. This is the day the cardiologists predicted. His vessels have clogged up. He is only 47...Wait a minute, that is how old his brother was when he died from a heart attack. Oh God, help us."

We headed to the ER. They immediately did a heart catheterization that revealed 80-95% blockage in four major arteries.

It was Friday afternoon so the surgeon scheduled open-heart surgery on Monday and began to admit him, but Don refused to spend the weekend in the hospital. Instead he went home, wrote instructions for his mechanics at work, and then we drove three hours to our river cabin for a relaxing weekend with our kids. We prayed and God gave both of us His "peace that passes understanding" that he was going to be okay, and he was.

Monday morning Don checked into the hospital and underwent a quadruple bypass. As I remembered how his brother Paul had looked, I tried to brace our kids for the shock of seeing their dad after surgery. They weren't prepared to see his ashen face, unable to talk with the breathing tube, hooked up to machines with wires and tubes protruding everywhere. Together we all continued to ask God to restore him.

As death loomed close, I thought a lot about how short life is. Our earthly stay is a tiny speck of time when compared to life in eternity. (I love how Francis Chan-Rope Illustration powerfully nails this on YouTube.)

I also paused to think about what the next life would be like. I knew I wouldn't be sitting on a cloud with a pair of wings playing a harp as I had once imagined. When I thought of all there is to explore and enjoy in this temporary earthly home our Father created for us, I realized that our eternal dwelling place He created us could not possibly be boring. Heaven will be incomprehensibly breathtaking, for it is the eternal home for our Father and those who love Him.

Soon the threat of death subsided as Don recovered quickly. After a few days at home my resilient hubby, unable to sit still, began building bathroom cabinets. I was relieved when he returned to work in just four weeks.

Stronger than ever, he pushed the throttle full speed ahead. So did I.

Training the Trainer

Soon I embarked on an exhilarating and demanding new career as coach and trainer of Northwestern Mutual financial advisors. What a marvelous time I had working for John Wright, my gifted mentor and boss for the next fifteen years. I learned so much from him and valued how he taught "true north principles" of building godly character and habits. As I flourished in this new professional environment, I was unsure which I enjoyed most – training or being trained.

Surrounded by colleagues eager to learn, I became a more voracious reader, soaking up knowledge from books, seminars, trips, and videos that shaped new leadership skills and habits in me. Being an effective teacher meant I must also be a lifelong learner.

Goal setting, a major priority of the firm, launched me into a lifelong habit of setting written goals. To evaluate, I learned to pay close attention to numbers and evaluating and analyzing to make things better. This has been a great strength but over-analyzing and over-thinking has also been a weakness at times. Quite often our weaknesses tended to be our strengths taken too far.

At age 48, my five-year goals were to 1) have a spacious home to entertain with a big shop for Don, 2) both have great jobs, 3) be free of credit card debt, 4) be actively serving God, and 5) weigh 149 #. Written goals are powerfully effective as they keep us focused in the right direction. I hit my targets, except the weight goal. Four out of five wasn't too bad.

In this new affluent world, I worked daily with clientele new to me: successful business owners, well-educated professionals, and influencers in the community. We made priceless new friends with so many of them and admired how they were making such a big impact with their generosity. Yet somehow I knew that we would not staying in this world long term.

An Audience of One

Father God was always showing himself close at hand. I remember an intimate interaction with Him on a spring evening at the Peoria Country Club where we honored our top producers at an annual gala black-tie affair. I was in charge of making it a night to remember and had spent weeks attending to every little detail. The event turned out spectacular in every way. Yet on the drive home I was cranky and felt bummed.

"So what is going on?" I asked myself. Then I realized I was miffed because all the credit for the evening's success was given to a young assistant. I couldn't seem to shake off the resentment.

When I got into bed, I took it to the Lord, "Honestly, Lord, I am so upset that I hardly got any recognition for my hard work. I think it is my people pleasing issue again, isn't it? It's way too important to have the praise of people. Deep down I really want to please you. Help me see this night from your viewpoint."

He answered immediately by shifting my paradigm as He showed me I wasn't the only one who had done a great job, and the other gal needed our boss' recognition more than I did. Then I sensed God's gentle voice inside say, "Well done, good and faithful servant." With those words, the resentment and hurt feelings melted away as quickly as they had come. I realized that His approval was enough. He was still teaching me to play out my life for an audience of one.

> *The LORD does not look at the things people look at. People look at the outward appearance, but the LORD looks at the heart.* (I Samuel 16:7 NIV)

Everybody Gets to Play

Life was good. We had bought a cozy little home, our nicest ever, and settled in. On weekends we hit the road to visit our kids in college or relax at the cabin. Yet at times I longingly remembered back when we had been more powerfully connected with God. I realized that our love of the world and its pleasures was squeezing Him out of first place. Lukewarm and no longer ablaze, the scariest part was that we were becoming content with that.

Don't love the world's ways. Don't love the world's goods. Love of the world squeezes out love for the Father. Practically everything that goes on in the world—wanting your own way, wanting everything for yourself, wanting to appear important—has nothing to do with the Father. It just isolates you from him. The world and all its wanting, wanting, wanting is on the way out—but whoever does what God wants is set for eternity. (I John 2:15-17 The Message)

Realizing how we missed our close connections with other passionate believers, we began looking for a church. On our weekends in town we randomly picked one of the 150+ local churches to visit, but we didn't feel at home anywhere.

Then one day we were driving down a main street when a small sign, *The Vineyard Church,* caught our eye. We visited and were drawn to the lively worship which seemed different as they sang songs *to* God not *about* Him. The people were warm and inviting; the message was practical and challenging. The church offered lots of small groups and places to serve. After the service a trained team of ordinary folks were available up front for anyone wanting prayer.

We liked that it was no one-man show but led by a team of pastors filling different roles. We found them to be vulnerable, authentic, and open to the Holy Spirit. They said, *"Everybody gets to play"* and meant it.

I had been the one in search mode. Don hadn't been enthusiastic about attending church for some time, but when he walked out the door that first Sunday, he declared, "This is home" and our search was over. We had found a tribe where we belonged in a new local church. It would be just in time, for we would need this strong anchor in the storms just ahead.

Life in the Fast Lane

College days passed quickly and our four adult kids walked across the stage graduating in four consecutive semesters. Shawn and Damon were now engineers, Jenny was a teacher, and Christy was a certified public accountant. Our kids had studied hard and helped pay for their education with jobs, student loans, and military service. Over the next fourteen years, we gladly paid off the $30,000 we had borrowed.

Our kids college educations have been our finest financial investment. We marveled how God had provided the funds when it had looked like such an impossible dream to get them all through college.

Amassing wealth has never been a big priority for us, and we were content raising our family living a very modest lifestyle. When I asked our grown kids if they remembered not having a lot of money growing up, they all agreed, "No, not really, but we sure remember our family having a lot of fun together." Money can't buy that. God had taught us that putting trust in money was not to be our aim.

> *Teach those who are rich in this world not to be proud and not to trust in their money, which is so unreliable.* **Their trust should be in God, who richly gives us all we need for our enjoyment**...*They should be rich in good works and generous to those in need, always being ready to share with others.* (I Timothy 16:17-19 The Message, emphasis mine.)

While we knew that money couldn't buy us happiness, we still wanted to have a chance to prove it. Mark Twain said, "*Money isn't everything, but it ranks up there with oxygen.*"

Seriously, we got wrapped up in what money could buy for a short time. It didn't take long to figure out that rich relationships trump money. Relationships with others brought us far more joy than what money could buy.

Our kids related well which led to a rapidly expanding family in the next six years as our daughter *Christy* was joined by another *Kristi* who married Damon; then *Chris* who married Jenny. We also added 5 grandkids in 6 years just like we had 5 kids in 6 years. Together we enjoyed the rich gift of a growing family.

Life Wrapped in Words

> *"The palest ink is better than the sharpest memory."*
> — A Chinese Proverb

At one time I was confident that I would remember the details of all the important things that happened in my life. I was mistaken. Fortunately much of my life is documented in a stack of notebooks that is over two feet tall, chocked full of events along with my thoughts and feelings and conversations with God. Writing has always helped me sort things out.

My life is like my garden. Unless I keep at it, it will be a garden full of weeds. Journaling helped me sort out the flowers from the weeds. When I didn't know what to think or do, when I didn't understand what was happening, I wrote. I grew more intimate with God as I penned my prayers and questions, His answers and revelations. I recorded the times that I got it right, and more frequently the times I missed it and what I learned.

Journaling and connecting with God seem to go together for me. One day I realized such writings were part of my heritage when I located this entry in my grandma's journal: *February 1, 1953. Becky & Cathy gave their hearts to Jesus.* I had known I met Jesus when I was young but had no idea when. Knowing the exact date I became a Christian isn't crucial, but it sure was fun to discover the date in Mom Kendrick's diary.

The priceless details I recorded far outlasted my memory. I had no inkling that someday my scribblings would provide accurate details for a book of never-ending GodStories.

A cheerful heart is good medicine, but a broken spirit saps a person's strength. (Proverbs 17:22 NLT)

Here are some playful excerpts written when I was in my 40's:

Cookies In My Journal

Wednesday, February 22: Did you know that oatmeal raisin cookies are in the Bible? Me neither, but there they were. I discovered them quite unexpectedly. It all began last Sunday.

Sunday: Trying to be a model loving wife, I baked a double batch of oatmeal raisin cookies, Don's favorites. Of course, they were all for him, a pure labor of love. Right?

Monday: I took four Texas-sized cookies to work. I hid the treats in the back of my top desk drawer as an emergency stash for the coming week. At 2 pm I reached in for another morsel. My hand searched far and wide but located nothing, not one tiny morsel. I pulled the drawer open wide. All four of them had vanished!

I was really annoyed. My first thought was "Who ate all my cookies?"

Then I sheepishly added, "Uh oh!" as I identified the cookie monster.

"How could I possibly have eaten all those cookies?"

God had been urging me to pay attention to my eating and how I went to food for satisfaction and made it an idol I worshipped. He wanted me to come to Him instead of sweets for comfort. I was appalled at my mindless eating.

"Oh well," I rationalized, "It's really no big deal. God won't notice. He has a big world to watch after. What are a few cookies in His big scheme of things?"

Tuesday: I opened my One Year Bible and was reading the daily passage, in the obscure four-page book of Hosea when this phrase popped out,

"For the Lord loves the Israelites though they turn to other gods and love the sacred raisin cakes." (Hosea 3:16 NIV)

Whoa, Lord. Are you talking to me? Israelites—your people, turning to other gods—sacred raisin cakes. Here I am, one of your people, worshipping oatmeal raisin cookies.

Busted! You are right. I often do worship food as an idol and turn to other sugary gods for pleasure. Forgive me. Help me turn to you when I am needy. In my heart I know that you alone satisfy my deep hunger. I just need to convince the rest of me.

And God, I do love your sense of humor.

I celebrated the good times with these fun stories. I also recorded stories of His provisions, answers, and miracles as I wrote down many conversations with God.

But I also agonized with God in the hard times as I poured out raw emotional words which described my hurting heart and helped it heal. Somehow in both good times and bad, journaling always helped me get closer to God.

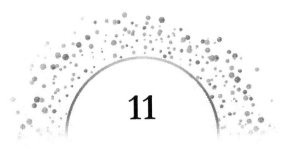

11

The Raging Floods of '93

I desire a smooth orderly life where I feel understood and am in control of what is happening. Does anyone else? That's too bad because it's just not going to happen.

Perhaps to compensate for my ADD tendencies, I often go to great lengths to bring order. I can be quite the planning junkie who sets goals, makes lists, and journals all the options. I like to google and google some more. I enjoy measuring and including actual numbers in descriptions. Being hardwired to analyze how to make things better is a great strength, but when taken too far, can turn into a weakness of overthinking almost everything.

Real life has made me face the stark reality that life is uncertain, and so much that happens is out of our control.

> Look here, you who say, 'Today or tomorrow we are going to a certain town and will stay there a year. We will do business there and make a profit.' How do you know what your life will be like tomorrow? Your life is like the morning fog—it's here a little while, then it's gone.
>
> What you ought to say is, "If the Lord wants us to, we will live and do this or that." (James 14:13 -15 NLT)

God wanted me to learn to let go of my fix-it mentality and walk with Him when life spins out of control. The problem is that we learn this most often while facing trials. It was that time for me...again.

> The seed that fell among thorns stands for those who hear, but as they go on their way they are choked by life's worries, riches and pleasures, and they do not mature. (Luke 8:14 NIV)

In the span of one very long week, two very different events converged to test our trust in God and put me in full crisis mode.

First, we found ourselves in the middle of an unprecedented natural disaster, the Great Flood of 1993.

Battling the Mighty Mississippi

The spring and summer of 1993 brought a 500-year flood to the American Heartland. For months we were glued to the CBS nightly news as we saw how unusually heavy rains and melting snow from the north had caused the Mississippi and Missouri Rivers to overflow banks and break through levees in nine states, ravaging homes and farmland in unprecedented fury.

This natural disaster threatened Pike County which had been our home for 35 of our 50 years; our hearts ached for all of our dear family and friends whose homes and livelihoods were at stake. For three long months the National Guard and hundreds of volunteers and residents worked together patrolling and sandbagging the levees in a 24-hour vigil to hold back the river. Don and I prayed daily that the waters would not break through the levees and flood the area. We also asked that our cabin would miraculously be spared.

In May as the danger heightened, we began making the 3-hour weekend trip from Champaign to help. Local farmers in the low-lying plains had evacuated along with residents of our hometown of Hull, six miles from the river as the crow flies. By July everyone was growing weary and starting to lose hope as the river breached more levees and flooded 75 towns up and down the river.

On July 25, the morning of the 152nd day, we lost the battle. The raging river burst through the water-soaked sand levee and swiftly flooded 40,000 acres of prime farmland and all the homes in its path as the weary fighters helplessly watched. In Hull the water rose to chest high. Our extended family lost eight homes in the flood.

It was a somber day as we drove in from Champaign to see the damage. We could only drive as far as the flooded ramp from I72 at the Hull exit. The scene is etched in my mind: we stood with lifelong friends and neighbors tearfully gazing across the muddy waters that had claimed their homes, farmsteads, and fields as far as you could see. Hope was hard to come by.

We had picked up our pontoon boat stored close by so that we could boat out to survey the damage. We launched the boat and boarded it; Don's brother Lester who farmed 2000 of these flooded acres came along with us.

It had only been a week since the flood waters had begun to subside, and there was barely enough room for our boat to pass under the tall electric lines, eerily draped with remnants of corn stalks from the cornfields which were now 4' under water.

We passed former thriving farmsteads now devastated with toppled grain bins, missing buildings, floating tanks, and houses with only rooftops visible. Our niece's two-story family home that had faced the north now faced west, sideways on its foundation.

Lester jokingly commented, "There is a nice field of corn under here." When we reached his house, we tearfully stepped out onto his roof which protruded from the waters.

Then we headed on to our cabin site to see if it might be still there. The levee had disappeared, and the water was raging back into the channel right under our cabin making the current too swift to get close. The four summer cabins next to ours were gone, having washed off their moorings and floated down the river.

But amazingly, there, sitting atop the flood waters, was our cabin, unscathed. We paused to give God thanks.

A Muddy Mess

Why are you down in the dumps, dear soul? Why are you crying the blues? Fix my eyes on God — soon I'll be praising again. He puts a smile on my face. He's my God. (Psalm 42:5 The Message)

Cleaning up the muddy mess was a monumental task for thousands along the river. Most houses were too far gone to salvage; the repairable ones contained thick layers of foul mud, piles of soggy trash, and too often, dreaded mold in the walls. Homes had to be stripped to the studs and rebuilt. Most country folks couldn't afford to walk away from their modest homes, and farmers had to rebuild their farmsteads for their livelihood. Carloads of volunteers came from long distances to help. Still it took years for families to painstakingly restore their homes from the rubble.

Slowly the countryside was transformed. So were the people. We saw firsthand how catastrophes often bring out the best in people and witnessed countless stories of generosity as people sacrificed their time and resources to help the needy like God designed humans to do.

Our own restoration project was slow going. We could see our cabin was still standing for several weeks before we were able to reach it. Meanwhile the seventeen inches of muddy water inside its walls subsided, leaving behind an inch layer of greasy mud. So much was destroyed. But praise God, a cabin full of gooey muck is better than no cabin at all.

Stepping inside, we carefully waded through the treacherous slime to avoid slipping, leery of what we might find as the dim light of the flashlight scanned the rooms. There would be no electricity for months. Then I saw what I had feared the most as I pointed to a corner of the living room, "Look, a snakeskin!"

Shawn pointed to the other corner, "Look, a snake!"

The men chased the snake into the sofa, pulled it out by the tail and killed it. This began a string of sleepless nights at the cabin while we were rebuilding as I lay awake imagining the rest of the snakes coiled up hiding close by. There were none, thank God. It was one more thing I feared that didn't happen.

Soon the initial shock of the disaster passed, and in its wake came long days of cleaning and restoring. Don and I made the 6-hour round trip to the cabin almost every weekend with bleach, cleaning supplies, tools, and yard sale treasures to rebuild our family sanctuary.

Sometimes when things look overwhelming, the best thing to do is to trust in God's goodness, roll up your sleeves, and go to work. That is exactly what Don did as he cleaned up the cabin, replacing soaked insulation, drywall, flooring, and cabinets, rising at dawn and working long into the night.

Don was used to hard physical labor and found it therapeutic. For me, it was just hard. Here was one more calamity to hit us and one more job that I couldn't do well. Fortunately, I didn't know the restoration project would drag on for two years.

On the Rocks

The LORD is my rock, my fortress and my deliverer; my God is my rock, in whom I take refuge, my shield and the horn of my salvation, my stronghold. (Psalm 18:22 NIV)

The first few weekends I didn't want to make the trip to the cabin, but Don encouraged me to come along, take it easy, and do only whatever I felt I was up to. I was certain that wouldn't be very much. When we first arrived, Don began steadily plodding through the muddy mess, one small step at a time.

And me? I climbed the stairs, walked slowly through the cabin, turned around, and walked right back out the door, down the steps onto the riverbank. I plopped down on a big boulder and sobbed for hours.

Outwardly, I was dreading the months of grueling work ahead. Inwardly, I was drained, dreading life itself. I felt like I was losing grip of God's hand and was slowly sliding down the sides of a deep muddy pit of despair with no way to climb out.

It wasn't only the flood I was grieving but also the other major losses in a short span of time. Our house wasn't bustling with the lively laughter of kids. Our finances had taken a major hit first from our business and then the farm. I lacked a sense of purpose as I was no longer teaching in the Christian school or leading small group or helping pastor people. I also missed our long-time close community and the comfortable Christian bubble where we had spent most of our Winchester years. Then there was the loss of Don's dad and brother. The last straw was when I nearly lost Don, the love of my life, first with a heart attack and then with a midlife crisis.

Let's face it. I no longer had a sweet little family as a sweet little wife in a sweet little church with a sweet little life.

I did a lot of soul searching, playing through the scenarios as I wondered how we had gotten here. How much of these struggles were my fault? Regrets ran rampant as I rehashed what I might have done differently and how I had missed it again and again. As I dwelt on my past, I felt shame and depression pulling me down. My deepest pain was feeling that I had failed God and had lost my intimacy with Him.

This mental turmoil churned inside as I sat on the rocks looking up at the remains of our cabin. I cried, pouring out my heart, trying to make sense of it all. I asked God for strength to go on, to climb out of this pit. Like King David, *"I almost lost my footing."* (Psalm 73:2)

Slowly I realized that even when I thought I had let go of His hand, He was still had mine. God had never left me but was waiting for me to turn my eyes from my problem to my provider. I felt Him holding me, giving me strength.

If I rise on the wings of the dawn, if I settle on the far side of the sea, even there your hand will guide me, your right hand will hold me fast. (Psalm 139:9:10 NIV)

While I didn't know how to handle all the internal challenges, I did know what to do with the external challenges right in front of me. So I crawled off the rocks and climbed up the stairs to come alongside my man and go to work. God highlighted His recovery plan: ask for His strength, look in front of me and start doing what I saw to do, taking the first step, right foot then left foot, as I trusted Him to guide me and heal me.

Our family pitched in to help us over the months as did many others whom God sent to encourage us and lend a hand to rebuild this summer place. Little by little we got the job done. Keeping hope alive and having the strength to keep on was difficult, yet God's presence steadied my hope and gave me strength.

When you pass through the waters, I will be with you; and through the rivers, they shall not overwhelm you; when you walk through the fire, you shall not be burned, and the flame shall not consume you. (Isaiah 43:2 NIV)

The Mississippi River wasn't the only flood to hit that week. There was a more private event that was also strongly contributing to my rocky lament, one that appeared to threaten our family unity and touch us at our core. This challenge would especially cause me to wrestle with my basic Christian beliefs and require work far harder than the physical work as God taught me how to be real and vulnerable and gave me an unprecedented opportunity to love like Jesus. There was only one question: As a Jesus lover, would I walk my talk?

Out of the Box

As our kids transitioned into adulting, each of them went through at least one major crisis which is not mine but theirs to tell. I like Beth Moore's wise words, *"Be authentic with all, transparent with most, intimate with some."*

However, I do include the following life story we lived with Shawn because it so greatly impacted us and because it addresses a common experience that many families face today. I do so with my son's blessing.

To help you get to know our son, I pulled out a few stories to share from the large treasury of our kids' growing up stories.

Shawn is independent. He proved it often as he relished walking on the border of any boundary we set while careful to not cross the line. When he was 6, our new sitter greeted us at the door with, "Do you let Shawn walk on the kitchen counters?"

"Uh, no. Why do you ask?" She shared how he had convinced her otherwise and had spent most of the night walking the counters, hopping down with a big grin on his face right before we walked in. She suspected she might have been duped.

Shawn is smart and inventive. His 11th summer, he and Damon made a 6' tall working Ferris wheel for their little sisters and talked his Dad into helping them build an electric go cart from scratch that clocked at 35 mph (blowing off the tires). Then they created a full-scale ethanol still from *Mother Earth News* blueprints and used some of the fuel to race their garden tractors.

Shawn is resourceful. Also at age 11, he changed the heating element in our dryer by himself. When left with a new baby sitter, he installed a 3-way switch to turn off the basement lights at both the top and bottom of the stairs.

Shawn is inquisitive and free-spirited, traits which stood out often as he pursued his own interests and continued to refuse to confirm to others' expectations. This was very evident in later years when he got sidetracked into exploring the whole college party scene.

During this crucial time for him, Don and I were struggling with our own issues and not alert to all that Shawn was wrestling with during this transition period so many miles away. I wish we'd been more aware. It may have made a difference, but then again, maybe not.

Then came the week of the epic flood, when we made a new discovery about our son. Shawn is gay.

The Gay News

We were totally taken by surprise to find out that our 27-year-old son was living a gay lifestyle. As rural conservative Christians this news shook us to our core. We had barely heard of the gay lifestyle in this pre-2000 era. What little we had heard from the pulpit was that this lifestyle was outside the church norms and counter to our Christian family values.

Then came the conversation with the three of us. At first, Don was totally silent, unable to respond in words. On the other hand, I responded with way too many words. We were all in such emotional pain that we left no room for the other's views. Don and I shared our concerns. We felt that our son was rejecting our family values which included our belief that God's ideal family plan begins with marriage between a man and a woman.

We argued with the handful of Bible passages we could find. Most of all, we didn't want to see him to miss out on what we had found to be most precious in life: children to enjoy and a spouse at his side to enjoy life and grow old with. We wondered how this would impact his future and what stigma and rejection he would face. We also wondered how it would impact our life.

I don't remember all that was said, but I do know what Shawn heard, "You don't accept me. You don't value my beliefs. You don't want me around. You are rejecting me. I have let you down. I have failed you. We can't be close anymore."

Strange as it may seem, this is what Don and I were hearing him say, "You don't accept us. You don't value our beliefs. You don't want to be around us. You are rejecting us. We have let you down. We have failed you. We can't be close anymore."

These observations are from the vantage point of some twenty-five years later as none of us could articulate our feelings at that time. That was a lot of the problem. Our conversation ended in tears after too many painful words and too little empathy, too little understanding, and no resolution for the future. Instead, we had opened wounds that would defer hope and make healing long and difficult.

> *The tongue can bring death or life; those who love to talk will reap the consequences.* (Proverbs 8:21 NLT)

As I wrote this chapter, I asked Shawn to read it and offered to leave this story out if he objected, but he agreed that the pain of vulnerability would be worth it to offer hope to others. He gave not only his permission but agreed to also add his input.

The Turmoil

As devastated as I felt, looking back I can't imagine how hard this time must have been for Shawn, for I was wrapped up in my own despair. Don and I wish we would have been more compassionate and done things differently. More 20/20 hindsight. But this book is about what actually happened, not what we wish would have happened. I can only tell what it was for me to go through this time as a mom.

That day I learned my son was gay is etched in my memory. This was not a possibility I'd considered or explored. At first, I couldn't seem to switch off the endless questions that swirled through my brain... *"How could we have a gay son? I know nothing about this. We don't know one person that is gay. Well, I guess we do know one, don't we? What went wrong? He is a Christian. Can Christians be gay? I don't even know. Was this our fault? How can we fix it? How will our family respond? What will people think? of him? of us? What if he never marries or has a family of his own? He loves kids. Will he miss out? How will this lifestyle affect him? How will it affect us? Will life ever seem normal again?"*

Then I directed my questions to God: *"Where were you? Why didn't you protect him? We had him in Christian schools. We've prayed your best for him since he was born. Is this what you had I mind? He is one of your kids. Why, God? What do we do? What did we fail to do? I just don't understand. This is so beyond our understanding. O God, we need your help. Shawn needs your help.*

God Sent Help

He knew that we were going to need some help, and one couple fit the bill. On the Monday morning when the river levee broke, I fell apart, so I called our good friends who were also our small group leaders. This couple came right over to talk with us and pray. On Wednesday I had called them in tears again about another devastating family event that I'm not at liberty to share. Again our leaders came over. As they left I quipped, "Thank you so much. It can't get any worse." I was wrong. On Friday they were back to process this third crisis.

This couple stuck close over the months and helped us sort through our emotions, beliefs, and responses; they prayed with us as we tried to figure out how to navigate this foreign journey. This friendship forged by doing life in small group was now a lifesaver. We all need each other. We just don't know when a need will come nor whether we will be the one helping or needing help.

As I calmed down, I began to ask for wisdom to walk through this journey with God's love and understanding.

That is when the Lord showed me that this came as no surprise to Him for He had already given me a guidebook before I knew there was an issue. Lying in plain sight on our coffee table was Barbara Johnson's *Stick a Geranium in Your Hat and Be Happy,* a book I'd bought before the flood. I had skimmed through it in the bookstore, and it looked like a fun story chocked full of quotes I could share with flood workers. But God had me buy it not for the workers but for this desperate momma.

The next weekend after the floods hit, I felt I could use a geranium and a little *happy,* so I opened Barbara's book and began reading her GodStory of how the Lord gave her joy and strength to overcome several crises. First, she told the story of losing one son in his twenties in an accident; then she lost a second twenty-year-old. Next, her husband, an engineer, was disabled after being hit by a car (and later healed.) But she also wove through the stories how she found joy in Jesus right in the middle of it all. She shared how the hardest trial came next when she discovered that her third son, an outstanding Christian leader in his college, was gay. I couldn't believe what I was reading. Another mom with a gay son sharing her story?

Barbara's reaction was very similar to mine: incredulous, judgmental, feeling like a mom failure. She shares her healing story of reconciling her love for her gay son with her walk with God. I needed her sense of humor. I needed to see the path someone else took to healing. I needed to hear how to love. I needed hope that I, too, could make it.

I had picked this book out of the hundreds of books in the store, oblivious that the story was mainly about a gay son and clueless that I had one of those too. God knew what would soften the blow for this stressed-out mamma and provided help before I had asked. He was right there, holding us up, loving us and answering my prayer for help. He knew that nothing could have helped me more at the time than hearing from another mother.

God is our refuge and strength, an ever-present help in trouble.
(Psalm 46:1 NIV)

However, like a typical momma, I wanted to get in there and "fix it." We could work this out. We'll talk about it, and it will be fine. We'll just pray, and it may take a little time, but soon God will change him.

That quick-fix idea was only a wish and not a reality. Over the months Shawn and I talked more calmly about what the scriptures said and discussed what this might mean for his future. He also assured us this was not because of something we had done or not done. I wasn't totally convinced.

However, we did have to face the fact that it was his choice to decide how he would live his life. Freedom of choice is a gift God gives to us all. As parents, our choice was how to navigate our part in our son's life, and that would be a big enough job. We agreed to disagree as we tried to connect and care for each other. On the outside, the days went on as usual.

Choosing Misery

Yet inside all was far from normal; I felt torn apart for some time. We often have no choice over the things that happen, but we always have the choice of responding with joy or misery. I chose misery. Added to the other losses, once more I felt I was losing connection with someone I loved dearly, my precious Shawn, and I spiraled into a depression which lasted for months. I could hardly think of anything else. I had failed once again.

During this time, Don and I didn't talk much at all, and then only on a superficial level. We didn't understand the deep pain each were feeling inside as we felt the shame that somehow we had failed our son. We just kept busy with work and activities, avoiding the subject.

This struggle during the weekends of cabin cleanup meant more time sitting on the riverbanks sorting through this great sadness, wrestling with my thoughts, my God, and crying out for help and strength.

If the enemy can isolate and get us alone, he can lie to us and lead us astray. When Don and I could finally talk to each other about how we were feeling, we began to experience healing. We weren't nearly as vulnerable to share our weaknesses with others back then when appearing like we were doing fine was more important than being real with others.

It took a long time before we told anyone except our small group leaders and a few of the family. We believed the enemy's lie, "If people knew what was really going on, what you are really like, they would reject you." This was not true at all. To our surprise, when we opened up and shared our thoughts and feelings with others, we got better much quicker and were set free to move on with our lives and release Shawn to live his. I began spending less time on the rocks.

The Lord didn't answer all of our questions quickly. He still hasn't answered some of them. Some things we just have to walk through on earth, regardless of whether they get resolved in this life or not.

He was very clear about the basics during this journey with our son.

He is God. He is present.

He loves Don. He loves me. He loves Shawn. Equally.

The rest? We would figure out the rest over time.

He has shown you, O mortal, what is good. And what does the LORD require of you? To act justly and to love mercy and to walk humbly with your God. (Micah 6:8 NIV)

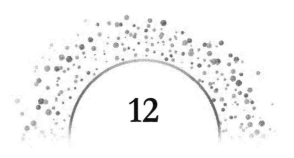

12

Gay Reflections

Looking Back

Now that you have heard our gay story, let me add some gay reflections now that twenty-five years have passed. How do I see things now? The biggest change is how we view our son. We no longer see his identity as being gay. This is only a part of his life. There is so much more to this amazing man who is also independent, smart, inventive, resourceful, inquisitive, and free-spirited.

Shawn is a gifted engineer highly regarded at work. He is fun, energetic, and compassionate towards people in need, often housing a myriad of people who live with him through tough times. Daily he makes a difference in people's lives. He is also a loving child of God with great value. He quickly responds to my texts during crises with an immediate, "I'm praying for you, Mom" which means a lot to me and to God. We are proud of the man he has become.

He is still our son whom we love passionately just as we deeply love our other treasured children, Damon, Jenny, and Christy. Over the years we have been learning the delicate balance of being there for each other, yet giving each other space to live our own lives. We deal with the issues that come up the best we can, sometimes better than others. We're far from perfect parents, but we continue to love and help each other grow.

Jesus didn't promise His followers an easy life but quite the opposite:

Here on earth you will have many trials and sorrows. But take heart, because I have overcome the world. (John 16:33 NTL)

We are still trying to let Jesus help us overcome in our little world.

Reflections as a Mom

I will no doubt rile a lot of people as I comment on this volatile hot topic of today. My thoughts won't line up with what many people think, but these are my thoughts for what they are worth. I encourage readers to keep an open mind.

Twenty-five years ago I had this all figured out and if anyone had asked, I could have explained exactly what God thought about homosexuality by quoting the six verses that mention the topic out of the 31,173 verses in the Bible. Today I am much less presumptive to speak for God. I have read a lot about how both sides interpret the scriptures which was a first step to understanding, but I'm not going to delve into theology. I have seen my understanding of God's will on other key issues change as I grow, so I am not so adamant about expounding His views as I used to be.

When I was young in my faith and striving to be righteous, we went overboard for several years making a strong stand against "abominations" such as television which we were certain was a tool of the devil, trick or treating on Halloween, and of course, the biggies, Santa Claus and the Easter Bunny. One Christmas we refused to have a Christmas tree because someone had told us of an obscure Old Testament passage that spoke against worshipping tinseled idols (Jeremiah 10).

I'm sure that God saw our heart motives, but looking back, we wish we had been wiser in helping our kids recognize truth without legalistically forbidding so much. The kids still remind us how super-religious we got every Halloween and how they felt they missed out. We are really sorry about that, kids.

Our views have changed on another topic, drinking. My family of origin abhorred drinking. Before the age of forty I looked down on anyone who drank alcohol and was very proud that I had mostly avoided this evil, determined that not a drop would touch my lips. Not only did that viewpoint strengthen my pride and self-righteousness, but also I had to totally ignore passages of the Bible such as Jesus turning five 20-gallon jars of water into wine at a wedding.

I chose to focus more on obeying the letter of the law than how to extravagantly love like Jesus did. I realize we each must wrestle through our stance on subjects such as these, and I prefer to give room for other views as I question some of my own early beliefs.

Of course, I am influenced by the culture around me, but also I see the organized church changing on what it was so legalistic about in earlier periods. No, I am not old enough to recall slavery times, but I vividly remember seeing on television how Afro-Americans were treated as second-class citizens in the 1960s in many churches in the South. That was not God. It still isn't.

I also remember when the women liberation movement was seen as anti-God, and during my years as a teen and young adult, women could not be ordained pastors in our church. There was a time when anyone who was divorced was looked down upon. They could not be a pastor, and sometimes not even become a member of a church. In my opinion, wrong again! I am concerned that the current generation is viewing the organized church as judgmental, not loving.

While today it is no longer divorce but homosexuality that is viewed as a prevailing issue. Why do we pick one to highlight over another? Most people would probably agree that homosexuality is not God's ideal. Neither is divorce. If you study Jesus' teaching, He addresses divorce several times, but doesn't mention homosexuality. What's with that?

Some people do have an inherent same-sex attraction, just as people often have a strong attraction many from the opposite sex. I feel that there is no sin in having an attraction, but from what I understand in the Bible, God does not condone sex outside of marriage, heterosexual or homosexual.

As I consider how not all in this imperfect world is in God's perfect will, I find it hard to navigate what to think. I find it even harder to know how to *live*. What is my place in all this?

I don't have all the answers, but this sums up what I try to live out when dealing with relationships with others: It is God's job to judge, the Holy Spirit's job to convict, and my job to love.[4]

What the Father is looking for in me is how I love. Love trumps, and I believe God's primary mandate is to love people and help them, not to judge them. For me, that is taking an entire lifetime. Thank you, Shawn, for helping me learn to love. I am so proud of you.

I love you. Mom

Judgment without mercy will be shown to anyone who has not been merciful. Mercy triumphs over judgment. (James 2:13 NLT)

As Shawn reviewed this chapter, I asked him, "Since so many families struggle with this issue, would you be willing to share about this season through your perspective?" The next morning, I received the following response from him. His opening words describe my godly mother's response which demonstrates what it has taken me many years to learn as being the most important response of all.

Reflections of Our Son: *Shawn writes…*

Unconditional Love

You have to love my Grandmother Mary. She is a piece of work. I figured she and people of her era wouldn't be typically understanding of homosexuality. But she always made sure I knew she loved me, no matter what. She always made sure my friends felt welcome. I invited some more colorful friends to a few large family functions, and she made sure they felt welcome even though some family members were less than enthusiastic about their presence. She still today asks me how my "friends" are and prays for them daily. I know that she knows God has someone or something in mind for me. Her ability to love unconditionally has influenced me greatly.

Coming Out

My coming out to my parents came in a unique circumstance. I remember it was a Saturday, and I went boating with a friend. I remember coming home that day with mom and dad sitting on the couch in tears. I remember a rough conversation with them. I remember some comments about what friends and family were going to think. I remember thinking before this, when my parents find out about me, Mom will be OK with things and Dad will go through the roof. As I recall that day, Mom was the one that came apart at the seams, and Dad stayed relatively calm.

I remember going to some counseling and the counselor saying that maybe I was ok, and some people have these kinds of feelings. That counselor, as I remember, didn't last long. My parents wanted me to talk to people from church that took my parents' view about this lifestyle.

I don't remember finding much common ground during this time. I felt a separation from my parents. I don't remember much about my younger sisters finding out, but I remember when my brother heard, his wife made it pretty apparent she didn't have a problem with it.

Separation and Resentment

I don't know who said it or how it was made known to me, but at one point I remember it being put out there that my friends weren't allowed at the river cabin. It may not have been an absolute thing, but it was generally put out there. I was extremely hurt by this. The cabin was my home and had become a fun great experience growing up there. I remember frustration and resentment over it even today. I remember saying to myself "if my family doesn't want me around, I have family that does." This was a hard one to deal with and led to a lot of years of further separation from family. I would tell friends about the river cabin, and when they got excited about going there some time, I would add, "I don't go down there much anymore."

Rebuilding

I feel under construction at this point. My guess is there were about 7-10 years (1993-early 2000's) of destruction and now about 10-15 years of reconstruction. My parent's views on things, I would have to say, have changed, maybe not during first few years so much, but after some time I started seeing more acceptance of things.

I had a life-changing incident in 2000 where I got beaten up more or less because of my lifestyle. I had a rough time for six months to a year. My parents were there for me. They were there when I don't remember: the first week to surgery then to court a year or so later. I felt like something changed during that incident. I had family members at court that I didn't expect, and ones that I did expect, nowhere to be seen.

My Faith

I believe in God and have accepted Jesus as my savior. I know where I'm going, and I'm totally comfortable with that. I feel like my early upbringing in the church, home groups, and Christian schools was a lot to take as a youngster.

Once I had the ability to make decisions on my own and decide my own path – I may have swung hard left field (preacher's kid syndrome?) It has taken a little while to find some balance in my life. I talk to God – not enough. I don't believe He would burden me with these feelings unless there was something to it. I try not to be bashful about my faith – I pray for friends and acquaintances. Most of all, I believe that God loves me for who I am.   Shawn

AUTUMN HARVEST

His Mission—My Purpose

All of our life seasons were dramatically different. During the lush springtime, God planted a bountiful supply of seeds of faith in His love and power as He introduced us to His Spirit and the supernatural. Then came the long dry summer and His hard lessons on how to love which ended with me flooded with emotions and at a near breaking point, good soil for His seeds to grow.

Then came Autumn, a time to enjoy the harvest. We needed a major overhaul before we could reap the ripening fruit in our lives. He gave us one. This season looked nothing like the others and would require our knowing Him at a deeper level to successfully navigate the challenges ahead. At the same time we would enjoy the new treasures He had hidden for us to find in our lives.

As the fall began with my sitting on the rocks, I wondered what lay ahead: What now? Who would I become as I waited? Shawn had moved on with his life, and we had moved on with ours. My faith was shaky. Although I knew that God was still powerfully at work within me, I questioned how He would get us through the strong winds that continued to hit us and tried to knock us down. I was experiencing how "the darkest hour is just before the dawn" at this juncture as I faced possibly the greatest crisis point of my lifetime.

Life is never really about our troubles; it is about how we learn to navigate them. God showed me how to travel through this time trusting Him to do more than all I asked or imagined. In this season He re-awakening my passion for Him as He shaped me and helped me make His mission my purpose.

> *Now to him who is able to do immeasurably more than all we ask or imagine, according to his power that is at work within us, to him be glory in the church and in Christ Jesus throughout all generations, for ever and ever! Amen.* (Ephesians 3:20, 21 NIV)

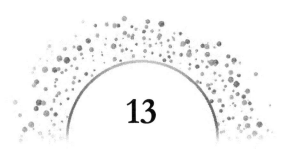

13

Give Me a Break

I entered the autumn of our life with some trepidation. Would I regain my connection with God? Would our future still be full of powerful adventures together? Honestly I wasn't overly confident in what lay ahead. My thoughts were more along the line of "Good grief. What is next? Will these troubles never end?"

My Bionic Man

The next year Don turned 50 and faced another heap of troubles. While he was actively trying to stay young and fit, his aging body wasn't cooperating resulting in surgery more than once.

First, he jammed his finger and broke it while playing basketball with a young buddy. The doctor installed a surgical pin that protruded ½" from his finger; he assured Don that when he removed the pin in three months Don's finger would be as straight as a pencil. Today that finger is as crooked as a fishhook.

His second surgery repaired a torn meniscus from who knows what activity. In a few months his knee felt strong, and he was eager to get active again.

The next mishap began with great intentions. Don bought a classy 10-speed bike, a real bargain, at our neighbor's yard sale. He said, "I'll get a helmet, but first I think I'll take a little spin. One little bike ride won't hurt, right?" as he rode off in the country on his maiden voyage.

After ten miles he turned back and was cruising down a short hill when the bike chain jumped off the sprocket. Looking down to investigate, Don jackknifed the bike and landed face down on the concrete pavement. Dazed, he got up and walked his bike the final mile home.

Hearing him come in, I called out, "Dinner is almost ready. How was your ride?"

He calmly replied, "I think we probably ought to run by the ER before dinner."

I looked up and saw blood streaming from the open cuts on his bruised face. In the ER the doctor stitched him up, and Don sported two black racoon eyes for weeks.

His third surgery soon followed to repair his cracked facial bones with three metal plates held together by 23 screws. Don still has no feeling in certain spots on his face although I still find him quite handsome.

His fourth and final surgery that year came a few months later when an ENT surgeon diagnosed and repaired a deviated septum from the accident.

But the surgeries were not what stood out that year, but rather the revelation of God's celestial help. On the night after the bike spill, I lay beside Don, thanking God for protecting him from serious injury. I prayed, "Lord, I sense there was more happening here. Reveal the unseen."

A picture of Don pedaling the bike played in a movie in my mind's eye. Running alongside him was a well-built angelic being perhaps seven feet tall. When Don fell headfirst to the ground, this angel reached down and cushioned Don's head in his hand just as it met the pavement. I thought, "Oh my goodness. That kept him from cracking open his skull."

The next morning as I told Don that story, I looked at his tan face and saw what appeared to be a white thumbprint on the skin of his right temple. I sensed God saying, "There is the thumbprint of the angel who lifted his head." Don went to the mirror, and he began smiling too as he saw the distinct thumbprint. Did an angel just deliver Don from a fatal fall?

Later that morning I got my answer as I read these passages in my One Year Bible:

But you, LORD, are a shield around me, my glory, the One who lifts my head high. (Psalm 3:3)

You, who through faith are shielded by God's power... You greatly rejoice though now for a little while you may have had to suffer grief in all kinds of trials...Even angels long to look into these things. (I Peter 1:5-13 NIV)

Wow! The prior night I had wondered if I just had an active imagination, but the next morning I felt God's confirmation as I read His Word– shielded by God's power, the lifter of my head, suffering grief in trials, angels—all reassuring me that God had given us a *glimpse* into the unseen realm.

Are not all angels ministering spirits sent to serve those who will inherit salvation? (Hebrews 1:14 NIV)

Four years later my journal read,

Today Don got a bright red sunburn and the white thumbprint showed up again on his right temple. It appears sometimes when his face is especially tan.

Now over twenty years later, the thumbprint comes and goes, but I see it more frequently as he ages as a visible reminder of the invisible realm around us.

Thank God that four surgeries in a year was only a short season, and I got to continue doing life now with my bionic man.

Oh No, Not Suicide

I thought, "What a year! Surely this string of trials is over." But then one morning the phone rang at work, and I heard my brother's shaky voice on the other end. I knew immediately that something was wrong but in no way expected the shocking words that I was about to hear.

"Cathy, I just don't know any easy way to tell you this. Dad is dead. He just shot himself."

"No way!" I thought, "This just cannot be happening." Life once more was proving unpredictable. We knew Dad had been increasingly depressed, but none of us thought he would take his own life. Our family was reeling. There are no easy words to explain such a time when it is someone you love deeply. It just doesn't make sense.

People always enjoyed being around Dad, for he enjoyed visiting with everyone and knew no strangers. He had been a good father but was human and obviously had some shortcomings like the rest of us. He had always been proud of being a very strong and capable man.

But as he aged, his health declined, and at 72 he became depressed, painfully aware of his failing mind and body. He began to feel hopeless. The thought of not being in control and actually being a burden seemed unbearable. He wrote a suicide note to my mother saying how we would be better off without him, drove into the country with a shotgun, and ended his life.

From that moment on there were far too many questions and too few answers for our family. Some asked the question, "Why? Why would he do this to us?" Others asked, "What if...?" that took them on a dead-end futile trail of thought of how they might have stopped him.

While the pain was over for him, the pain would go on for the loved ones he left behind. God helped us cope during this time, but the pain that accompanies such a tragedy can go on for a lifetime. Each of our family dealt with grief in different ways and intensities, but it was devastating for all of us.

Suicide was not a good answer. It never is.

The Time of Great Sadness

That year was a real struggle as I dealt emotionally with the losses, surgeries, and rebuilding the cabin along with our relationship with Shawn. At times it appeared like the devil was winning. No wonder I sat and cried for hours on the river banks. We had been hammered hard. Over those next few years I'm sure that my life looked fine on the outside to those around me. I loved my job, the kids were prospering, and Don and I were enjoying a lot of new adventures. Many days I was convinced I was fine as long as I stayed busy. But inside, my heart was going through a time of great sadness.

The pain churning inside messed with my faith as hopelessness began to creep in. How could I have gotten in this kind of shape after all the powerful encounters with God's presence? When I saw how I had succumbed to being sidetracked by the allures of the world, I felt like such a loser though I knew failing did not mean I was a failure. It sure did feel like it.

As I stared into the future, I stewed about the likelihood of more loss and failure ahead. Yet I knew that worrying was as unproductive as fearing howling coyotes that never appeared. I knew from the past there was only one place I could go for help.

> *At this point many of his disciples turned away and deserted him. Then Jesus turned to the Twelve and asked, "Are you also going to leave?" Simon Peter replied, "Lord, to whom would we go? You have the words that give eternal life."* (John 6:66-68 NLT)

I needed once again to lay my inadequacies before God and allow Him to help me fight off this darkness. This was a defining moment in my life—Know God more or No more God. It was my choice. It is always our choice as he never forces us. Under the heavy weight I cried out, "Lord, I give up. I am overwhelmed trying to carry all this on my own. I am sorry. I feel like such a screw up and can't seem to keep my focus on you. I feel like I am slowly swirling down into a dark pit of despair. Keep me from drifting farther away from You. I know You are my one and only hope. Come to my rescue, Lord."

Then I added, "Maybe we need a little breathing space from our hectic pace to regain our focus on you and why we are here on this earth. Lord, we need a break."

Hawaii or the Amazon?

Over the years when we were asked, "If you could travel anywhere, where would you go?" Don always had the same answer, "Someday I want to take a trip to the Amazon."

When he brought it up again I laughed, "Fat chance!" as I suggested a more comfortable spot. "Not me, Honey. I want to go to Hawaii and sit on the beach and sip on a piña colada as we watch the sun set over the ocean. I can almost hear the strains of ukulele music floating on the breeze. Now that's what I'm talking about."

Two weeks later we were sitting in church, and I could not believe my ears. Pastor Ben Hoerr was speaking, " I just got a call from a missionary from Project Amazon or PAZ in Brazil. PAZ has a vision of planting 100,000 local churches, one in each village in the Amazon Basin, and they need help. Rick, the leader in Macapa', has asked me to gather a team to come help erect a church building. I am going. Who wants to go with me?"

Don was thinking, "Let's go!"

I was thinking, "Let's not."

Then my heart began to pound. "Oh dear. Maybe this coincidence is really a God-incidence." The music from Waikiki began fading. Could this be the answer to my "give me a break" prayer? PAZ does mean "peace" in Portuguese. Besides, my bionic man wasn't getting any younger, and here was a chance for him to both reach his dream destination and serve in his favorite role as Don the Builder. It was a no-brainer...for him. Isaiah's conversation with God in the Old Testament came to my mind,

> *Then I heard the voice of the Lord saying, "Whom shall I send? And who will go for us?" And I said, "Here am I. Send me!"* (Isaiah 6:8 NIV)

So I said, "Here am I. Send Don...Oops, I mean, send us... Ok, 'Here am I. Send me.'"

It looked like we were headed on another river adventure. The Mighty Mississippi had just brought a flood of destruction; hopefully this one would bring living waters of refreshment and restoration.

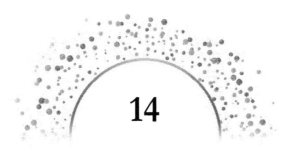

14

Up the Amazon River

Let those who fear the Lord say: His love endures forever. When hard pressed, I cried to the Lord; he brought me into a spacious place. (Psalm 118:4,5 NIV)

A New River Adventure

On my 52nd birthday instead of packing suntan lotion in a bag for Hawaii, I packed sunscreen in a bag for the Amazon. Uncertain how my indoor-loving, physically-challenged body would survive this trip, I hoped that Don's wonderland would not turn out to be my struggle land. Thank God, we would be on the outskirts of the jungle and we weren't going during flood season when the river raises thirty feet and spreads to 120 miles wide.

The Amazon River is the world's largest in sheer volume as it meanders 4000 miles through South America. I was praying hard that I was up to another big river experience, trying to trust God as I reasoned, *"This excursion only lasts for sixteen days. I can do anything for sixteen days, right?*

Soon we were flying into the unknown with our pastor Ben and an energetic young couple in their 20s. Thirty-one hours later we stepped off our plane into the Amazon Basin, a whole new world 3600 miles from home. Belem, Brazil, was definitely not a tourist destination, and only a few locals spoke English. Of course, we weren't the typical tourists either. We had brought only a few clothes and personal items so that we could lug along nine 70-pound boxes of supplies including an airplane propeller tucked away in the clothing. I also carried a lot of heavy baggage inside me which I hoped God would help me leave behind.

During this long layover in Belem a delightful missionary couple picked us up and showed us the city. That afternoon while the others got in a few hours of rest, I sat with the wife on her bed as we shared a private heartache we were both going through as we cried and fervently prayed with each other. This short intimate time together with her and God would have made the whole trip worth it for me. But there was much more to come.

Later as we sat waiting in the outdoor airport lobby I realized the bugs were really going to bug me. "There goes a mouse," I remarked, pointing to the critter darting across the concrete.

Don raised his eyebrow and retorted, "Look again, Honey."

"Ewwwh! It's a cockroach," I moaned. They were big ones!

I had pictured the Amazon as beautiful but uncomfortable, quite hot and humid, full of colorful iguanas, pesky bugs, humongous spiders, hordes of mosquitoes, and fat pythons squeezed around tall palm trees with not a piña colada in sight.

Many of my pictures turned out to be accurate: the beauty, hot humid days, iguanas, bugs, spiders, and mosquitoes galore. But there were surprises around every corner: swerving our jeep to miss a sloth slothfully crossing the road, walking a wide detour around a swarming waist-high ant hill, and staring at an alligator tail on the counter destined to our breakfast.

I could present an amazing travelogue describing the wonders of this exotic part of the world, but I've chosen instead to share what we saw God doing. For me, the most impactful story was the transformation He made in the heart of one comfort-loving, pleasure-seeking, affluent American momma, namely me.

I've chosen to paint a picture of the Amazon that may seem different than you would expect.

For in the Amazon Basin...I saw Jesus.

All in A Day's Work

We flew into Macapa, Brazil, to tackle our week-long building project. The first few days I barely noticed all the rare wonders of this world as I struggled to get my focus off my discomfort. I really wanted to navigate our first third world experience with some measure of joy. I was thinking, "Am I ever spoiled! This might prove harder than I had imagined."

The daily weather was always around 100° with 99% humidity, so there were no weather forecasts or thermometers. No need. Our daily schedule was just as predictable. After a 6 a.m. breakfast we gathered our tools, pushed our two-ton truck to jump start it, and then hopped in the back and onto a bench bracing ourselves for a harrowing ride weaving through the heart of the bustling city to reach the building site. The sights and sounds were captivating as we passed the colorful open-air market teeming with such things as fresh caught-fish, meat hung on a hook, tropical fruits and vegetables, handmade baskets and clothes.

In a half hour we reached the site nestled in a primitive remote area where the forest and city met. People were daily streaming in and clearing brush to build huts for their families and search for work and a better life. Sprawled out along long dirt roads with no trees were 8x10' one-room dwellings for families of five or six. Most of the men were gone all day trying to find a little work. The kids played contentedly in the dirt while the women hauled water from long distances. In the evening they prepared their family meal, a little rice, beans, and manioc root boiled in a pot over a fire made with sticks the kids had gathered.

The shanties had no plumbing or electricity except for when someone would "borrow electricity" by throwing a wire over the main electrical line to light a single light bulb. My heart ached for the families who spent every single day of their lives working just to meet their most basic needs of food, water, and shelter. In this close-up view of poverty, God was changing my understanding of what is essential.

Don the Builder thrived in our ten-hour days as we erected the 14" concrete foundation for the 35'x75' church building. The team laboriously dug shallow trenches in the clay ground using a pick and spade and then filled the footings with hand-mixed concrete.

Cathy the Comfort-seeker was surviving more than thriving. As the oldest member of the team, I was assigned the easiest job, drawing water from a 50' well. It was all my 52-year-old body was able to do. I lowered a five-gallon bucket into the well to fill with water and turned a wooden hand crank to wind up the rope that drew the bucket to the surface. Then I carried the 41.5-pound pail of water to the concrete mixing trough…repeat…all day long. This was grueling labor for me. Water is heavy!

Each morning we worked hard and stopped at noon for a light lunch although we were rarely hungry in the scorching mid-day heat. What we cherished was water and lots of it. Then we took a two-hour nap along with every man and his dog as all shops closed and all movement ceased until 2 pm. I looked forward to this sweet siesta as I quickly learned to fall asleep on a narrow wooden bench without falling off. But too soon I was the water girl again.

After my first full day working in the blazing sun I looked forward to a quick shower before dinner in the cool rainwater collected in an overhead roof reservoir. My first shower in the steamy bathroom ended quickly when I noticed that I was not alone. An 8" iguana was climbing across the shower wall. He was a beauty but way too close to admire. As I dried off I noticed a large black spider which filled the sink bowl, and I quickly vacated the bathroom. But I am happy to report that I didn't step on a single snake nor even see one, big or small during the entire trip. However, I was certain they were there lurking in the trees ready to drop at any moment to squeeze the life out of me.

Evenings were spent with our missionary host Rick and his wife Sandra who had prepared us a delicious simple meal. We were unaware how they were sacrificing for us until one night when one of Rick's little boys crawled up on his lap asking for a little more juice in his small cup. Dad said, "No, I'm sorry, buddy. You have had enough." We looked at our large cups and how we had given little thought to having refills, unaware of our indulgence. We saw their love as we learned their story of how God had called them to this remote area to make Jesus known to these precious people.

Rick shared that they now had a handful of new believers who they were discipling in small cell groups across the expanding city, and he had called for our help for the next phase which was a church building for gathering new settlers on the outskirts. We felt privileged to help bring these people hope as together we prayed for His joy and peace to appear in the middle of their toil.

As I witnessed the sacrifice and compassion of these servants…I saw Jesus.

The World's Worst Missionary

At bedtime Don and I walked across the dirt road to sleep at another house with some of the young new believers. We didn't speak the same language so conversation was minimal. I tried to ask a question about the wet clothes I had hand-washed and hung to dry in the backyard that morning. Laboriously I smiled at our hostess and pointed to a few words in my Portuguese-English dictionary, "Leave clothes overnight?"

She vigorously shook her head pointing to the words "Nao, ladrao" or "No, robbers."

Now I realized why Julio pushed his motorcycle into the living room at night before he bolted the door. We were told of the crime and vice accompanying the poverty all around us and were aware of our defenseless state. We relied solely on God for his protection. I had to remind myself more than once,

> *For God has not given us a spirit of fear and timidity, but of power, love, and self-discipline.* (II Timothy 1:7 NLT)

Totally exhausted, Don and I fell into bed, thankful for our rolled-up sweatshirts that served as pillows. I lay very still to avoid feeling the wooden slats underneath the 2" mattress as I tried to ignore my sunburn, aching muscles, and the bites of the tiny mosquitoes swarming through the window openings with no screens. What the pests lacked in size they made up for in numbers and ambition, but we learned to disregard these little pests that were just part of normal life for these folks.

We all still struggled with giving up the comforts we were used to at home, especially in the evenings as we passed by a vendor stand displaying two or three enticing liter bottles of Coke. After the sweltering heat of our work day, we really craved a Coke. Each of us had enough pocket change to buy a bottle, but how could we indulge in this luxury unaffordable for so many around us? We held out for eight days but then caved in and shared a cold one.

To fight off the thoughts of how I had to be the world's worst short-term missionary ever, I turned to a habit I had learned to do when I felt distressed. I turned my focus to consider God's provisions and began thanking Him for each simple pleasure, beginning with the fact that we slept in a bed as I remembered to pray for a good night's sleep for Ben swinging in his hammock.

My woes at home were seeming smaller, and I told God I was sorry for taking so much for granted. We drifted into a deep sleep until the rooster crowed before dawn. After a week this incessant wakeup call began to annoy me, so at breakfast I quipped to Rick, "I wish that rowdy rooster would sleep past 5 am just one morning."

Rick frowned, "What rooster?"

Then he burst out laughing, "Do you mean the parrot next door. He just thinks he is a rooster. Definitely an imposter!" Duped by an early rising parrot!

His Glory in the Heavens

During the week people stood by observing our daily progress, so on Saturday night their curiosity was peaked when our truck surprisingly returned to the building site at dusk. Our team began hanging a large sheet above the dirt road and setting up a makeshift projector in the back of the truck with some "borrowed" electricity. We were preparing to show the renowned "JESUS" film translated in 1500 languages to share the gospel.

My assignment was to go invite everyone in the large neighborhood to come see the movie. Limited by my vocabulary of ten words in Portuguese, I was relieved when a young Brazilian gal offered to go with me even though we couldn't communicate with each other. As we approached each hut, we clapped our hands twice and invited the people who came out. I tagged along, clapping and sharing a big smile on my very white face, quite a novelty. The building site had long disappeared, and the farther away we went, the more lost I was and the more anxious I was becoming as I tried to ignore some growling dogs and a few uncomfortable stares as the night darkened.

I shifted my eyes upward and was suddenly struck by the splendor and glory of God's handiwork. The velvety black sky was filled with a brilliant display of stars, more than I had ever seen I was so overwhelmed with what a tiny speck I was in this vast universe and felt somehow all alone.

> *Lord, our Lord, how majestic is your name in all the earth! You have set your glory in the heavens.* (Psalm 8:1,3-5 NIV)

But then all at once I was more overwhelmed how the Creator of this splendor was right there with me, my Father who intimately loved me and sent Jesus to walk with me. His very presence swirled around and through me.

I knew that I was not alone... I saw Jesus.

A half an hour later I was relieved when we arrived back at the base where the projector was hooked up, the sheet was hung, and 70-80 people sat in the dirt ready to view the movie which was a first-time experience for most. The powerful message of God in Portuguese resounded in the night air. While we couldn't understand the words, tears streamed down the faces of our team as we watched this account of Jesus' rescue mission to Planet Earth.

Then 40-50 came forward to receive a free Bible and many began their own walk with Jesus. What a privilege to live out Acts 1:8 and witness some of the first fruits of this new church tribe at the ends of the earth.

Once again…I saw Jesus.

> *You will be my witnesses in Jerusalem, and in all Judea and Samaria, and to the ends of the earth.* (Acts 1:8 NIV)

Up the River

To begin the last leg of our adventure we flew to PAZ headquarters in Santarem to spend time with the team who had moved to Brazil to oversee the mission. Our plane set down at 3 am, and at 6:30 am we boarded a 15' x 45' two-story medical boat with two missionary families for an unforgettable 8-hour trip up river. How refreshing for my aching body after all that labor. As the boat chugged up river, we enjoyed becoming friends with two dedicated American missionary families as we heard their stories.

We also basked in the sun on the breezy roof deck as we journeyed through the rain forest. The scenes we passed looked like pages of National Geographic: thatched huts nestled under palm trees with chickens and cows and kids wandering free. Men with their sons fished with homemade nets from their hand-carved canoes. Women washed clothes on rocks along the banks as the children bathed and played in the river. Life was simple but far from easy.

Our destination was the site of a special three-day Congresso or camp meeting in a large village of 1500 Brazilians. The massive river and its tributaries were the only highways to this remote area as no roads went through this part of the thick rain forest. Over 300 believers and their families walked for days carrying their hammocks and a little food. They cleared a path through the jungle with machetes so that they could gather with other believers to worship and be encouraged by hearing the Word of God preached.

Again I thought about back home and how easily we hop in our cars and drive to a church service on Sunday, oblivious of what a privilege we have. I thought of the times I had been irritated by little things like a mediocre sermon, the service going too long, or those times I just slept in and didn't go. But here I saw a people had an intense passion for more of Jesus as they took this command to heart:

> *And let us not neglect our meeting together, as some people do, but encourage one another, especially now that the day of his return is drawing near.* (Hebrews 10:25 NLT)

Tarantulas, Piranhas & Sting Rays

We arrived, tied up the boat, and then waded through knee-deep water. On shore we climbed a makeshift terraced stairway up a steep 100' bluff. On top, all the locals and lots of children excitedly gathered around as Becky Hrubik, a familiar missionary, who gave us a tour. In the center of the village was a 150' deep well that PAZ had dug so that people could draw clean water with a hand pump which helped eradicate disease from drinking contaminated river water. Then Becky used her nursing skills to serve the people's medical needs.

As she served… I saw Jesus.

That night a generator lit a few light bulbs as everyone turned out for the camp meeting. The Portuguese worship music was lively, and we joyfully sang along both in our own language and also in tongues since all our words were a different language to those around us anyway.

Jeff Hrubik, the PAZ director, gave a powerful message in Portuguese as his wife Becky translated to our team. As she spoke, she smiled pointing to the large tarantula resting in the rafters a few feet above our heads. After that I had a hard time listening. After the message, Jeff invited us to come forward to pray as those hungry for more of God rushed to the front of the makeshift. We laid hands on around fifty people, praying mainly in tongues since we knew no Portuguese and didn't know what to pray.

We saw how God is still powerfully working as we are willing to partner with Him as the Presence of His Spirit began to come. Some were dramatically touched by God, falling backwards to the ground as His power healed them and set many free from oppression as they testified afterwards. None had never before witnessed this phenomenon. We were as surprised as they were although such unusual phenomena has been recorded throughout church history. Sometimes it is hard to stand in His Presence.

In this place on this night filled with His power...I saw Jesus.

Later after we waded back to the boat, a ten-year-old missionary's son went fishing off the side of our boat and caught a couple of piranhas and three 18" stingrays. I was thinking, "And we just waded through that water." Soon we fell asleep in hammocks strung across the open roof deck while admiring God's splendorous sky full of stars.

We awoke at dawn and were surprised to be shivering cold and drenched with dew. As we looked out of our hammocks, we saw nationals using long poles to rid the river bottom of stingrays. When all was clear, we joined in with the crowd who came out to celebrate the baptism of fifteen new believers from the prior night. Thank God, the piranhas and stingrays did not join us.

Our boat returned to PAZ headquarters, and the next morning we joined the staff for their 7 am prayer meeting at their boat shop where back then craftsmen were building 6-8 small river boats a year for native boat pastors. Together we prayed for these men who live with their families on boats traveling upriver to reach remote people who have never heard the good news. The previous month a pastor and his wife lost their five-year-old son when he fell overboard trying to get a bucket of water one dark night.

> *"He is no fool who gives what he cannot keep to gain that which he cannot lose."* [5] —JIM ELLIOT

Despite their incredible sacrifice these disciples experienced great joy and contentment from the Lord, thriving while surviving as they worked alongside the loving missionaries who trained them and modeled how to humbly follow Jesus. When Don offered Becky his extra tall sweat suit for Jeff, she was so elated, "One of our river pastors could really use these during cold nights on the river." These servant-leaders were always thinking of others before themselves.

In these servant leaders...I saw Jesus.

Hearing their stories caused me to think about how much of my life was spent on things that don't count and don't bring real joy. What do I sacrifice to make Jesus known? A sobering thought.

A Message in the Stars

The missionaries had discovered the richest treasure of the Amazon, its people whom God holds dear. These leaders loved God who loves all people; at the same time they loved all people and helped them love God.

Their disciples continue to multiply, and today 60,000 people meet weekly in the city of Santarem alone in cell groups of 6-10 people for 1½ hours to pray and study the Word. Meanwhile disciples reach more people and plant new churches in the remote up river villages.

In their passion...I saw Jesus.

During our short time together we had bonded with the PAZ leaders and were sad to see our last day together arrive. In the evening we gathered with the leaders on a white sand beach, built a campfire, and watched the sun go down while we worshipped God. Among us was Christine, the young widow of Luke Huber who had the vision of PAZ and had led the work until he was killed in a plane crash while spreading the gospel up river just six months prior to our arrival.

As I lay there gazing upward with my head on Don's lap, Ben led us in worship with his guitar and read a scripture and gave a few brief words of encouragement.

The star-studded sky reminded me of the scattered twinkling lights in the black expanse of darkness that we had seen from the airplane as we flew over the Amazon. I shared what I sensed God saying, "Whenever you look up at the night sky, see it as a picture of Luke's vision. You are planting thousands of churches that will be lights shining in the darkness of the Amazon."

Christine spoke softly, "God is so powerful tonight and confirming that PAZ is still His vision. Ben, the scripture you shared was the very one Luke had been studying when he died. Cathy, what you saw was the same thing the Lord showed Luke a few days before his plane went down a few months ago. I feel so overwhelmed with His love." Her words touched our hearts.

As we were gathered in one accord...I saw Jesus.

We were humbled that God would use us to encourage these mighty warriors who had indelibly impacted us with their sacrificial example here. Soon we boarded the plane for the long trip home never to return to the Amazon. But as we flew up out of this exotic place, we took a piece of it embedded in our hearts.

For in this the incredible place... I saw Jesus.

Finally Home, But Not at Home

I shudder to think how close I had come to allowing my obsession for comfort to rob us of the most amazing trip of our life. I will have all of eternity to be comfortable.

Coming home we faced reverse culture shock. I did not expect to return to my familiar world and find it strangely unfamiliar. As we landed in the US, the Miami Airport overloaded my senses with smells, sounds, and sights, such as the colorful artwork, boldly painted walls, and vivid carpets that shouted out luxury in every square foot. I had never noticed before.

On my first trip to the grocery store I was home but no longer at home. As I walked down the aisles, I began to weep out loud as I stared at shelves brimming with every food imaginable. Hundreds of cereal choices lined the shelves whereas in the Amazon there was one choice of cereal and not a single jar of peanut butter to be found anywhere. How could this be?

I realized how spoiled I was as a privileged American who gave no thought to how others in the world live. Over three billion people, nearly half of the world, struggle to exist, living on less than $2.50 a day.[6] While we were far from the American definition of wealthy, we were quite rich as are most Americans compared to the rest of the world. We just don't see the truth of this when we are inside our own little bubble wrapped up in pursuing the American dream.

Perhaps God didn't send us there for a break from our trials but to show us the trials others face as they daily toil for minimal food, water, and shelter. Many will never once experience a hot shower, indoor plumbing, electricity, a ride in a vehicle, or clean water to drink. Perhaps He sent us to give us new eyes to see.

> *Then they will reply, "Lord, when did we ever see you hungry or thirsty or a stranger or naked or sick or in prison, and not help you?"*
>
> *And he will answer, "I tell you the truth, when you refused to help the least of these my brothers and sisters, you were refusing to help me." (Matthew 25:44,45)*

15

Ground Zero

Hitting The Pause Button

Our trip sent aftershocks through my life creating my own ground zero. The week we arrived home I began experiencing major chest pain and abdominal cramping and suspected a heart attack. The examining doctor asked if I had done any strenuous work lately. When I told him of my well water job, he laughed, "You aren't having a heart attack. You bruised your chest wall muscle from all the strain. You'll recover in a couple of weeks." He was right.

Recovery at work took a lot longer as I felt disoriented and was unable to go back to business as usual. In light of the world I had just returned from, my work tasks and goals didn't seem as important. With a new paradigm of life I had to learn how to navigate with my new lens in my old world.

Little by little, I was shifting from a busy brisk run to a slow simple walk with God. I could hear the words of our missionary friend Pablo, "Just slow down. You Americans are always in a hurry even when you're not headed anywhere."

Taking heed I began to say *"no"* to more activities, shortened my *"to do list"*, and served simpler meals. My shopping list shrank as my prayer list expanded. Our bank balance wasn't expanding, but it certainly appeared to be bigger.

God was also changing my *stinking thinking* as author Joyce Meyer puts it. I no longer wanted to live a life all about me. We had an abundance of the basic needs—food, clean water, shelter, sleep, and health. During this Amazon pause I realized the problem was all the other stuff we'd spent or time and money pursuing over the years: more stuff, more experiences, and more success, the things which brought only fleeting pleasures. It was time for a life change.

The rich and satisfying life we hungered for was appearing as we pursued God and loved those around us. I pondered a whole new set of questions:

Who is needier? Believers who have given up everything or believers who have everything and are sidetracked with over-abundance?

What is real poverty? Not having enough or having way more than enough and missing out on God's best?

What is worse? Living with next to nothing and fulfilling great purpose or living with everything yet pursuing no purpose?

"Father, thank you for being here through all my trials when I was losing heart. Forgive me for not keeping you the center of my life, for getting sidetracked and captivated by other interests. I realize that only You bring abundant life. Restore my passion for You. Show me your purpose for me.

"Give me Your compassion for people. Thank you for opening my eyes to their needs. Never let me close them again. Lord, I love you. Amen."

I had seen what it looked like to make Jesus known in the Amazon, but it was time to work out what it was to look like in my own world. God slowly showed me my specific *mission, message,* and *methods* to make Jesus more fully known.

Standing On the Rock   *my mission...*

He lifted me out of the slimy pit, out of the mud and mire; he set my feet on a rock and gave me a firm place to stand.
(Psalm 40:2 NIV)

Our trip had been challenging, and I was thankful that I was no longer in a pit or crying on a rock. Now I was rejoicing, standing on the solid rock, Jesus, the living stone.

As you come to him, the living Stone—rejected by humans but chosen by God and precious to him (I Peter 2:4 NIV)

It felt like being at ground zero ready to build all over again. I realized my life story would never be valuable as a model of how to perfectly go after God but rather as a real picture of how He perfectly goes after us, rescues and restores us. It would tell the story that no matter where we are or in what condition our life is in, we can always start over in our life journey with Him, for He never lets go of us or quits loving us.

> *You did it: you changed wild lament into whirling dance; You ripped off my black mourning band and decked me with wildflowers. I'm about to burst with song; I can't keep quiet about you. God, my God, I can't thank you enough.* (Psalm 30:11-12 The Message)

The billions of people on this planet matter greatly to the Lord. He desires a close relationship with each one. I had seen how God was so delighted in the missionaries who gladly sacrificed their own welfare to bring His love to His precious people in a foreign land. I also knew that God was overjoyed with the ordinary local believers I had seen who contentedly served others with joy while living in poverty too. Now it was my turn to intentionally sacrifice my welfare to love on others in my very different world as I focused less on seeking blessing for me and more on blessing others.

My Amazon "aha moment" was seeing that a richly satisfying life boils down to knowing Jesus intimately and learning how to let Him love others through me.

My *mission* could be simply stated: Love God. Love people. Period.

My Life Anchor   *my mission,* **my message...**

Life is such a mixture of ups and downs, trials and triumphs. As soon as I clearly saw my mission, He gave me a specific *message* that I was to convey to others through our GodStories, indelibly imprinted it in me in a unique way. I had come to know Him as a God who enjoys talking with each of His kids in a million unique ways customized for each in the way we are most likely to hear.

His message appeared on an ordinary Saturday morning when I was out "sailing," a hobby that might seem odd to some folks since we didn't live anywhere near a lake. I didn't need any. I sailed down the city streets, yard sailed, that is. I discovered a choice yard sale route when we first moved to Champaign and found bargains to refurnish the cabin and clothe our new crop of grandbabies. It was my favorite "girls just want to have fun" outing as I found bargains like my $250 KitchenAid mixer I bought for $25. Yet the most priceless treasure that came to me while yard sailing was not something that could be held in my hands, but it would bring me great joy for the rest of my life.

It happened like this: one Saturday I was paused at a stop sign. "God, I'm having so much fun. Shouldn't I be home working or helping someone? Is this selfish? Is it okay that I enjoy yard sailing so much?" My eyes then darted to my car radio clock which displayed 10:10. I recalled the familiar scripture that I had read that morning where Jesus says,

> *The thief comes to rob, kill and destroy, but I have come that you might have life in all its abundance.* (John 10:10 NIV)

I could picture Jesus tossing His head back and laughing, enjoying how I was getting such a kick out of this pastime. He was answering me in His unique way. Yes, He wanted me to have an abundant life in a variety of ways. Oddly for me that includes yard sales. He has provided for us all kinds of things to enjoy and ideas to explore here on earth and likes for us to have fun as long as it is in *addition* to keeping our main focus on loving Him and others.

That night as I turned out the bedroom light, I looked at our digital clock at exactly 10:10. I slowly proclaimed John 10:10 out loud again as I sensed His presence. Somehow I recognized that this was no small day, no trivial treasure from Jesus. For this was the day I was imprinted with the life message I was to share with others: Jesus is present wherever we are, in our everyday ordinary surroundings. He wants to give us extraordinary abundant life as we walk intimately together, regardless of the destruction the enemy tries to bring.

Even as I walked in my own ordinary life...I saw Jesus.

For over two decades now, my eyes have repeatedly been drawn to the clock at 10:10, most often when I need to be reminded of the unseen spiritual war raging around us. Satan, our enemy, has constantly attempted to rob us of joy and peace, to kill us with disease and accidents, and to destroy our walk with God. God used this verse to constantly point out this truth.

Yet when I've turned and prayed for help, I've seen Jesus true to his Word creatively turning blows into blessings as He bring abundant life.

We Are Better Together *my mission, my message,* **my method**

Now armed with my mission to love God and people and my message of how Jesus gives abundant life, He began showing me what *method* I was to use to impact my world as I partnered with Him.

There was one thing He made very clear. We are better together. We were called to work together as His church, his tribe of people on this earth. Before this trip we loved God but attended church sporadically, taking off on weekends to visit our kids in college. Of course, we wanted to be with our kids, but quite frankly, we were burned out on church and had almost given up hope on His people. When we did make it to church, we'd arrive late and slip out early to avoid people. With unhealed church wounds, we didn't want to risk getting hurt again.

In Brazil the Lord began to change our hearts towards His imperfect people called the church. He especially gave me a new heart for leaders as we got to really know our own pastor. Ben was delightfully imperfect, but he was the real deal. He loved Jesus, worked hard, and still had boatloads of fun. He vulnerably shared his own struggles as he listened long and helped us sort through ours. We saw how he took time to engage with everyone, especially the least and the lost. As we got to know, to like, and to trust this authentic servant leader, we formed a lifelong friendship that would lead to a lot of serving together in the future.

We journeyed to the Amazon to help build a church building and came back ready to help build the Church.

One Sunday at our local church Don felt God say, "Look around. This is as good as it gets."

God was changing our views toward the church to line up with His own. He loves His church made up of imperfect people whom He intimately calls us His body here on earth:

Christ is also head of the body, the church... (Colossians 1:18 NLT)

We were seeing what a privilege it is to connect with other believers. We were realizing how the key to our having lasting contentment wasn't found in more money, more stuff, or more success. We flourished when we nurtured and served others. So we began intentionally surrounding ourselves with other God lovers as we began to get back on track.

I'm convinced that we would not have gotten so sidetracked earlier if we had stayed closely connected to God's family. It was too late to go back and change things, but it wasn't too late going forward to change the rest of our lives. So we began to connect with the 300+ believers who gathered at the Vineyard Church (which has now grown to a church of over 1500.)

Fresh Fire

I love the way how in different seasons God causes fresh gifts to bubble up from within. One such gift, a new specific *method* to deliver

His message, came about as a surprise.

At age 52 I was working as a trainer and headed out of the office to catch a plane for a business trip to Milwaukee when my daughter Christy called. She shared a crisis her fiancé was facing, "Our adult singles retreat this weekend that Orestes is in charge of has 120 singles coming. That is good, but our speaker for Sunday morning just cancelled. That's not so good. It's so late to get someone else. We don't know what to do."

I jokingly said, "I could speak."

She said, "Oh, Mom, would you?"

"No…Are you serious? I don't know. Let me pray about it and call you back."

As I hung up the phone I realized that when I wrapped up my trip on Friday that I would be an hour away from their retreat location in Wisconsin. Was this a coincidence or a God incident? "Could this be you, Lord?"

I listened…and a half hour later I called my daughter and said, "Yes" as I grabbed my laptop and headed to the airport. On the plane it began to sink in. Here I was, a married, middle-aged, country gal speaking to a crowd of single, young city slickers from the Evanston Vineyard in a Chicago suburb.

What could we possibly have in common? Well, there was one thing: hearts hungry for God. Was that enough? I felt like I had signed up for a marathon before completing a 5k run. I was in over my head, and God and I both knew it. I was right where He wanted me. Arriving at the retreat on Friday afternoon, I was greeted by Orestes, who barely knew me and was really hoping that he could trust Christy's recommendation. He rushed over to greet me and eagerly inquired, "So, do you have your talk ready for Sunday?"

I smiled confidently, "Not yet, but I will."

Saturday morning at breakfast he briskly walked over and asked again. I assured him, "Not yet. I'm waiting for God to tell me what to say, but He will." I can't imagine his anxiety.

God's timing was much later than mine, and it wasn't until late Saturday night when I heard His message. In the morning I shared powerful stories encouraging how He is present and wants to walk each day with us. I don't remember the talk as much as what my Lord did after it people streamed to the front for prayer, many in tears, asking for more of Him.

This was the day I felt God's calling to be a speaker who changes lives through sharing GodStories.

The Glory Glider

The very next week a Vineyard pastor, Pam Larson, surprised me with another invitation to speak to over 300 at our upcoming women's conference. Feeling even more outside my comfort zone, I said *yes* again and then began asking God what I was to say. While I sometimes share some of the same powerful GodStories, I believe God has a very specific message for the people at each gathering. This means spending time with Him until I sense I hear fully what He wants me to say.

At first, God only gave me the title, *Glimpses from the Glory Glider* . It appeared on the printed fliers weeks before I had any idea what I was going to say. I thought I might need a glider so I upped my search for a porch swing glider, an item that had been on my "want list" for a few years. I had hinted I wanted one to Don around Mother's Day and then again on our anniversary in June. But still no swing swung in the yard.

Finally he got the hint and said, "Honey, I'll just make you one." I rolled my eyes and said, "No thanks" and kept searching. I called the unseen swing *The Glory Glider* which was beginning to unfold into a message from God.

Then one day I was yard sailing and again saw the clock turn to 10:10 right before I found an old glider at a yard sale for $15. If you are thinking, "I'll bet that was a piece of junk" you'd be right. It had weathered many storms, outliving its usefulness and was ready for the junk pile. It was ideal.

I scrubbed it down, and Don replaced the boards and stained them, boldly tattooing *The Glory Glider* on its curved back. Then I began to understand what God wanted me to share. The glider was a picture of so many of us weathered by storms, not seeming to have purpose until we encounter our God who transforms us to reflect His glory and give us His abundant life. I love the way this version of the Bible says it:

> *We carry this precious Message around in the unadorned clay pots of our ordinary lives. That's to prevent anyone from confusing God's incomparable power with us. As it is, there's not much chance of that.* (2 Corinthians 4:7-9 The Message)

At the conference I went on stage and sat down, gliding back and forth as I shared a few of our never-ending GodStories of how the Lord had used our struggles and weaknesses to transform our lives. I shared how God loves to use ordinary people like us to bring Him glory, not because of who we are but because of His Spirit who lives within us.

These two events were just the beginning of a barrage of invitations to speak at banquets, conferences, women's groups, motivational business meetings, and training sessions. I had discovered my niche of changing lives with spoken words. I loved equipping listeners with tears and laughter as I shared how God changes the ordinary into extraordinary. I still delight in speaking to audiences, and He still delights in sending me fresh stories to share.

> *Come and hear, all you who fear God; let me tell you what he has done for me.* (Psalm 66:16 NIV)

Equipped to Serve

As a passionate teacher ever hungry to learn, I constantly read books and went to every conference and training course I could such find such as Healing Journey (Celebrate Recovery), Master Your Money, Beginnings, Encounter God, Learning to Minister Like Jesus, and three years of impactful Bible Studies by Beth Moore.

Don and I both began to get charged up again for God. While the training was wonderful, we grew even more from connecting with others passionate for God, especially in small groups. A dozen or so of us met weekly to learn how to live out what Jesus taught. When the two of us struggled, others helped us; when the tables turned, we helped them.

Within a year we began servant leading our own small group once again. We joined other groups in the church in an eight-week study based on one of my favorite books, *The Purpose Driven Life* by Rick Warren.

I journaled a purpose statement which accurately predicted my future.

> My *purpose* is to glorify God with my life, to love Him and bring Him pleasure. My *calling* is to love and serve others, make disciple makers, and help strengthen His church. My specific *gifts* are encouraging, teaching/training, sharing prophecy, and telling stories.
>
> If we could have enough income to pay the bills, I would spend my time *pastoring*. I would spend more quality *family time* enjoying my kids and grandkids and enjoy my golden years modeling how God is powerfully present throughout an entire lifetime.

Fasting and Feasting

To handle all the busy on the outside and issues on the inside, I constantly prayed, "Lord, make me a daily overcomer." I felt sometimes that He sent too many opportunities to practice. I was also discovering more and more ways to walk closer with Him which has turned into an endless quest.

One way over the centuries that disciples have drawn closer to God is through the discipline of fasting. When our local church had a large building campaign, I joined some other leaders in a ten day "liquid only" fast, a really big deal for me. Before this, I had fasted by drinking only water for a few days or had given up chocolate or a distraction like TV or internet for a period of time to focus and pray. Jesus assumed that His followers would practice fasting.

"John's disciples came and asked him, "How is it that we and the Pharisees fast often, but your disciples do not fast?"

Jesus answered, "How can the guests of the bridegroom mourn while he is with them? The time will come when the bridegroom will be taken from them; then they will fast." (Matthew 9:14-15 NIV emphasis mine)

I knew that fasting would heighten my sensitivity to God. But ten days? This fast turned out to be extraordinary for me, and so was the outcome. God uniquely answered my long-time request to pray continually. He gave me a gift of unceasing worship. One night I woke in the middle of the night with a worship song playing in my head, and in the morning a different song was playing. This has gone on 24-7 for over twenty years.

If I wake up without a worship song playing in my head, I check my connection with Him. Once in a while I will hear some secular song playing in my head which makes me aware that I have distanced myself from His Presence. But I simply "change channels" as I began to sing in worship and autopilot kicks in. The song changes frequently and is often a worship song I haven't thought of for decades. Though I don't voluntarily do this, it is how I experience I Thessalonians 5:17 "pray without ceasing" as the Spirit worships the Father from within me where He dwells.

During this fast I also noted interesting physical changes. Not only could I live without my former friend, chocolate, but also after a few days, my craving for food disappeared. Fasting knocked down my food idols and exposed them as false gods as I became keenly aware of how I had turned to food looking for comfort and pleasure instead of hunger.

But over the years I would find this food fight to be an ongoing struggle very hard to overcome. Jesus was constantly planting seeds of His kingdom principles in me but my life wasn't always good earth to grow them. I wasn't always good soil. The seed to make healthier food choices usually fell prey to the gravel described in the parable of the sower.

Study this story of the farmer planting seed. When anyone hears news of the kingdom and doesn't take it in, it just remains on the surface, and so the Evil One comes along and plucks it right out of that person's heart. This is the seed the farmer scatters on the road. The seed cast in the gravel—this is the person who hears and instantly responds with enthusiasm. But there is no soil of character, and so when the emotions wear off and some difficulty arrives, there is nothing to show for it.

The seed cast in the weeds is the person who hears the kingdom news, but weeds of worry and illusions about getting more and wanting everything under the sun strangle what was heard, and nothing comes of it. The seed cast on good earth is the person who hears and takes in the News, and then produces a harvest beyond his wildest dreams. (Matthew 13:19-23 The Message)

This little seed landed in the gravel where my enthusiasm waned and I went back to my idols of sugar, flour & processed foods. It seemed too difficult to overcome these addictions, but I had no clue how much harder it would be later going through the resulting health issues. I could have saved myself a lot of agony if I'd persevered in overcoming in this arena.

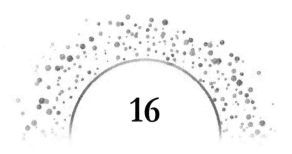

16

Let Freedom Reign

As we were more involved in serving, we experienced quite the tug-of-war in our personal life as the devil came to try to steal, kill and destroy us and block the abundant life we were proclaiming from John 10:10. But Jesus was true to His word and kept bringing good out of evil, resulting in more stories to share of His goodness.

Ironically, our family battled for abundant life over the enemy on two different 4th of July weekends as our nation celebrated freedoms also won by fierce battles. These fireworks hit way too close to home.

4th of July Mommas and Angels

My momma whom everyone in town affectionately called Grandmother Mary was quite a firecracker born on the 4th of July, and every year we lavishly celebrated this holiday with lots of family, piles of home-cooked food, and our own fireworks display on the river.

One year when five of our grandbabies were still toddlers in tow, our family gathered at the cabin for the 4th of July weekend. On Saturday two-year old Toby awoke from his nap in the boat wailing and covered with hundreds of mosquito bites. He was soothed with some prayer and lotion. Later in the day he drank a bottle of Baby Tylenol, and Momma Kristi raced him to the hospital. A little syrup of ipecac induced relief, and he was safe and calm. Thank God for happy endings.

But the weekend wasn't over. Kelsey, almost 2, climbed up on a chair next to the picture window to watch a passing river barge. As she leaned against the screen, it popped out of the window. So did Kelsey. We all heard her screams and ran around frantically trying to locate her. Then we saw the open window. Our hearts pounded as we pictured her having plummeted fourteen feet to the ground. But she had only fallen three feet onto the narrow walkway surrounding the cabin. Momma Jenny jumped out the window, scooped up her screaming baby, and headed to the hospital to check out her swollen shoulder and huge bump on her forehead.

Soon our second toddler returned safely from the hospital with her badly bruised head wrapped in a bandage sporting a bright blue shoulder-to-wrist cast to stabilize two broken shoulder bones. We were so thankful God had protected her from falling to the ground.

A month later we learned how. Joanna, her 13-year-old cousin, was visiting and was with Kelsey in her room when Kelsey stared and pointed upward, "Look. Angels."

Curious, Joanna asked, "Where are the angels?"

Kelsey pointed toward the corner of the ceiling, "Right there."

"Can you touch them?" Joanna asked.

"No, they too far." Joanna went into the kitchen to tell Jenny. Stunned, they just looked at each other. Was this toddler able to see celestial beings?

The next week as their family made a weekend trek to the river, Kelsey and her sister were fussing in the back seat, so their father said, "Kelsey, so tell me about the angels."

She instantly became very quiet but did not reply. "Where are the angels?" she asked, expecting her to say she saw them in her room.

Instead Kelsey answered simply, "At the cabin."

Confused, her folks looked at each other. Her dad asked, "What? At the cabin? Where?"

She answered, "Out the window" as she excitedly described the "owies" on her arm and head. It was then they realized that God had sent angels to catch her on that 4th of July and to protect her from falling. Kelsey had seen them.

> For the angel of the Lord is a guard. he surrounds and defends all who fear Him. (Psalm 34:7 NLV)

At Halloween that year, Kelsey was riding in a shopping cart at Wal Mart. She looked up at a demonic mask in the costume aisle and said, "Look, mommy, an angel." This little one had no knowledge of the

Bible's revelation of how the devil and a third of the angels rebelled against God. They weren't attending a church that mentioned angels and certainly didn't discuss demons or fallen angels. Jenny couldn't figure out where she had heard about angels. However, Kelsey recognized the face on the mask as a fallen angel. It convinced us that God had allowed her to see into the unseen spiritual realm in a very unique way.

Kelsey didn't mention seeing angels again for a couple of years until she was four, riding along with the family in their van. All of a sudden she said excitedly, "Look, there's an angel!"

Jenny said," Where?"

Kelsey got all excited. "Can you see him, Kasey?"

"No," her little sister, replied.

"You're too little to see angels. Can you see him, Mommy?"

"No."

She explained, "It's okay. Some people can see angels and some people can't. Daddy, open the window and see if he'll come in." Chris opened the window and let him in.

"There he is, by Kasey's seat. Now can you see him?" Kelsey asked.

After a couple of minutes she announced, "Oh, he's gone now. He must have gone back to Heaven to be with God." And that was it, no fanfare, just part of her normal life.

> *Beware that you don't look down on any of these little ones. For I tell you that in heaven, their angels are always in the presence of my heavenly father.* (Matthew 18:10 NLT)

That Christmastime Kelsey was coloring a picture depicting the multitude of angels appearing to the frightened shepherds. She asked, "Mommy, why were the shepherds afraid?"

"They probably weren't used to seeing angels, so they were afraid."

She replied, "Oh. I'm not afraid when they are around me."

She rarely talked about angels, but once in a great while would say something that made us realize they were visible to her. A friend tried to get her to tell him about her angel encounters, "Kelsey, have you seen any angels lately?"

She paused to think and replied, "No" and left the room to go play. Angels were nothing unusual to her. She stopped mentioning angels when she was four. Yet she made us aware of how angels are all around us, unseen except for those rare glimpses God sometimes gives us into the spirit realm.

4th of July Deadly Attack

A few years later another story unfolded on a memorable 4th of July weekend when our family faced death once again. The river had recently overflowed its banks, and the cabin was not yet accessible by road. We had to trudged 100 yards through slimy mud, suitcases and supplies in hand, to get to the cabin. Being together was worth it. We kept an especially close eye on all our little ones, but this time the enemy would strike elsewhere.

After a rousing deck conversation with our kids, Don and I called it a night around 1 am. As soon as my head hit the pillow my cell phone rang. At that hour it could not be good news. It was the nightmare call that all mommas dread, even when your child is 34. Our son's friend was on the line, "Come to the hospital quickly. Shawn has been badly beaten. Hurry." Then he hung up.

Our minds raced as Don and I waded back through the mud to our car for the 45-minute trip to the hospital in Quincy. Fearful of what we might find, we cried out, "Oh God, be with Shawn. Let him be all right. Help, Lord. We need You." Numb with shock, we had heavy hearts. We were stuck for words to pray. Then His Spirit began to well up in us, and we began to pray in the Spirit together for Shawn, interceding in tongues, as His Word describes:

> ...The Spirit helps us in our weakness. We do not know what we ought to pray for, but the Spirit himself intercedes for us with groans that words cannot express. And he who searches our hearts knows the mind of the Spirit, because the Spirit intercedes for the saints in accordance with God's will. (Romans 8:26 NIV)

As we reached the ER, we were rushed to a room bustling with doctors, nurses, detectives and policemen. My eyes fell on the body on the gurney, not recognizing the person lying on it. I thought, "This must be Shawn," as I looked into his bruised face covered with blood. His head was a swollen mass like a large melon ready to burst, and he had no definable nose, chin, or neck. Blood streamed from his nose and mouth, and bruises covered his body.

As the police explained what had happened, they pointed out the well-defined tennis shoe imprint on the right side of his face along with boot prints on his head, chest, and knee. Shawn was immobile due to severe back pain, and he drifted in and out of consciousness. His breathing was extremely labored, and he could only mutter a few words. He tried to focus to see us, but his blackened eyes were nearly swollen shut.

The team of doctors and nurses were in and out working on him all night. The police took sixty or seventy pictures of his injuries and guarded Shawn 24-7 from his attackers still at large should they return and try to kill Shawn to keep him from identifying them. Despite the chaotic swarm of people, God's presence felt like a thick blanket of calm putting us at ease. I was deeply concerned but not overly-agitated or panicky as might be expected. Instead we felt strangely confident that God was in control.

Shawn sensed His presence too. Later he told us when he squinted open his eyes and saw us walk through the ER doors, he breathed a sigh of relief and knew everything was going to be okay. Shawn's friend had also called Grandmother Mary, my 80-year-old prayer warrior momma who drove herself to the hospital at 2 am. We stood by his stretcher, gently laying hands on him and holding his hand as we prayed quietly in the Spirit. We again experienced how Jesus gives His peace when everything around is still amiss, just as He described:

> Peace I leave with you; my peace I give you. I do not give to you as the world gives. Do not let your hearts be troubled and do not be afraid. (John 14:27 NIV)

We were confident that God was working on Shawn powerfully throughout that night although there was no way to measure how much internal repair He did. When the sun came up, the swelling had gone down, and we could recognize him. Although he was badly bruised, the only major damage the doctors could find was a concussion and a broken nose and thumb.

His doctor shook his head, "I can't really explain what happened here; this is very unusual. As severely as he was beaten we expected to find broken limbs and ribs, but they are fine. Usually we see signs of internal bleeding or organ damage, but there are none indicated. He does have a concussion, but he is quite lucid and shows no sign of major long-lasting brain damage. I can't explain how it happened, but your son is in remarkably good shape. It just doesn't make sense."

We told him that we knew that God was looking after Shawn. Despite the severe beating, he had no lasting injury. Was His power at work as we prayed in the Spirit? We felt a partnership with God as Shawn responded with major healing during that horrible night and we experienced His calming peace and hope. For the next three days we stayed at Shawn's side in the hospital. Almost hourly he would wake and ask, "Where am I? What happened?" and we would have to rehearse the whole ordeal with him. We felt like we were in our own "Groundhog Day" nightmare.

Down a Dark Alley

We thanked God for coming through for Shawn. Our Creator has given each human the incredible gift of free choice, and choices come with consequences. Sometimes we are victims of the choices of others, sometimes of our own choices, and often a combination of both. When that incident happened, Shawn had been at a gay bar at 1:00 a.m. That had some consequences. A gang of four young guys had made the choice to have a little fun and shoot Roman candles off into the crowded bar, holding the door shut so patrons couldn't escape. Shawn went after them, bursting through the back door in pursuit and chasing them until they turned on him and drug him down a dark dead-end alley where the gang beat him severely, stomped on him, and left him for dead before they ran off.

Curious to know more details, Don and I went to the police station on Sunday afternoon to see if we could talk with the officer who had found Shawn. The desk person said, "He is off duty, but he just happened to drop by the station. I'll take you back to talk with him."

The officer shared with us the rest of the story,

I was five blocks away when I responded to the police call saying someone had set off fireworks at the bar. I saw people running so I just kept driving. A lady in a phone booth pointed toward a dead-end alley, and I drove around the block and into the alley and saw a Caucasian lying in a pool of blood. It was your son. As I approached him I realized I was too late as I watched him gasping for air–he took a couple of deep breaths and then stopped breathing. I just knew that this was the end for him. As a police officer, I have witnessed many people die in scenes like this. I knew that he was gone.

Yet I had this glimmer of hope and kept saying, 'Hold on. Hold on,' as I glanced at my watch, aware that his brain would be severely damaged if he weren't revived within six minutes. Four minutes later, the ambulance pulled up, and paramedics quickly intubated his throat, and brought him back to life. I am amazed that his brain was not severely damaged.

We thanked him and left the station so grateful that God arranged for us to hear the rest of the story. We praised him over and over for sparing our son's brain and his life in those critical minutes.

For the next two weeks I stayed with Shawn at his place. Nights were tense. His attackers were still at large, and we feared they might try to come finish the job. I was wide-awake praying most of that first night. Shawn jumped at the smallest strange noise and awoke with a jolt as people celebrated the 4th with firecrackers that sound a lot like gunshots. I still am not sure.

Within the week, all four attackers were found and arrested, and we rested easier. They didn't need to have worried about Shawn identifying them because his last recollection was bursting through that bar door. He still has no memory of the beating in the alley, the pain, or the first week of recovery. That is a good thing. During Shawn's recovery I read this:

> *God rescued us from dead-end alleys and dark dungeons. He's set us up in the kingdom of his Son he loves so much, the son who got us out of the pit we were in, got rid of the sins we were doomed to keep repeating.* (Colossians 1:13 The Message)

During those tough times we cried out to God for complete restoration as we waited for Him to intervene. God's presence was powerful as we thanked Him for His gracious restoration of Shawn's mind and body. As I recalled that horrendous night sitting by Shawn and lovingly looking on His swollen and disfigured face, I was better able to visualize the prophet Isaiah's vision of Jesus on the cross:

> *Just as there were many who were appalled at him – his appearance was so disfigured beyond that of any man and his form marred beyond human likeness.* (Isaiah 52:14 NIV)

Shortly after this I watched the movie *The Passion of the Christ* I thought, "*Jesus had to have looked much worse than Shawn.*"

Then I wondered, "*God, how could you let Jesus hang on a cross. I would never have chosen for my son whom I love so dearly to go through His horrible experience. How could you choose to allow cruel torture and even death for Your son?*"

His answer was simple, "I allowed my son to die so that we could live forever with humans we created and love."

What love they had for us to have made such a sacrifice. Things aren't always as they seem.

Waiting on God

Though rescued from death, Shawn's ordeal was far from over. He struggled with severe short-term memory loss, and at times we were uncertain if he would ever think right again. He had to carry a small notebook in his shirt pocket to record every detail like ordering a part because after a few minutes he couldn't remember doing it. As a plant engineer who normally handled complex situations, this was quite a challenge. We kept crying out for healing, and God gradually improved his memory. Nine months later Shawn's normal memory returned.

For years he became startled at an unexpected noise or when someone touched him. Fireworks still startle him. In the coming months, Shawn had two surgeries in Champaign, the first one to reposition his nose and septum (a definite improvement to his Vincent nose) and another to reconstruct his crushed thumb. The orthopedic surgeon said Shawn would not regain full motion. Wrong again. His healed thumb moves quite normally.

God also arranged some emotional healing. Shawn and I were at a stoplight driving by our church late one afternoon after a doctor appointment when I sensed God prompting me to ask Shawn if he would want to stop and have our pastor Ben pray for him. Shawn had not been going to church, so I wasn't sure what his response would be, but he said "Sure," so I pulled the car into the church parking lot. I looked at my watch and realized it was after hours, but in God's timing two pastors, Ben and Brian were just leaving the office. Shawn shared how he had been depressed the prior five years and was headed nowhere. He didn't want to go five more years and still be in the same place.

The pastors encouraged Shawn and asked questions to help him process things. Then they prayed, first thanking God for delivering him from death and then for the depression to leave and a new courage to choose wisely. They also prayed for God to show Shawn the root cause of the depression. Then Brian encouraged him with a prophetic word he felt the Lord saying, "Choice, choice, Shawn. I chose. I chose to raise you from the dead. Now the choice is yours. You must choose."

Then Ben shared, "God loves you, Shawn. He is not angry with you. He did not send this your way. This was not judgment. This was from the enemy. What the enemy meant for evil, God will turn for good. He loves you very much and you were born for such a time as this."

This brief encounter was a human touch from a gentle and compassionate Father who used these two men to immerse Shawn in His love. Sometimes in this life we need some Jesus with skin on.

Afterwards Shawn shared, "Wow, they really hit the nail on the head." He is still healing today, and we continue to share his story to bring hope to others.

Forgiving Our Enemies

In October we began driving across the state to attend the trials of the gang members who had beaten Shawn. Sixteen members of our extended family sat with us through the long days of the trials to support him. I'll never forget. Once more we were conscious of God's presence as He gave us strength to listen to the grueling testimonies. While Shawn still could not recognize any of his assailants, their testimonies were revealing enough. The attackers were each sentenced on several counts for other incidents of that night and sent to prison for a few months before their early releases.

At one of the trials I felt that the Lord wanted me to encourage one of the fathers who was so broken after his son's sentencing. As I walked past him in the courtroom aisle, I told him, "I want you to know I feel so sorry about all of this happening. We forgive your son. I know I could just as easily be in your shoes and you in mine. We will be praying for your son that God somehow uses this in his life." The father thanked me and told me he was a Christian and then introduced me to his pastor who was with him. We would be praying the same prayer in the months to come.

We found it strange that Shawn, Don, and I did not feel any animosity or hatred toward any of Shawn's attackers. Nor did we want revenge. How could this be?

I believe that God gave the three of us a special gift of forgiveness and compassion for his attackers and again, God showed Himself faithful. First, forgiveness is an action which God tells us to do. We are to speak forgiveness for wrongs done because God has forgiven us so much.

Be kind and compassionate to one another, forgiving each other, just as in Christ God forgave you. (Ephesians 4:32)

But often our feelings don't line up with our words of forgiveness. Yet we were experiencing a peace and forgiveness in our hearts because God took away any animosity and replaced it with compassion. Often these accompanying feelings of forgiveness come in stages over time. But if we continue to speak forgiveness and ask for compassion, unforgiveness will leave as compassion bubbles up from the Spirit inside of us. This time God gave forgiveness to all three of us at the same time.

So if the Son sets you free, you will be free indeed. (John 8:36 NIV)

A year later I had traveled to Quincy where Shawn and I went out for our semi-annual lunch rendezvous. When we were seated, Shawn glanced over at the next table five feet away and realized that he had looking into the eyes of the gang leader whom we thought was still in prison. Both men were startled. Though we avoided further eye contact, God turned it into a healing moment as Shawn realized he was facing his attacker without fear or hatred.

I wished later that we had told the young man that we had forgiven him, but that small window of opportunity passed quickly. Within a month he was dead from a gunshot wound during a dispute with one of his "friends".

Gremlin Attack—Envious Eyes

Have you ever made it through a big issue and been surprised that it was not the big struggle you expected but then shortly afterward let some little thing trip you up? I was so grateful to God's grace in getting us through Shawn's big ordeal but then got tripped up by a little envy. During one visit to see Shawn I felt sad that he lived in such a modest house. Then I felt worse when I told him that he would have to wear his old glasses that were scratched from the attack until we had an extra $400 to pay for new ones. Shawn understood, but I didn't.

After leaving his house I stopped by to see the new office space some dear friends had helped their kids equip. As I sunk into a plush office chair I thought, "I bet this chair cost more than those $400 glasses." Suddenly overwhelmed with envy, I lost it. I hurriedly left and burst out crying in my car because we couldn't give to our kids like that. It didn't seem fair.

On the way home I stopped by our other son's home and shared my discouragement that we didn't have much money to help our kids. Damon said, "We don't care about your leaving us any money, Mom." His wife Kristi continued, "Having the river cabin has been the best thing you could do for us." I knew deep down that it was okay, and I went away having to remind myself that things don't bring lasting joy. I have found that true contentment comes to both the wealthy and the poor; so does envy and dissatisfaction.

So again it was my choice to thank God for what we had or be discontent by comparing our lot with others who had more. God was changing me, little by little, not to compare our lot with others or envy them. It is not about what we have; what matters more is my attitude about it.

Gremlin Attack – Feeling Rejected

During the months of Shawn's recovery I fought another gremlin, rejection by others. I remember receiving very little support from our Christian friends. For a while I was upset that during the three weeks I spent by Shawn's side hardly anyone from the church contacted us. Afterwards, most acted like nothing had ever happened. Of the six small group leader couples we were overseeing, only one mentioned the incident and tried to encourage us. Maybe it was because our son was attacked at a gay bar and they were at a loss for words, or maybe they were just caught up in their own busy lives. Regardless of why, our friends kept their distance from us during that time.

But God used it for good. First, I came to peace that for whatever reason people just aren't always there when we need them, even caring friends. I forgave as God gently reminded me of times I hadn't shown up for others in tough times. I thought of when I had been too busy to go to the hospital when a friend needed me and that time I didn't call when she lost her job because I didn't want to take the time to listen. Realizing I had fallen short, I tried to put myself in the shoes of others and understand.

> Do not judge others, and you will not be judged. Do not condemn others, or it will all come back against you. Forgive others, and you will be forgiven. (Luke 6:37 NLT)

Secondly, through this, God gave me more empathy for Shawn as I realized how he must also face rejection. This helped me become more welcoming and compassionate toward him and his gay friends.

I thought about what response I had hoped for from others. I think I just wanted them to say, "I'm so sorry. I care. This must be very hard. I'm here for you." God was showing me how to support others in crisis even if I had no wise words to share. I had needed someone to just show up. I need to just show up.

My presence is the most valuable present I can give. We believers carry His Presence inside, and He makes a difference wherever we go. When the Holy Spirit nudges me, I try to pause and make that phone call, send an email or text, share a scripture, bring a meal, or most of all, pray with friends in need...right then. A tiny bit of encouragement goes a long way if it is inspired by His Presence within. I don't always come through for people, but I keep at it.

All praise to God, the Father of our Lord Jesus Christ. God is our merciful Father and the source of all comfort. He comforts us in all our troubles so that we can comfort others. When they are troubled, we will be able to give them the same comfort God has given us. (2 Corinthians 1:3,4 NLT)

I like how comfort is mentioned four times in that scripture, showing us how important it is to God. Depending on my friends' support is great, but it just is not enough.

One who has unreliable friends soon comes to ruin, but there is a friend who sticks closer than a brother. (Proverbs 18:24 NIV)

That friend is Jesus who wants me to go to him <u>first</u>, before I go to people. Like Joyce Meyer says, "*Run to the throne— not to the phone!*" He is the One with power to help anyway."

I wish that I'd learned these lessons once and for all, but I still have to daily choose to actually live out Jesus' words as I imperfectly live my life, openly share my struggles, and love people with Him. Praise God our lives can be very rich and satisfying as we experience His Presence.

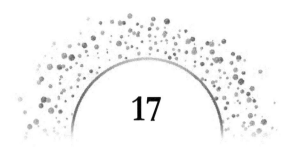

17

Out of My Comfort Zone

When I turned 58, change was in the air as I asked, "What is ahead, Lord?" Then I journaled what I felt God was saying,

The next step will be out of your comfort zone, in a land foreign to you, a place of great risk and great reward. Be willing.

Right on! This predicted the nature of my next very tough assignment that would that would further equip me for the future.

Losing Confidence

It began with another odd encounter when I was trainer/coach attending a Northwestern Mutual Conference in Chicago. I had arrived at a downtown hotel when my daughter Christy who worked downtown called, "Mom, come to my house tonight. You can take the elevated train (the L) back in the morning." Going to the suburbs sounded great, but coming back downtown the next morning did not, especially when I found out I'd be alone. I had only ridden the L once, and now I was considering this 45-minute trip on the L and then finding my own way to my hotel in the windy city. As a country gal from Small-town, USA, this sounded scary. I asked, "Should I go, Lord?"

I felt Him answering me, "Risk it. Get out of your comfort zone, and trust me," so I did, even though I was nervous (more like terrified) about my adventure. But I took the challenge and invited Confidence to come along as my companion. The evening began well as Christy and I stopped for a quick dinner downtown as the January skies began to dump several inches of snow on the sidewalks. I struggled walking in my heels while Confidence slipped away on snowshoes. At dinner I mentioned having

$500 cash in my purse which Christy insisted I hide in my bra to keep it safe. I would certainly hope so.

When we boarded the L, my eyes were drawn to a very distraught woman. Christy explained how she had obviously boarded the blue line, not the red line, and it would take her ninety extra minutes to get aboard the right train. I thought, "That will probably be me in the morning." As we stepped off the train Christy insisted we stay on the brightly lit platform until her husband picked us up because the street was unsafe. Confidence was now out of sight.

The next morning my daughter explained the easy fifteen-minute walk from the L to my hotel, "Just get off the train downtown, turn left, go up the steps and head right toward the Lake.

After brushing my teeth I repeated the instructions, "Get off the train, turn right, go up the steps and head left toward the Lake."

"No, Mom! Listen..." Confidence vanished.

Angel on the L?

As Christy dropped me off at the train station I boarded the L, looking around for a friendly face to no avail. Had I entered a train of zombies? No one was talking or smiling or even making eye contact. As the train moved out, I sat down, read a chapter in my Bible, put it back in my briefcase, and nervously stared out the window. Ten minutes later a young woman walked up behind me and whispered in my ear, "May I suggest Psalm 20?"

Wow! Could God talk to me in this scary place? I got out my Bible and read:

> *May the Lord answer you when you are in distress; may the name of the God of Jacob protect you. May he send you help from the sanctuary and grant you support from Zion...May he give you the desire of your heart and make all your plans succeed.* (Psalm 20:1, 2, 4 NLT)

Instantaneously the Lord took away that apprehension and flooded me with His peace with these comforting words from the Psalm. I turned around to thank her. She was gone! I thought, "Have there been any stops on the way into the city where she might have gotten off?" I couldn't recall any. "Was she an angel, a special messenger from God for me?"

Don't forget to show hospitality to strangers, for some who have done this have entertained angels without realizing it! (Hebrews 13:2 NIV)

Whether she was an angel or not, God answered me in my distress as He sent her to help me and give me support from the Word that brought me total peace.

As I arrived and stepped off the train, everyone scurried away. I stood there trying to get my bearings and realized I was alone on the platform except for the three burly guys about ten feet away who I just knew were gang members. Fear rose with a flashback of Shawn's attackers. I pondered, "How can I get away from them?" I know I had just been calmed with Psalm 20, but my spiritual attention deficit disorder (S.A.D.D.) was kicking in. I hurried faster, and the men picked up their pace right behind me. I tried to look calm as my heart pounded. As I reached the escalator, they were closing in. Then one guy said, "I don't know how it works, but the Word cleanses us from all sin…"

I breathed a long sigh of relief, and then I noticed Confidence had returned and gotten on the escalator with me. Relaxed, I really enjoyed overhearing their conversation as once again God pointed out, "No, you are not in control, but I am. You are in my hands, and I am sufficient."

Turning the Switch

Of course, I turned the wrong way at the top of the escalator, and that fifteen-minute walk to the hotel took forty minutes. On the detour I thought about the "Mastering Your Money" class I'd taught at church where I saw a future problem with our small nest egg. We didn't want to be one of those couples who had saved enough to retire at 65 and live comfortably for six months.

So I began talking to my Provider, "Lord, show us if there is something else you want us to do with our lives–any new ventures, a new business, maybe marketing one of Don's inventions? Just tell us. We are willing to change course at this late age if you have something else in mind. There's time for getting prepared for our golden years…isn't there? Help, Lord."

This time God answered me speedily in a most peculiar way. At my first conference session, a "Run to Success" luncheon for women financial planners, He showed me what was next with a "once in a lifetime" experience with His Presence. As I listened to a panel of women share tips on running their business, I kept thinking, "That is what I'll do in my practice." Then I'd try to correct my mind, "Wait a minute. What practice? I'm not a financial planner."

It was as though I no longer was hearing with the ears of a trainer but with the ears of a financial planner. For the next thirty minutes I was fascinated by the tug of war in my brain. Could God be supernaturally transforming me to see my future from a new paradigm? As I shared with a friend next to me, she smiled, "It sounds like God to me." I couldn't remember anything they had said but only what He was saying. All weekend this phenomenon continued.

When I arrived home from the conference, before I took off my coat, I told Don this wild story and finished with "Well, what do you think?"

He sighed, "Sounds like God. What choice do we have?" Got to love that man!

"To Be or Not to Be, That is the Question"

Of course, I actually did have a choice. While most normal folk start winding down in their late 50's, I would be ramping up in a brand-new risky business. Over the past ten years I had trained several hundred financial planners and had not once considered the career for myself. Yet I couldn't ignore God. One minute I was not the least bit interested; the next moment I was strangely drawn to this difficult path. Just because it looks difficult doesn't mean it is not God.

For eight days I weighed the pro and cons of the freedom and risk of starting my own financial planning business. Did I want to be a woman entering a male-dominated commission-based profession at my age? Did I have the energy? the health? the discipline? the guts?

The practical answer was *No Way*, but the conviction that God was calling me to this adventure tipped the scale to *Yes*. Even if my career were short-lived, who knows what impact I would make. I considered how Jesus accomplished all His earthly ministry in three short years.

So I moved into this great career with eyes wide open, fully aware what a crazy choice it was in my situation. While I had no idea where the path would lead, I was sure of the One who was leading me as the angelic words from Psalm 20 rang through my being:

> Some trust in chariots and some in horses, but we trust in the
> name of the Lord our God. They are brought to their knees and
> fall, but we rise up and stand firm. (Psalm 20:8 NIV)

Be Strong and Courageous

On the first day as a financial planner, I felt lost. Nervously flipping through my cards wondering whom I should call to meet with, I feared being rejected. I felt inadequate and ill-prepared to handle SEPs, IRAs, 529s, DI, CLU, ChFC– Tilt! God kept encouraging me to be strong and courageous as I learned what I needed to know. It was okay that life was hard because I was being held by Him.

> *Have I not commanded you? Be strong and courageous. Do not be afraid; do not be discouraged, for the LORD your God will be with you wherever you go.* (Joshua 1:9-11 NIV)

So I overcame fear with obedience as I began doing the work in front of me. on I was looking forward to meeting people as I learned better how to help them protect their future with insurance and investments. When someone died, I not only brought condolences to the family but also the funds to help them carry on living. When a dear 60-year-old friend turned out to be my first client to receive long term care benefits after he had a stroke I saw firsthand how my work would reap benefits far into the future..

One of my favorite perks of this career was being in charge of my own schedule. Daily I kept my first appointment at 7 am with the CEO of the universe. My biggest challenge was to consistently make daily phone calls to set appointments, a hard task for a people-pleaser like me. This weakness kept me close to God as I constantly went to him for strength for the next five years. I would love to tell you how I overcame my fear of rejection. Except for short-lived spurts of success, that didn't happen. But I did get closer to God.

All of my life, my ease and comfort mentality has been an issue, especially with physical challenges. When I'm called on to make my body uncomfortable, I don't like it one little bit – skiing, rebuilding the cabin, planting flowers, mowing, or cleaning house.

This business was no bed of comfort for someone like me. I was often on my knees, praying different versions of this prayer,

> *Today I call on you for strength. Someday I may be called on to do the uncomfortable for you, Jesus. Let this time strengthen me for the future, even if full of risk and discomfort.*

> *Lord, I know you love me and accept me just like I am, but I have problems loving myself when I don't measure up to my own performance standards. Please*

fix my faulty thinking. Help me slow down and enjoy this. I am powerless to heal myself. I surrender to You again.

A Successful Failure

My first two years in business went remarkedly well; the last three years, not so much. First, I ended up crippled by my phoning phobia. Then gripping hip pain caused me to have to stand to finish any client appointment lasting over a half hour. Awkward! After two hip replacements in thirteen months, I ran out of steam and fizzled out. This wonderful challenging financial planning career lasted all of five years.

I was a very successful failure. I helped hundreds invest in their financial futures. At same time I also helped many others invest in their heavenly future as my flexible schedule freed up time to work with the church. Both endeavors further equipped me for another unexpected career change that lay further ahead.

> *Trust in the LORD with all your heart; do not depend on your own understanding. Seek his will in all you do, and he will show you which path to take.* (Proverbs 3:5, 6 NLT)

"Write a Book"

The year I began my business, I was still doing some public speaking when God called me to another *method* to share His good news. For years I had heard people say that someday they want to write a book. Not me…until that day God changed my mind.

I was cruising along on my way to work when out of the blue, God's voice interrupted my thoughts with three simple words: "Write a book."

I was surprised, but I had no doubt that I was hearing His voice from within. The words were clear and bold, almost audible, the first of two such vivid encounters in my life. God's instructions sounded outrageous, yet intriguing.

I laughed out loud, "Write a book? Are you kidding?" I jotted the words down on a notecard to ponder later. Right now, I had to get some work done.

That evening I reclined in my easy chair and stared at those three words, "Write a book" as I wondered how I'd go about that. Then more details began to flow, "No hurry…Just begin…Gather your stories and share them…Let them flow…Tweak them later…Put down your heart feelings. Share your issues. Be vulnerable."

So I sat down and began to write. My life verse, John 10:10, proclaims that Jesus came to give us abundant life. It came as no surprise that God said to write a book on 10/10/2001.

As I thought about this huge task, I asked, "Why me, Lord? I am nothing special."

He answered, "I know you aren't. That's the point. Tell them I AM."

So I began writing my story of how over the years Jesus has given us His rich satisfying life as we partnered together with Him to overpower the enemy's attempts to rob, kill, and destroy.

Me and Michelangelo

The following week I was talking with God again as I was driving home from work, "Lord, this task is exciting but also overwhelming. I don't know where to begin. Help me, Lord. Show me how to do this. What is the plan?"

Once more His Presence was real in my car (which was becoming our frequent meeting place.) With open eyes I saw a vision floating through my mind of the sculptor Michelangelo carving the statue of David from a massive slab of marble. He painstakingly chiseled away the extraneous pieces of stone until a glorious masterpiece of King David was revealed. I felt God show me that in a similar way I was to chisel away the extraneous pieces of my life story until it revealed Jesus, the glorious masterpiece hidden within.

I researched and discovered that in 1501 Michelangelo was commissioned to carve a 14' statue of David from a six-ton marble slab that had lain dormant for years. It took him three years to finish the task.

In 2001, exactly 500 years later, I felt God was commissioning me to first gather my stories lying dormant in dusty journals into the marble slab of my computer and then chisel away until I saw Jesus revealed in my overall life story.

Gathering the stories would take months; seeing how the puzzle pieces fit into the big picture and chiseling away the extraneous would take years. I had always longed to know what my life story was saying, and little by little, He gave me insight along the way and added even more stories.

For the next eighteen years I assembled the slab of words and chiseled out the form within, hurrying along at a snail's pace. As I was sidetracked by other important and not-so-important tasks, months sometimes went by with no new written words. But God was still constantly at work sculpting as He revealed His mysteries in stories old and new.

Every block of stone has a statue inside it and it is the task of the sculptor to discover it.[7] —MICHELANGELO

Just as it is the task of the sculptor to discover the statue inside, so it is the task of each one of us to discover the masterpiece God is creating in our lives and share it with the world. This is our purpose.

A-D-U-L-T-E-R-Y

Once in a while God likes to shake things up with the unexpected just so there is no doubt in our minds that He indeed is God. These fresh stories happened much more often for Don and me when we were hanging out with other bold believers who risked all by stepping out and acting on what they felt God was saying. Little risks often bring a little reward, but big risks often bring big rewards.

One such big risk for me happened at a local Pastor's Conference. During our worship time, my attention was drawn to a man in the row right in front of me. While I could only see his back, in my mind I could picture his forehead with the word adultery written across it. I thought, "Oh my. Is that you, God? Surely you don't want me to share that word." This did not line up with normal prophetic protocol as I understood it. It didn't sound very edifying which is the purpose of prophecy; it would be an awkward word for me as a woman to share with a man; and it would insult him and embarrass me if the word were not accurate.

"So what are the odds of this picture being accurate? Fat chance. What if I'm not hearing him accurately? Big mistake. But then again, what if I AM hearing God? Big risk, big impact."

I let the word simmer for a while and went back to worshipping. After the service, the man lingered, and so did the word, so I decided to go for it. I took a deep breath, tapped the man on the shoulder, "Excuse me, could I share something with you. "

He looked at me quizzically, "Okay."

"This is either straight from God or I am way off base! During worship, I saw the word *adultery* written across your forehead."

Silent, I waited for his response.

The man looked down at the floor for a few moments and then looked at me with tears in his eyes, "You heard right. I am a pastor, and I had an affair a few months back. It was a one-time thing. My wife knows about it, and she has forgiven me. I have asked for forgiveness, but I am really struggling. I just can't believe God will forgive me."

A wave of the Father's great love for him swept over me as I said, "God didn't show me this picture to condemn you. He wants to set you free." Then I prayed with him asking the Lord to assure him of forgiveness and to release the man from guilt so that he could forgive himself.

The next day he searched for me at the conference to share the rest of the story. "I called my wife immediately yesterday and told her what you shared. She encouraged me just as you did that God was setting me free from condemnation. Now I feel like I can go on with what I've been called to do. I am totally forgiven. I am totally free." Together we rejoiced in His love and power.

Does God normally use a woman to share such a word? I don't think so (although it happened in 2 Kings 22:14-20) However, I am learning not to limit Him to my expectations. He can do as He pleases even if it doesn't fit my norm. I think He likes doing things outside my comfort zone to see if I am willing to trust and obey His voice, no matter what.

A few years later I was reading in a book by John Wimber, founder of the Vineyard Church, about a similar incident where he described seeing the word *adultery* on someone's forehead. I was curious how we would see the same picture. Since then, I have heard of God showing the same thing to two other people.

Regardless, this word was right on. God enjoys being outside the box. I loved how He continues to give us both fresh stories and new places to share them.

> So we fix our eyes not on what is seen, but on what is unseen, since what is seen is temporary, but what is unseen is eternal.
> (2 Corinthians 4:18 NIV)

18
Touched by Story

Picture slipping on a cool pair of jeans in the ideal size and finding they are a dream fit. Oh what a feeling that must be! I haven't found any such skinny jeans yet, but at 58 I did find that ideal fit in Alpha which became my ministry sweet spot for years to come.

Alpha My Sweet Spot

So what is Alpha? It is a 10-week get-together for the spiritually curious to come explore Christianity. Others come mainly to find friends while most come to get grounded in the basics of faith. Alpha, a place to connect with God and others, is held in hundreds of churches across the globe regardless of their denomination.

Each church does Alpha differently. Our typical course went like this: we gathered on Sunday evenings to share a delicious home-cooked dinner. We sang a praise song and listened to a team member briefly share his/her story of connecting with God. Then we had a short talk on basic questions such as *How can I be Sure of my Faith? What about Evil? Is Healing for Today?*

The rest of the evening we spent in discussion groups of 10-12 facilitated by several team members. Throughout the course people learned to trust each other as they got real and shared problems common to humans. They shared their issues with bad relationships, marriage, divorce, kids, addictions, physical issues, pornography, alcoholism, gambling, and mental challenges like neglect, anger, fear, abuse, loneliness, and legalism. You name it. It came up.

At the core, people were struggling to fill that God-sized void inside which they'd tried to fill with worldly things that didn't satisfy. Inside they wondered, Am I <u>loved</u>? Do I <u>belong</u>? Am I <u>significant</u>?

Amazed, I watched the Lord help them answer *Yes* as they saw how Christianity is the only religion that reveals how they are <u>loved</u> unconditionally by God. As they responded to Jesus, now they knew they <u>belonged</u> to His big family and they found new <u>significance</u> and purpose for living.

Some were radically changed in a specific transforming moment. Most were changed little by little as they took baby steps toward freedom. Regardless of the speed, people began experiencing for themselves His joy, His love, and His peace.

The Saga of Big Red

Don and I realized that this course was another powerful *method* to fulfil our *mission* to love God and love others and teach the *message* of abundant life, so we served together on the Alpha host team for the next fourteen years. As Don led a small discussion group, I helped oversee the program and taught with two other leaders, Burnsey and Dianne, who became dear friends.

This was a season in which God gave me a fresh new crop of common yet incredible GodStories to share. One Monday morning Don prayed a short prayer: "Lord, give Cathy a new story to use as she teaches on *Does God Answer Prayer* this weekend."

That Friday at dusk I was driving on a road that I rarely traveled and spotted a big red truck parked in a cornfield with a *For Sale* sign. The fleeting thought ran through my mind, *"That is Don's truck."* I recognized God's voice which often comes as a knowing that resonates within, often a surprising thought that seems to come totally out of the blue.

The next morning I eagerly told Don, "Honey, I found your new truck."

He asked with a skeptical frown, "You what?" as he began down his checklist: "Is it a Ford F350? Diesel? 4x4? One-ton pickup? Crew cab? In good shape? Around $10,000?"

I interrupted him. "Heavens, I don't know. All I know is that there is a big red pickup sitting in the cornfield a few miles up the road, and I think God says it is the one you've been looking for."

My description was less than convincing, but we'd been searching over a year, and his old truck had 250,000 miles. We both knew how much God loves to provide, so we went to look at the truck. Don was amazed that it was everything he was looking for. The sign said $11,500, which was in the ballpark.

The next question was "So can we afford this rare find? Lord, show me the mo." I figured we might have to borrow a little, but I hoped not. Don had just been paid for a large fabrication project giving us some extra money in the bank. I expectantly added up our personal and business bank accounts.

"Unbelievable!" I exclaimed. My eyes widened as I checked my math. Yes, we had $11,581.27 in the bank, enough to buy the truck with $81.27 to spare. (I can't ever remember having $11,000 in our bank accounts before.) We gladly paid the asking price to the owner, who happened to be a pastor, as we praised our Lord who cares, who speaks, and provides all our needs.

That Sunday night I taught the Alpha lesson, "How and Why Should We Pray" with fresh fire as I told the story of how God had answered Don's prayers, both to find a truck and to have a story to illustrate this talk. I finished, "We plan to buy it in the morning."

Then I asked, "So did God answer these prayers so miraculously because Don and I are special, and He loves us so much? The answer is *Yes* and *No. Yes,* we are special in His eyes and He loves to show us favor and give us upgrades as we trust Him. But *No,* it wasn't just because *we* are special. He also did this for you who hear our story so that you would know that YOU are His special kids. This is the kind of loving Father He wants to be for both me and you.

The following Sunday evening we drove to Alpha in Big Red, our new truck and more than a few guys were gathered outside to check out the illustration. God was speaking in their language I quoted John 10:10, my life message as I shared the rest of the story at Alpha along with one interesting fact:

I found the truck on 10/10.

A Lost Finger

We continued loving to do Alpha courses where we shared stories of how Jesus is present and wants to enjoy life with us. During another ten-week Alpha course, our whole Alpha tribe was involved with another of our family crises. One morning I walked down the hallway and stopped to lay hands on the wall portrait of our little grandchildren as I prayed that God would protect them that day. I also asked Him to deepen their parents' faith and trust in the Lord. God answered both prayers, but it took me a while to see that as He answered in a way quite different than I anticipated.

That afternoon we received a frantic phone call from Jenny who was at the hospital. Their almost one-year-old Kassidy was a climber who crawled up onto anything and everything. As Jenny was out jogging, Kassidy climbed up onto a wooden kitchen chair and tipped it over, crushing two of her fingers under the chair rim. Hearing her screams, Poppa Chris quickly picked her up and wrapped a cloth around her blood-covered hand, gathered their other two girls, and picked up Jenny on the way to the hospital.

The doctor found that one of Kassidy's fingers was smashed and the end of her ring finger was missing, so Chris drove back home in twelve minutes flat to retrieve the rest of her little finger to sew back on. After a tedious surgery, the doctor told them, "I've done all I can do. In four weeks we'll remove the bandage and see what happens. She'll never re-grow nails on those two fingers. She'll probably need more surgery and a skin graft to repair her finger later."

In tears Jenny said, "Mom, it's her ring finger. Someday she'll want to wear a diamond on that finger." I shared the story at Alpha and asked our eighty new friends to pray with us for a miracle.

Four weeks passed. Two days before my Alpha talk on *Does God Heal Today?* it was time to remove Kassidy's bandages. Jenny was hopeful yet nervous as she held her baby girl in her lap. The doctor reached for her hand. He slowly unwrapped the bandage and then broke out in a big smile, shaking his head in disbelief. There were five healthy fingers, all intact, fully restored, complete with fingernails. God left a tiny curl on the end of her ring finger nail as a reminder of His miracle. With fresh confidence I shared at Alpha this example of how God *does* heal today.

Holy Spirit Day

Each week at Alpha we heard evidence of God at work in people's lives as people shared in the small groups how God was becoming real to them. Near the end of the course we enjoyed a Saturday retreat called "Holy Spirit Day" at a nearby forest lodge. On this day we all brought food to graze on; we laughed and shared stories; we listened to three talks on the Holy Spirit and discussed them; we spent relaxing time outdoors. At the end of the day we gathered in our smaller groups and prayed "Come, Holy Spirit" asking God to fill and refill us with His Spirit.

Most guests cite this day as their favorite part of Alpha on course evaluation sheets, not only because of the stories others share, but also because they experience their own stories as He shows up in unexpected ways. I have witnessed God's power at work in hundreds of people.

So what does it look like when the Holy Spirit comes and people experience His presence? They become more animated about life as they realize that their Father really loves them just like they are and that He has a purpose for their lives. Some invite Jesus into their lives for the first time. Most people develop a more intimate relationship with Him.

On Holy Spirit Day, God moves powerfully and often supernaturally delivers people from long standing emotional problems. We spend time inviting everyone present to listen for impressions from God on what He wants to do and to share them out loud. Many times people who had never felt they had heard from God shared what they felt God was saying. For example, during such a listening time someone shared this word of knowledge, "I sense God is saying that someone here is being healed of a broken heart you have lived with for seven years.

Immediately, a woman raised her hand and said, "That is me. My husband left me seven years ago and I've never gotten over it." We prayed for her, and God flooded her with His peace and healing that has lasted over the years.

A former cocaine addict commented, "This is better than any high I ever experienced." A former alcoholic added "And there is no hangover the next day, just more peace and joy."

On one Saturday, a woman lost her diamond necklace. Imagine her delight when we held the necklace up on Sunday evening at Alpha and asked, "Did anyone lose a necklace yesterday?" We had found the necklace when cleaning up, unaware that the diamonds were real.

She exclaimed, "I am so glad to get it back. It is worth $3000 but more importantly was a precious gift from my husband. When I realized that it was gone, I thought to myself '*My experience on Holy Spirit Day was well worth the value of that necklace.*'"

I am still in awe how God answers people's prayers. As we gathered expecting to experience supernatural encounters with God's Spirit, He didn't disappoint as we witnessed many powerful prophetic words, healing, and other encounters.

Another Saturday at lunch I felt God nudge me to go up to a couple and ask, "Does the word *barren* have any special meaning to you? That is a word I heard for you."

They looked at each other, and the husband said, "Yes. We have longed to have a child together, but I had a vasectomy last year." So we prayed together that God would cause them to conceive a child anyway. In the spring they shared their GodStory in Alpha of the arrival of a little miracle baby. Her name was Faith.

Another time God gave me a prophetic word to share about how someone was building, and the foundation was laid. It was now time to take the next step. A young man named Ryan was having a house built and the foundation had been laid that week, so he sensed the prophetic word was for him. He also realized the word applied spiritually, for he had just taken seven weeks to explore faith at Alpha. He said that now his foundational knowledge was solid, and it was time to take the next step. So he did. He asked Jesus into his life.

Powerful Spirit Words

During the rest of the Alpha course, God continued to give lifechanging words to many of us. One morning I awoke at 2:30 a.m. and began praying for someone from Alpha who was to be baptized the following Sunday. I heard the word *marijuana* and then forgot about it as I fell back to sleep. That Sunday as I was walking with him as he was getting ready to be baptized. I remembered the word and quietly commented to him, "Oh, I forgot. When I was praying for you this week, I heard one word *marijuana. Does that mean anything to you"*

He turned pale, "Who told you? No one knows I smoke. I haven't even told my wife."

I replied, "Evidently God knows. Earlier this week I woke up in bed and heard that word as I was praying for you. Don't panic. He doesn't want to expose you or shame you. He just wants to release you from that addiction." God did set him free from his habit along with his old life as he was baptized.

Each Alpha course produced a variety of transformations as people became rooted in the Lord's love and power and filled with His fullness.

Then Christ will make his home in your hearts as you trust in him. Your roots will grow down into God's love and keep you strong. And may you have the power to understand, as all God's people should, how wide, how long, how high, and how deep his love is. May you experience the love of Christ, though it is too great to understand fully. (Ephesians 3:17-18 NLT)

My favorite role helping with Alpha was taking my turn to teach the evening's lesson. In the movie, *Chariots of Fire*, Eric Liddell, a 1924 Olympic runner, said, "When I run fast, I feel His pleasure."

I know the feeling. *When I teach, I feel His pleasure.* It fulfils my calling and purpose to make Jesus known.

Year after year I have seen God transform lives and became aware of how involved He was with every detail. Don and I wanted more people to know Him better so we began doing Alpha in other locations—a Salvation Army halfway house, home groups, as well as at other churches an hour away. It was so worth the effort.

Alpha has been a favorite *method* of making Jesus known as I've been with over 3300 people passing through the 50+ courses I've helped with. I watched God bring His abundant life to thousands as they came alive in Him and were healed in different ways. They learned to love God and people in their own unique way and share their own stories.

The GodStories of all those touched by Him during Alpha could not be contained in even another book.

Winter Wonderland

Leaving a Legacy

Seasons rarely arrive overnight but more often come slowly over time. The beginning and end of our life seasons are also hard to pin down. As Don and I headed for our 60th birthdays, we seemed to be slowly transitioning into our winter season. I call it our *winter wonderland* for it would be filled with wonder as we saw what He had been up to in our lives and continued to experience His Presence.

Wondering how we were to proceed, we desired to finish our earthly mission well. Neither of us were eager to slow down and retire like a lot of older folks we knew. We still wanted God to actively use us as long as possible. We longed to live transparently and model finishing life not perfectly but purposefully walking with God. We determined to live a story we could not explain outside of God's intervention.

I've heard of an accurate test for determining if your mission on earth is finished. It is a one question test: "Are you breathing?" If your answer is *yes*, your mission isn't finished.

Yes, we were breathing deep, and life was far from over. Many winter winds lay ahead to batter us, but we were determined to stay on fire with His Presence.

This seemed like a fitting mantra for the season:

For I know the plans I have for you," says the Lord. "They are plans for good and not for disaster, to give you a future and a hope. (Jeremiah 29:11)

Still I wonder when I am eighty-five years old if I'll look back and say, "I miscalculated. Winter has just arrived."

Regardless, in this final quarter of life we wanted more than ever to make a difference in making Jesus known.

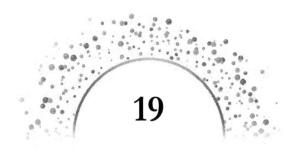

19

A Rough Stretch of Country

Winter began with quite a rollercoaster of ups and downs as we faced more fierce battles. Is response, God packed this season with never-ending adventures with Him.

Gone Country

During our ten years of city living, Don had often shared his dream of living in the country. When he shared this desire again at our small group, they encouraged us that since he was almost 60, it was time for dreams to come true. So we upped our prayers and contacted a realtor to begin searching for a space in the country with a large shop for my country boy yet close to town for this city girl. We both wanted an open spacious house where we could serve others with the gift of hospitality the rest of our lives.

Such a place was nowhere to be found, at least not in our price range. Over a year passed as the search dragged on. It looked hopeless, yet we stayed hopeful as we kept believing and praying the promise Jesus had given us to stand on during our house hunt:

> *Keep on asking, and you will receive what you ask for. Keep on seeking, and you will find. Keep on knocking, and the door will be opened to you. For everyone who asks, receives. Everyone who seeks, finds. And to everyone who knocks, the door will be opened.*
> (Matthew 7:7, 8 NLT)

Then one day I drove by a *For Sale* sign on a farm house only seven miles from town. Could this be it?

I turned the car around and peaked through the windows of the vacant house. It was just what we were looking for, a spacious ranch with a wide-open floor plan and plenty of space to construct a shop building.

I thought, "This has to be way out of our price range." We looked up the listing and it was. No wonder our realtor hadn't mentioned it.

Recently a favorite author spoke words that articulated what we were finding to be true:

Every problem we face comes with a promise and a provision from God. —GRAHAM COOKE

We prayed together, "Lord, you told us to *'Keep on seeking and you will find.'* Then we found this ideal house. But we can't afford the asking price. Please bring your provision. Show us what amount we should offer."

Afterwards we both wrote down on a piece of paper what we felt God was saying to offer. Don showed me his number and I showed him mine. We grinned as we saw the amounts were the same, a little above our price range but far lower than the asking price.

We prayed that the sellers would accept the offer and called our realtor. He laughed.

He called the owners with the offer, and they laughed. "No way."

They counter-offered and we refused, peaceful with our bid we felt was from God. We told our realtor to let the property go as we held onto the promise "keep on seeking and you will find" and just kept on looking.

Three weeks passed. Then one morning our realtor called, "You're not going to believe this, but the owner wants to know if your offer is still on the table."

"Yes, it sure is," we replied. We laughed.

Within a month we had moved into our spacious new country home prepared to practice the hospitality encouraged in Romans 12:13. The day after we moved in, our pastor Ben and his wife Tina came to share a meal and dedicate this place to our Provider.

Hit By a Mac Truck

Soon we faced another major "rob, kill, and destroy" attack. On December 23 we were hit with a fierce snowstorm in the night with 30-

mph winds as the temperature plummeted to 5° F. Snowplows piled up snow banks on each side of our country road up to four feet tall.

As I headed to work in the morning, the high prairie winds swirled the snow into a formidable whiteout. No longer able to see the hood of my car, I was surrounded by a wall of white and slowed to a crawl to attempt to stay on the now invisible road.

BAM! A powerful force rammed the rear of my car. The air bags failed, my car seat snapped and folded flat as I was thrown onto my back. Dazed, I pulled myself up with the steering wheel and gazed out. All I could see was the blinding white cloud of snow.

What on earth had hit me? I turned to see that my rear window was a heap of shattered glass, and snow was piling up in my back seat. Then I saw a two-ton garbage truck in the road ditch. Now I know what hit me.

"So this is what it feels like to be hit by a Mack truck."

I kept looking for some sign of life in the truck but saw no movement. I wondered, "Is the driver dead?"

Disoriented, I couldn't figure out exactly what was happening. Every few minutes an oncoming car would appear in front of my windshield in the whiteout and swerve to miss me. But it would go around my car on the passenger side. I was really confused until it dawned on me that the garbage truck had pushed my car over into the oncoming lane where it now sat facing morning traffic. It was entirely possible that the next car would not be able to see me in time. I knew that my life was in grave danger.

I cried out, "Jesus, You are my rock and my fortress. Please protect me!"

Within a minute another vehicle clipped the front of my car. I glanced out the rear window opening to see the driver keep driving, disappearing into the wall of white. Hit and run.

Three more cars appeared and swerved at the last second to miss me. I decided I would be better off to lie back down, put my scarf over my face, and pray in the Spirit. It was the best I could do.

Suddenly another car hit me head-on, shoving my car partly out of the traffic lane and onto the side of the road. Again I looked out the back window to see if this driver had stopped to help. He was running up to my car.

He opened my car door, shouting, "Come with me. We have to get you out of here before you get killed! Let's make a run for it."

I jumped out of my car and ran to his waiting vehicle. He drove to a nearby gas station to wait for the police. Soon the Mac truck driver walked in, alive and well. Thank you, Lord!

The police promptly closed our treacherous county road, a tow truck hauled away my totaled car, and I went to the hospital to check for injuries. The ER doctor prescribed strong pain meds, saying, "You might look fine, but you won't feel so fine in the morning. You can just plan on staying in bed tomorrow. Your entire body will be aching."

As I left the hospital the severity of the ordeal hit me, having been rear-ended by a two-ton truck, clipped and spun into oncoming traffic and hit head-on twice. Yet there I was, unscathed, at peace, and having experienced no fear whatsoever. God IS my peace, and He had protected all of us. There could have been serious injuries or fatalities had He not been on the scene, but He was at work as I cried out to Him.

Leaving the ER, I praised Him and prayed for healing. The next morning I felt great with only a few mildly sore muscles. I took advantage of the day off and got ready for all of our family to arrive for Christmas. I was aware that God had spared my life. I was one thankful momma.

Always an Open Home

That Christmas we celebrated with our first big family gathering in our new home. We were also eager to start sharing it with others, so on New Year's Day we shot a quick email to invite friends to a spontaneous Open House.

Three days later, 48 friends arrived, and I had them all sign a guest book. After having 137 visitors in our first two months, I laughingly closed the guest book for good, confident that God would send a steady stream of people to love.

What a great gathering place it has been as God has brought all sorts of people–singles, couples, families, students, old and young, believers, seekers, even some temporary live-ins. We've enjoyed fun parties and big celebrations, intimate dinners, overnight stays, weekly small groups, meetings, and simply hanging out together. Hospitality would be another method to make Jesus known.

Offer hospitality to one another without grumbling. Each of you should use whatever gift you have received to serve others, as faithful stewards of God's grace in its various forms. (I Peter 4:9-10 NIV)

Death Comes Knocking

John 10:10 helped us to deal with the mixture of good and bad, trials and triumphs, and to make sense of what was happening as we faced new trials. Eleven years had passed since Don's bypass surgery with no heart issues. Zilch! We were grateful.

Then one morning I woke up at 4 am and saw him stretched out on the recliner. I knew what was up.

"Are you okay, honey?"

He replied, "Yes, I'm just having some chest pains."

"How long have they been going on?"

"They started yesterday morning."

"What? Are you serious? We need to get you to the doctor."

"No. That EKG treadmill test the doctor ordered is only a couple days away, so I'm just going to wait. If it gets any worse, I'll go in." He went to work Thursday and Friday morning.

Friday afternoon the cardiologist examined him and said, "First of all, you have stage IV angina which is very unstable and the most dangerous kind. There will be no treadmill for you today – it could be fatal. I'm fairly certain I know what is going on. Your four arterial bypasses are failing. It's been over eleven years. Grafts normally last seven to ten years before becoming severely clogged. You're overdue. I'll give you nitro patches to wear this weekend. So take it easy. Don't do anything strenuous. Call me immediately if it gets worse. Monday morning we'll do a heart cath and probably put in some stints."

We went home, and Don took it easy, by his definition. Saturday morning I peeked in the shop to check on him. There was my man standing on top of a 14' extension ladder hanging fluorescent ceiling lights. He quipped, "Honey, I'm just changing a light bulb."

Saturday afternoon I began thinking how death was a real threat. Heart attacks and strokes had claimed the lives of Don's father at age 70, his mother at 74, his brother Paul at 47, and his nephew Paul Jr. at 29. I was starting to get uneasy. I obviously wasn't the only one. The pain caused Don to realize he might have only a matter of days left, so he composed letters to all four of our children, describing the special deposits that he had seen God place in each of them.

Saturday night after church Don was the first one to the altar when invited for prayer. Several gathered around him and asked God to heal Don's heart and clear his blood vessels. After five minutes Don said, "Amen," and we began to leave, but a dear friend Mark said "No, God isn't done yet." We continued for another ten minutes to pray for clear blood vessels, no blockage, and clear thinking. When we finished Don sensed peace and felt that something powerful had happened, but he still had some lingering chest pain.

On Sunday morning three other friends gathered with us to pray again. In the midst of their prayers Don said that although his eyes were closed, he sensed a fourth person joining the group. Don knew it was Jesus. Opening his eyes, he could only physically see the three friends but was quite confident that Jesus was right there. And the pain left for good.

On Monday morning Don headed to the heart cath, confident and eager to see proof that God indeed had cleared his blood vessels. He was semi-awake with eyes on the monitor. As the dye passed through the first grafted artery, the doctor said, "Hmmm. I don't see any blockage at all. That vessel is totally clear."

As the dye passed through the second graft, he shook his head in disbelief, "Amazing. No blockage here either. Well, I'm not going to make any money off you here. Let's look at the third...Clear.

It must be the last one...Clear too. All four grafts are clear. Your arteries are all totally free of plaque." The doctor shook his head. "Unbelievable. These grafts are over eleven years old and look like they were done two weeks ago. Go home and enjoy life. I can't explain it."

Don grinned, "I can, but you probably wouldn't believe me."

"Try me," said the doctor. Don shared his story and left his doctor pondering. We drove home to enjoy this precious gift of life. As we pulled into the garage Don said, "When we left this morning, I thought I might not come back home. Now I think I'll live another ten years." That was 16 years ago.

Now those grafts are 26 years old. Recently Don's nurse mentioned, "In my thirty years in cardiology, I've only seen one person still alive with grafts that old." I think that is really good news, isn't it?

Still Greater Is He

Most of our health challenges weren't life threatening. Picking which few healing stories to share is hard, for there were so many. Many accounts lie penned in my stack of journals as thanksgiving offerings to my heavenly Father. Those records may remain there for His pleasure alone just as the millions of wildflowers blooming in remote places give Him glory, seen by Him alone.

For me, health crises seemed to pop up more often when I was preparing for a major speaking engagement. Could it be I have an enemy who prefers to silence my words?

Four days before I was to speak at a large women's conference, a nurse called for me to come in for further tests after a mammogram. "Did you find a suspicious lump?" I asked.

After a short silence she said, "Well, actually there are four lumps, two on each side."

I gasped, "Seriously?" Immediately I realized the timing and felt that the enemy was trying to steal my focus and dampen my confidence in the abundant life Jesus gives us, the message of my talk.

I hung up the phone and boldly addressed the situation in His authority, "I stand against this attack. I refuse to be distracted by the enemy's wiles *No weapon formed against me will prosper.*[8] Worry, go in Jesus name. I command any cancer or pre-cancerous cells or any other foreign thing that doesn't belong in my body to go in Jesus' name."

I had the tests, kept my focus on Him, and got a good report...three weeks later. This was another test of faith, no doubt–the audacity of the enemy. Sometimes I'm just sick because humans get sick, but at times like these I suspicioned a culprit was at work trying to derail me and steal my hope and testimony in God's goodness. Then again if you ever wonder, "Is this a test? the answer is Yes. Everything we go through in life is a test of our trust and follow through.

Two days prior to the conference, I felt attacked again when I was hit with the flu and dizziness, and I slept until noon. He also attacked my family as my daughter called in tears. Jenny asked, "Mom, do we have any history of seizures or epilepsy in our family?" I sighed a big sick sigh as the ceiling kept swimming around. Jenny went on to explain how our granddaughter was having issues with allergies and symptoms of OCD and ADD, and the teacher suspected she might be having seizures in her classroom. The school psychologist suggested her doing 3rd grade in a special education classroom the next year.

Her momma and I prayed fervently over the phone, binding the enemy and asking God to intervene for our little girl's health and future. I wrote in my journal,

> OK, no you don't, devil. I recognize your tricks. You are going to lose. Kelsey is going to be set free of this junk and have a healthy normal childhood.

I doubt it was any coincidence that part of my upcoming talk included a story from years ago how our powerful God delivered both our one-year-old daughter Christy and me from epilepsy. This all transpired days before I was to speak.

> *You, dear children, are from God and have overcome them, because the one who is in you is greater than the one who is in the world.* (I John 4:4 NIV)

But God prevailed. The flu vanished that evening. The women's conference was wildly impactful, and I was amazed at God once again. Kelsey had a fun active childhood in regular classrooms all twelve years as she learned to work hard and overcome. We watched with great joy as she graduated from Texas State University with honors—another victory over obstacles, all praise to Him.

> *My child, pay attention to what I say. Listen carefully to my words. Don't lose sight of them. Let them penetrate deep into your heart, for they bring life to those who find them, and healing to their whole body.* (Proverbs 4:20-22 NLT)

Don's Dream Shop

As this season began, Don was loving his new life in the country. His work life was a different story. He had lost his job of ten years in a major company downsizing and then had gone through several short-term jobs and was feeling very vulnerable. Like most men, Don had always found value and identity in his work. His job situation took a major hit on his confidence and required trusting God. The struggles were real, and the road was long.

As he worked various jobs, Don envisioned owning a business where he could solve mechanical problems, do ag repairs, and create the dreams people brought to him. To run such a business, he needed a shop.

So at age 58 he began constructing a 40' x 60' machine shop. At first, I was a little miffed that the shop was bigger than our house, but I got over it. Don exhibited the slow and steady work ethic he had learned on the farm. All winter long after a full day's work he would come home, eat supper, bundle up, and go outside to build on his shop until around 10 p.m. in wind, snow, and ice. He finished in the spring, and friends came to help set the roof trusses in the air. The building was ready for final siding.

Then early one morning a fierce March storm rolled in with 60 mph wind gusts. A loud crash woke us both at 4 a.m..

"Thunder? Oh Lord, please let it be thunder," I prayed.

Don sat up in bed, "Do you think that was the shop?"

"Yes." Dazed, we peered out the window into the darkness. The flashes of lightning illuminated what was left of Don's shop framing, folded flat on the ground.

Despite the howling winds and sheets of rain still pelting our bedroom window, we sensed God's calm presence in the storm. We couldn't do anything in the night so we turned out the lights, headed back to bed, and fell asleep, holding hands. At daybreak we surveyed the devastating debris, the remains of his long winter labor.

At breakfast we paused to hold hands and ask God's blessing on our food and the task before us. Don tearfully cried out, "Lord, you own everything we have. We are your stewards. This is your building. Help us get it back up. " Then he added, "And may this bring You glory."

I was in total agreement until he tacked on the glory request. Being a mighty woman of faith, I looked at him incredulously, "Bring Him glory?" For some reason, I totally snapped and lost it. Peace suddenly left me numb with shock as I faced incredible disbelief. I didn't try to hide how I felt from my heavenly Father since he knows what I am thinking anyway. I knew that He would rather I come talk to Him in my anguish instead of turning away from Him.

As soon as Don headed outside, I began to vent, "God, why did you let this happen? He worked so hard this winter. Why didn't you protect his shop? How could you possibly work good out of this disaster? Bring you glory? I'll have to see that to believe it."

I thought of the words of Joyce Meyer, "*You can't be pitiful and powerful at the same time.*" I definitely chose *pitiful* for several days before I could snap out of it. I'd tell myself, "*Focus on God, Cathy.*" Slowly I quit glaring at the pile of debris that I could see and began focusing on my God whom I couldn't see, the one who had always been there in our crises, the one whom we had always counted on. I cried out to Him, "I believe. Lord, help my unbelief." I didn't want to end up in a pit of despair again.

I cried out, "I am slipping!" but your unfailing love, O Lord, supported me. When doubts filled my mind, your comfort gave me renewed hope and cheer. (Psalms 94:18-19 NLT)

Slowly I began to believe with Don that somehow God was going to bring glory out of this rubble in our life. How? I had no clue, but deep down I knew somehow God would come through again. We had the easy part of trusting Him. He had the hard part of resurrecting that building in a manner that would bring Him glory. Just because the building fell into a heap didn't mean our lives had to also.

We lived on a very visible S curve on a major county road and had been unaware how many commuters who drove by our house were intrigued by my man's steady progress. The floodlights he had put up to work in the dark had lit the sky each night for miles. The morning after the crash when people passed by and saw the shop in a pile on the ground, one car after another slowed to a crawl as they stared in disbelief. One stranger stopped and rang the doorbell, "We are so sorry to see this disaster. I called my wife on the way to work and said, 'Honey, it blew to the ground.'"

She knowingly replied, "The shed?"

"Yep," he replied.

For days people drove by, honking and waving in support. Soon I was able to see blessings in the rubble. The building missed landing on Don's pickup by six inches. We survived the destructive storm unscathed as did our house. Members of our family came to help us for a week along with many from our church family.

God's Glory Crew

Then God answered Don's prayers for this disaster to bring Him glory and had it published in the local Fisher, IL newspaper to make sure

I didn't miss it:

> God was glorified this past Saturday, March 23. Many helpers from the Fisher/Dewey Council of Churches & Mennonite Disaster Group went to the aid of Don & Cathy Vincent, who live on the curves on the Fisher/Dewey Road. Don had a dream and a vision of a large workable garage/shed. He worked day and night mostly by himself...diligently putting up board by board. It looked pretty good. But on March 9th, those dreams were blown down to the ground.
>
> But many prayers were answered! People's hearts had compassion for this man and God knew it. He put together a work crew and a food crew. Praise God the dream is going back up! To those who lent a hand, whether it be a hammer, advice, food or prayer, we thank you.

On that Saturday twenty-six strangers pulled into our drive with pickups and tools to clean up rubble and begin reframing, raising up one side of the building as the women prepared a delicious home-cooked lunch. Channel 3, our local tv station, came out and interviewed the workers for an evening documentary. Many workers gave glory to God on the broadcast.

The following week I wrote the editor:

> Dear Karen,
>
> One of my clients from Fisher brought the paper that had the article about our building. We weren't aware that it was even in the paper until then, but we wanted to say, "thank you".
>
> On the morning the shop blew down, we held hands at the kitchen table, and prayed, "God, you own everything we have. We're just your stewards. It's your building. Help us get it back up, and above all, help us bring glory to you as it goes back up." Imagine our delight when your article begins: "God was glorified this past Saturday..."
>
> We just want to personally thank you for being courageous enough to allow people to express their faith in your newspaper. So much of what we hear in the news is depressing and discouraging. What a bright light to see a paper with encouraging news. Thank you.
>
> Don and Cathy Vincent

The following week the editor published our letter in the paper. To God be more glory!

The Lord was still not done with His upgrades. We had been running out of funds to finish siding the shop. Then it looked like we had lost everything, for we doubted that our homeowner's insurance would cover the loss, but it did. The generous settlement was enough to rebuild the frame *and* purchase the siding.

God, the master builder, restored our shop leveled by the storm, the same God who restores lives leveled by the storms of life when all seems hopeless and beyond repair as we to cry out for help.

Rebuilding was difficult with our new awareness of how fragile and out of control life really is. Loss will come again. Things will not last. People we trust will let us down. Ventures will go awry. Life will be hard at times. Yet in it all, we knew we could trust in a God who always shows up.

God's Provision

Being affluent had never been very high on our goal list, so we had not saved enough for a rainy day, let alone the golden years. We had a few tough financial years of transitioning to being self-employed. For a while we struggled with covering basic needs, and God encouraged us with surprise provisions.

For several years our house had needed a fresh coat of paint which seemed too costly. Then one fall, a couple from our small group told us that they felt God wanted them to help us get our house painted before winter and handed us a sizeable check for paint. Others came to prep the siding and help Don paint our house which made it more inviting, recharging our hospitality.

The following February our heat pump chugged one last time and died leaving us without heat or air conditioning for the summer. Fortunately, spring arrived early and we got through the remaining cold days with auxiliary heat. Spring was okay, but summer was not so fine. We prayed for a solution while we braved the hot summer days with open windows and fans, joking how in the "good old days" nobody had air-conditioning. We also recalled surviving the Amazon laboring in the humid 100-degree weather, content with just a little shade. But that was only a few weeks. This hot Illinois summer stretched out a bit longer.

We weren't trying to be martyrs. We had gotten a quote for $6300 to replace our system, $6200 more than what we had, so that job went on the bottom of our TO DO list and the top of our prayer list. We got along in the summer heat, but when those fall gusts turned chilly, we knew winter was right around the corner. We asked for help and trusted in His promise:

And my God will meet all your needs according to the riches of His glory in Christ Jesus. (Philippians 4:19 NIV)

In September when we got a call from our son-in-law Orestes who shared, "You're not going to believe this. This morning a co-worker (whom I'll call Joe) told me, 'I just won some money that I don't need. I wish I knew someone who needed some extra cash. I'd like to give some of it away.'"

Orestes jokingly said, "I need a new shotgun." Joe was not moved!

Then he added, "Actually, I do know an older couple who is having a hard time affording a new heating system for this winter. But I'm sure you will find some good place for those dollars."

Joe left. A half hour later he was back holding twenty $100 bills, "Would you give this to them for me?" That weekend Orestes brought us the $2000. I don't know Joe's real name, but the Lord used this stranger to provide for us. We also received an unexpected $500 check in the mail that week, and with $300 in our bank account, we ordered the $2800 heat pump. Don installed the system in our crawlspace, saving all the labor costs. We now had both heat and air-conditioning. I was so thankful for my talented patient man and the help of Joe and Orestes. We profusely thanked God all winter for His provision.

My Unhappy Birthday

Age has never been a big deal to me, and I still freely share my age with everyone. I had celebrated birthdays as I turned 30, 40, and 50 with hardly a glance wondering why they bothered so many people. It seems to be one particular year that gets us, different years for different people.

When I hit my 59th birthday, I got it.

Painfully hobbling along in sore need of a hip replacement and almost 60, I began to feel old. Obviously my concern was showing as Don so painfully reminded me one night as we settled into bed. He quietly commented, "I don't want to talk about it right now, but two times in the past two weeks you were really a lot of fun." Stunned at what that implied, I asked, "Really? When was that?"

"When we went to Menards and again in the kitchen when we were goofing around."

Silence followed as Don drifted off to sleep and began to snore. I lay there wide awake, eyes staring at the ceiling, heart and mind racing.

Really? I'm not fun to live with anymore. I thought that was my normal life. When did I quit being fun?

His words tumbled over and over in my head for forty minutes. I realized that anxiety had become my normal state of mind as I was constantly overthinking and over planning everything, working too many hours, and often worrying about too much month at the end of the money. I was feeling more like a human doing than a human being.

I tearfully cried, "Lord, Don is right. I'm not fun to live with at all. Restore my joyful spirit." And I promptly drifted off to sleep and snored along with him.

I wish I could say that was the end of that, but this is no fairy tale, and many days in my early 60s were not exactly *happily ever after.* Worry and anxiety peppered my journal during a long funk as I wrestled with more haunting questions:

> Will life continue to spiral downward? Will we die too soon as health fails until we are frail? Will we live too long and run out of money? Or will we have a full life fulfilling our calling and leaving a legacy?

The stressors of work, health, and wealth lined up like dominoes, each toppling the next until all were flat and I lay under the pile. Times were tough, and I fought to keep upbeat.

While I wanted God to remove all the hardships, I realized if He did this for everyone who became a believer, people would flock to Him but for the wrong reason. Love has to be a choice. He wanted me to choose to love Him and trust Him to meet our needs when times were good and especially when they weren't.

I was hoping to finish living my life as a good example of what *to* do, not as a bad example of what *not* to do. He kept encouraging me as I read.

> *We now have this light shining in our hearts, but we ourselves are like fragile clay jars containing this great treasure. This makes it clear that our great power is from God, not from ourselves. We are pressed on every side by troubles, but we are not crushed. We are perplexed, but not driven to despair.* (2 Corinthians 4:7,8 NLT)

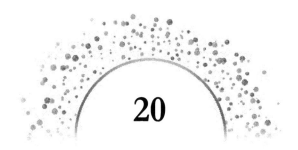

20

Fulfilling Our Mission

Mission In Mexico

At age 63 we served on another short-term work mission trip, this time in Mazatlán, Mexico. While Don poured concrete for a community building, I was assigned to help pull teeth in a makeshift outdoor dental clinic for the poor. (Going to the dentist is one of my least favorite things. Go figure.)

In the hot dusty winds, our team dentist served the poor by pulling 122 decayed teeth. I held the flashlight in each patient's mouth as I prayed for them in the Spirit and cleaned the instruments with some alcohol to be ready for the next person in the long waiting line.

I'll never forget our trip with the missionaries to feed the poor at the city dump, a tall hill created from years of rubbish. Along the winding road, we passed families living in tiny cardboard shacks who scavenged through the fresh trash dumped atop in hopes of finding some food for their family and pieces of cardboard and scraps to sell. We served them a lunch of pancakes, oranges, and refreshing water as we encouraged and prayed for them. I felt overwhelmed by the hopelessness reflected on their sun worn faces.

In the evening we joined in the local church service and saw a sharp contrast in the hopeful faces of the joyful local believers who rallied to serve the needy around them while living in poverty themselves. I saw again how living a rich life doesn't require having loads of money or possessions. I saw true riches, often unnoticed in our modern world, at work in the lives of the poor as they loved like Jesus loved.

We returned from this trip humbled again by how we had taken for granted how our daily luxuries far exceeded our needs. We were recharged to fulfil our mission to serve others, to love God and the people He created and loves.

Mission at Home

Soon a new adventure awaited us. In our ninth year of doing Alpha, we met Momma D, a fun-loving forty-two-year old biker with tattoos, a big Harley, and a colorful past. Her husband of thirteen years had just left her for a younger woman. Angered by the betrayal, she began to devise a plan to kill her husband and his girlfriend. Then her in-laws invited her to the Vineyard Church one Sunday morning and urged her to check out Alpha where she could ask God all her questions. The first night she was hooked. Momma D kept coming and asking questions. Slowly she saw that God loved her just as she was.

For years she had suffered from severe asthma attacks and avoided spending any length of time outdoors which would often lead to a hospital stay. One afternoon she began fuming again about the situation and decided to go outside to mow the overgrown grass in her large country yard. As she mowed, she ranted and raved at God with choice expletives. Shaking her fist in the air, she shouted, "Why me? Why have you made me so miserable? Just give me an asthma attack. Go ahead and kill me. I don't care. I don't want to live anyway."

Instead of killing her, God gently reached down and touched her, healing her from her lifelong asthma on the spot. He quieted her spirit and gave her new hope as she calmly finished mowing the yard with no symptoms while she wondered what had just happened. She soon radically gave her heart to Jesus and began telling everybody she knew about how he had taken away her anger and replaced it with peace and joy and given her a reason to live.

Momma D had a big heart for people, so when she decided to get baptized, she invited all of her family and biker friends to come watch. Thirty friends showed up, most of whom hadn't been in a church since childhood and a few who'd never stepped inside a church their whole life.

But they did know how to party. I was invited to the Saturday night baptism after-party at her place way out in the country. Don was working so although I was feeling wimpy, I decided to go alone. I got more anxious when I heard the rock music jamming a half-mile away. I thought,

Cast all your anxiety on him because he cares for you. (I Peter 5:7 NIV)

I parked my four door sedan among the Harleys and walked past a growling Rottweiler in his pen as I climbed the steps and entered a new unknown world.

Inside a warm welcome awaited me as I was escorted to the dining room where the party was going strong. A huge cake decorated with *Congratulations on your Baptism* sat on the big oak table surrounded by empty wine cooler and beer bottles. Other not-so-empty bottles were in the hands of the celebrating crowd.

As I mingled, a delightful woman said how she had enjoyed church, "But that didn't seem like church. That was a lot of fun!" She went on, "And I loved the karaoke," her description of the worship song lyrics projected onto the big screen.

Then Mamma D graciously gave me a tour of her large country home and proudly shared that she had twenty-six guns in the house, pulling out several for me to admire. While the party was out of my comfort zone, I'm sure Jesus felt right at home in this house full of pre-Christians, with the large celebration cake, beer and wine coolers, loud music, and all. The Bible tells how Jesus often enjoyed people in their unreligious extravagance like when He turned thirty gallons of water into wine at a wedding. (John 2) Jesus was, no doubt, delighted in this gathering where his brand-new child was on fire and sharing with everyone how He had set her free. So was I.

Biker Alpha

Don and I were drawn to this vibrant woman who so freely loved and gathered others. We invited Momma D over to dinner to get to know her better. Although rough and tough and clad in a black leather jacket, this woman had a soft heart of compassion. We shared our stories, and she asked questions, soaking up everything about God like a dry sponge.

At dinner she shared, "At Alpha last night I laid hands on Kim and prayed for her to be healed. My hands got red hot and I jumped back; I was afraid I was going to burn her skin."

Don explained, "That gal is more likely to get healed than to get burned. Feeling heat as you are praying is often a sign of healing in your hands, that the Spirit of God is working."

Then Momma D shared with us her grand plan. She was going to do a Biker Alpha. Since many of her friends wouldn't set foot in a church, she'd invite them to her place each week, cook up some fried chicken or other delights and then have an Alpha session. We said, "We will help you. Count us in!"

After she left I was thinking, "What have we gotten ourselves into?" I was a bit fearful about entering this new unknown world. I lay awake, allowing my mind to conjure up how dangerous it could be, how we might be robbed and pillaged in our home, not realizing how I was listening to lies of our enemy, the devil, who was trying to steal one of our greatest adventures before it had begun. None of my fears materialized. Instead we gained some of our dearest friends and were transformed along with them.

One summer evening we headed out to coordinate the Biker Alpha. Momma D had spread out quite the feast of fried chicken, mashed potatoes and gravy, and "all the fixings." Three guests arrived. We waited and waited for rest of the crowd.

Momma D was annoyed, "Where is everyone? They were coming. I wonder if there is a problem." She made a quick phone call. Yep, there was a problem. On the way to Alpha, one of the guys had changed his mind about coming and was stopping cars headed to Alpha to search for his stolen pistol. Instead of proceeding to Alpha, the bikers loyally turned their cars around and headed to a local bar to help find the thief and retrieve the gun. Somehow, they ended up staying at the bar. So went the first night of Alpha.

Each week it was something else. But slowly over the following eight weeks, more people began showing up and openly asked lots of great questions. God revealed His love in unique ways for each of them. And what GodStories!

When we covered the topic, *What about Evil?* one woman shared how a ghost habitually pestered them, doing odd things like slamming doors in their home. We told her that she could command him to go in Jesus name. As time passed, her faith continued to grow. At the end of Alpha when we asked people what changes they had seen in their lives she mentioned, "Oh, you know that ghost that bothered us? He's gone. I don't know what happened to him."

God was changing people's lives even when they didn't understand everything about His ways. Jesus promised abundant life, and He was making good on His promise.

Another evening around 11 pm Momma D excitedly called from Chicago where she was attending a Harley Bike Show with a couple other Alpha friends. She explained, "We are at a bar, and B. just asked Jesus to into her life. We just had to tell you." There was Jesus lovingly at work...at night...in a bar...drawing those He loved to Himself. That is the Jesus I know and love.

I have come to call not those who think they are righteous, but those who know they are sinners and need to repent. (Luke 5:32 NIV)

Friends Forever

That Christmas, Don and I hosted a party that included these amazing new friends. The doorbell rang, and as I welcomed B in, her adult daughter she had brought along asked, "Would you save me?" She hadn't taken off her coat.

I smiled, "No, I can't save you, but I sure can introduce you to the one who can." That night Jesus did save her and free her from emptiness and disappointment and made her a new creation.

Eight lives were transformed during that Biker Alpha, including Six Pack Jack, their leader and still one of our dear friends. He commented, "On Holy Spirit Day, I felt the weight of sin like a freight truck sitting on my chest suddenly lift, and I could breathe freely, totally free."

This Biker Alpha saga continues as God is still at work as these believers reach out to their friends and their families who want to hear about this life-changing God. One Sunday morning we noticed the lineup of motorcycles in the church parking lot and were delighted by the twenty-one people sitting in the two front church pews because of the Biker Alpha.

Momma D continued to grow as a servant leader and is now an ordained pastor who travels to China to spread the good news. I love how uniquely God uses each of us when we catch His fire and partner with Him in His work. We serve a God who amazes us when we take the risk of faith.

Let all that I am praise the LORD; may I never forget the good things he does for me. He forgives all my sins and heals all my diseases. He redeems me from death and crowns me with love and tender mercies. He fills my life with good things. (Psalm 103:2-5 NLT)

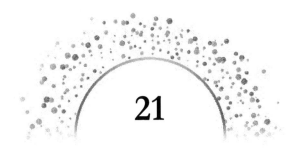

Dreams Do Come True

Tucked away in the middle of this roller coaster season is one of our favorite GodStories. Christy, our youngest, had married Orestes and pursued her career for a few years and was now ready to start a family. They anticipated a baby within the year, but several years passed with no baby in sight. They consulted a fertility specialist who ran extensive tests only to inform them, "I am so sorry, but it is impossible for you to have biological children." We were all devastated with this news at first until Jesus began building hope in us for the impossible.

Barren

We prayed and believed...for over five years...and our hope was starting to wane. Then on Mother's Day, our Vineyard pastor Dianne shared a message on hope and how God had healed her from barrenness and given her five children.[9] At the end of the service she offered to pray for anyone with infertility issues, and Christy responded to God's urging to go up for prayer one more time. Dianne laid hands on her along with several other of us women and asked for healing and a baby. Christy sensed nothing unusual, but one young woman who was praying shared later with those praying that she sensed that Christy would become pregnant within a month. I didn't mention it to Christy, but I wondered, "Could you be up to another miracle, Lord?" A month passed. No phone call of good news. Hopefully, the woman had heard God but missed the timing.

Despite indications that she was not pregnant, six weeks later Christy decided to take a pregnancy test before taking meds for a cold just in case. The test was positive!

She writes, "I can't tell you the thrill that knowing I would be a mother brought me. I have always loved my nieces and nephew, and now we would have a child too. Thank you, God, that you still do miracles today."

On February 8 their miracle baby arrived; they named him Mateo meaning gift from God. I was ecstatic to hold him in my arms. I thanked God for once again doing what man had deemed impossible.

With man this is impossible, but with God all things are possible. (Matthew 9:26 NIV)

No, Not Again!

Aunt Jenny was holding little Mateo when we noticed that his hands and feet were blue and his breathing was very erratic. I said to the nurse, "I don't think he is breathing right. Could you check him out?" The nurse whisked Mateo out of Jenny's arms and left the room.

Suddenly fear flooded in with a flashback of an almost identical scene in a hospital years ago when I handed our newborn to the nurse and uttered those identical words, "I don't think he is breathing right. Could you check him out?"

I never held my son Cory in my arms again. Would I hold my grandson Mateo again?

We all prayed as we watched and waited. The neo-natal specialist cleared the baby's airways several times, but Mateo could not get enough oxygen to breathe on his own. The next time we saw him he was in an oxygen tent looking so small and helpless with a breathing tube, numerous monitors, and an IV in his tiny arm. For the next week he remained on oxygen and intravenous antibiotics and a light for jaundice as his parents stayed by his side. Numerous times the staff had unsuccessfully tried to get our little one to breathe. Once more they pulled the tubes to see what would happen.

Don felt impressed to go to the nursery right then and found himself alone with Mateo. He prayed and then spoke to our baby, "Mateo, you can do this," and all at once, Mateo began to breathe on his own. Soon they took their little gift from God home, and we all continue to share this story of how God answered prayer and turned this test into a testimony.

Christy and Orestes wanted another child but once again the doctor said she would not be able to conceive. She couldn't...without God, but we knew that with Him, the impossible is possible. Two years later Raquel, our delightful baby of the family arrived, a fiery little beauty, full of passion for life. This one has no dreams of being Princess Leah; she wants to be Luke Skywalker!

> *Praise the Lord, my soul, and forget not all his benefits—who forgives all your sins and heals all your diseases, who redeems your life from the pit and crowns you with love and compassion, who satisfies your desires with good things so that your youth is renewed like the eagle's.* (Psalm 103:2-5 NIV)

Grandkid Camp – Leaving a Legacy

In our winter wonderland season we created one special family tradition that turned out to be another memorable method of making Jesus known *Grandkid Camp.* (Thanks for the idea, John and Deanna Wright) We called it Only the grandkids were invited, and they eagerly looked forward to it. So did we, and their folks didn't mind the little break either.

The first year of camp I arrived to pick up the current five grandkids at our rendezvous spot decked out in my special camp t-shirt, clipboard in hand with the four-day schedule and a whistle to gather my little chicks. I surprised them each with a camp T-shirt stenciled with their pictures. The kiddos learned our new camp cheer, and heartily cheered it together. Then we loaded up the van for our 90-minute drive home. The excitement was electrifying as I turned the ignition key, proclaiming, "Whoo hoo. Here we go!"

Toby, age 7, squinted up his nose at me and with a serious face asked, "Grandma, just how much sugar have you had today?"

Grandkid Camp #1, entitled *We Are Family,* lasted four days. In the mornings we all cooked breakfast together, and Grandpa made everyone his traditional "cocoa coffee" which is cocoa minus the coffee. We lifted our cups in the air, clicked them together and took a slurp, letting out a big collective ahhh. We started the day with a favorite Bible passage and a discussion led by Grandpa and then prayed for each kiddo. We sang from our camp CD, *The Fruit of the Spirit.* In the van, the kids would crank up the volume and sing through the whole album with gusto.

During the day we took learning excursions to nearby places, visiting an Amish community and touring a chiropractic/rehab center, and playing together at a water park and assorted playgrounds. In our scheduled instructional times we taught about relationships. Each day we had a *Once Upon a Time* story slot, and they never tired of hearing stories of their parents growing up. The final evening we made a big bonfire in the backyard and roasted hotdogs, toasted s'mores, sang and shared more stories. We modeled how we end each night as we begin each day, connecting with God.

Grandkid Camp # 2 lasted only three days the following year. We were getting older…and wiser. We again modeled daily Bible and prayer and shared more GodStories. We kept clicking cups of cocoa coffee. This camp included a backyard scavenger hunt, a petting zoo, and a swimming hole with boats, tubes and trampolines. The kids also created some amazing outfits from newspaper, scissors and duct tape and did a style show as we took pictures and made a photo memory book.

Grandkid Camp #3 was only two days on a weekend. As the kiddos got older, it was harder to fit a time in among summer sports, vacations, and activities.

The next two summers we missed *Grandkid Camp* altogether as I recovered from two hip replacements. Then we continued to have mini-camps at the insistence of the two youngest who missed out when they were only babes. When we took them to St Louis for a mini-camp we were surprised that Kelsey, now a college senior at Texas State flew in to join us along with our oldest, Taylor, now 22.

Over the years we made some priceless memories, and the kids can still quote the fruit of the Spirit from singing the song 50+ times. Some friends have begun having their own grandkid camp tradition. What a privilege to get to celebrate the gift of grandkids and to input into their lives. Thank you, parents!

My Bucket List

I delight in how God speaks powerfully through His Word, but it also blesses my socks off when He talks to me through everyday events like movies, news, songs, and conversations. When I ask Him to speak to me, I am on the lookout for His response and so much more likely to hear what He is saying.

My pastor friend Jeff says, "I come out of every movie with a message from God." This is because He expects God to speak to Him that way, so now I do too and usually am impacted by what God is saying in a movie.

One such movie that touched me when I was in my 60's was *The Bucket List*, the story of two men who were terminally ill roommates in a hospital room with little else in common. They become friends and create a list of things they want to do before they kick the bucket and die. Then they leave the hospital to travel around the world and check items off their bucket lists, discovering joy in doing life together.

Walking out of the movie theater I was stirred with another life lesson. I was realizing that I had a limited amount of time left, so for the next few weeks I worked on my own Bucket List. Many things floated through my mind onto the pages of my notebook such as places I wanted to visit or things I wanted to do.

But in the end I narrowed it down to only three things:

1) Get out of all debt except for mortgage and stay out of debt

2) Finish the book.

3) Weigh & stay at a healthy weight (159 # which was later revised upward)

These would be on my annual goal list for years. I believed God would give me these desires of my heart as I delighted in Him.

> *Take delight in the LORD, and he will give you the desires of your heart.* (Psalm 37:4 NIV)

However, I'm better at hearing what God is going to do than hearing when it is going to happen. I often expect Him to be quicker so I miss His timetable. I forget to factor in that precious space in the messy middle where He grows our faith. God just never seems to be in a rush. I'm a firm believer in Philippians 4:13 "I can do all things through Christ who strengthens me" but I often have to remind myself, "however, not necessarily in my time frame."

But in His timing the Lord did remember my bucket list containing three small seeds of hope. The most impossible item was # 1– getting out of debt. I'm embarrassed to say that our short-term debt load had soared to $80,000, mostly on credit cards. The major portion of the debt was from building the shop which we weren't able to fold into our mortgage until our new startup businesses showed stable profits for two years. We also still had some college debt, but the embarrassing remainder was from charging living expenses when we were making insufficient income. It was a test of faith.

Until the time that His word came to pass, the word of the LORD tested Him. (Psalm 105:19 NIV)

Four years after building the shop we again applied for a mortgage. We petitioned God for a large appraisal value which was highly unlikely as the housing market was in a slump. We were floored when our property was appraised $100,000 higher than four years earlier. With the mortgage refinance we paid off all short-term debt and lowered our interest rates. Suddenly bucket list item # 1 was checked off. This book checks off item # 2. Lastly, item # 3 is well in progress as my weight is descending, but that's another story for another time. God answers prayers in His timing.

Don's Dream Job

Thankful that our debts were cleared, we still were concerned that we hadn't saved well for the future and couldn't picture how God could change things around. But He did. After several years running a contracting business Don looked for a job with good retirement benefits. His dream had been to work for the main Kraft plant, so he applied there at age 63 with not-so-great odds of being hired at that age.

He heard nothing for three months after interviewing, but God made a dream come true when he was hired as a line tech in a job that fit his passion to fabricate and fix things. He enjoyed troubleshooting the production line for four years until his hearing made it too difficult to continue. By that time, our nest egg was replenished, and it was time to move on.

Another Impossible Dream

As a young girl listening to my Granddad preach, I dreamed of being a pastor. For years this seemed a closed door to me as a woman, but the passion didn't go away. When doing financial planning, my schedule was flexible so I unofficially began pastoring people as I oversaw small groups, taught classes, and helped lead Alpha. While I had hoped to be successful in my job and overcome my phoning phobia, that seemed to pale in importance as the work I was doing at church began captivating my heart. Soon I was volunteering 10-20 hours a week. My season of financial planning was drawing to a close and proved to be an ideal five year prep school for what God had in store for me next.

One dark evening as I drove home in the country, thousands of fireflies lit up the cornfields. God softly encouraged me that His angels were just like those lights, surrounding us in these dark times. I went to bed and saw 10:10 on the clock right before I closed my eyes. God was on the job providing abundant life. A new season was close at hand, and I prayed, "Bring it on, Lord."

The next day I received an unexpected call from our pastor Ben who asked if I would consider being his half-time assistant since I was already at the church working most of the time anyway. We set a time for me to come in and talk about it. Driving to the interview I got a call from another staff pastor, Jim, "I know small groups are your passion. Would be interested in a half-time position as a small group pastor?"

I replied, "Have you been talking with Ben about me?"

"No," he replied.

"Unbelievable. Right now I am driving into town to interview for a part-time position with him at the church."

Although they were from the same church, neither pastor was aware that the other one had called. It sounded like God. Both positions sounded so right to me. But I really wrestled with the Lord about whether to close my business, I journaled,

> Lord, I feel like I missed it big time. I questioned yesterday if I hear your voice at all. This job thing has me confused. You know I want to quit, but I don't want to fail or cave in to giving up. Would it be a big mistake if it didn't work out? It looks like I missed you, but deep down I don't think I missed you, but I am not infallible. I don't have enough time left to miss you again. Please, Lord, put me in the center of what you want for my life. This new possibility is swirling inside. I'd love doing work so valuable in Your kingdom.
>
> But what about my career? Am I done with this season? Yesterday I felt you spoke to me, "New season, new reason." Is this what you meant? Is this your plan? I am sensing right now that you are fine and could use me in either path. You know my future, my energy, my strengths and weaknesses, my opportunities and limitations. You know what's best, Father. Show me. And help Don and I be in one accord.

The following day I wrote what I sensed God gently speaking in my spirit,

> "This is a new season to serve and to live abundantly. Embrace this. You are called for such a time as this. Be yourself. You can do this."
>
> My response was, "Lord I would never for a moment consider this job without your presence and grace going with me, covering me. But here am I. Send me."

A few weeks later at the age of 63 my childhood dream came true. I became as a pastor.

The first year I wore several hats as Small Group Pastor, Ben's assistant and HR Director. It was a busy year of helping oversee small groups, making thirty hires, and setting up a new employee health insurance program. I went into work at 8 am and with Don working until 11:30 pm most evenings I got home late at night after meeting with people and teaching classes. I had found my calling, and I was reveling in it.

And More...

The next year I was asked to be full-time Connect Pastor to assimilate our new people in their first year at the Vineyard. I was intrigued since connecting was my passion. But the job would come with a high cost: working weekends, less time with our family, and the responsibility of getting newcomers rooted in our church family. This task would fill my days, my nights, AND my weekends.

I wondered, "Should I do this?" This led to a talk with the Lord as I drove home. It is hard to explain how I experienced this back and forth dialogue in my head, but I certainly knew who was talking with me.

I asked God, "Am I up to it?"

Then He asked me, "If you were forty years old, would you be willing to do this?"

I replied, "In a heartbeat."

Then it hit me, "I think I'm too old, don't I?

Then God spoke again. "What if you were 50?" ...Sure...

"55?" ... "Yes" "60?" ... "Yes." "65?" ... Dead silence.

I hesitated. "It's not a job I could do apart from you, Holy Spirit. I don't know if I am willing to commit to this big responsibility. Don't I ever get to rest?"

Dead silence again. I said "Yes" to the Lord that night to a role that would be all-consuming but so rewarding. Many people grow up in our self-absorbed culture not knowing how to openly relate to each other or God. They often come to the church battered, weary, discouraged, wondering, "Is this the place I will find answers? hope? Will someone tell me that I matter?" It became my privilege to help new people get connected and find friends so that they would stay and find their answers in God and his family, the church.

What an awesome job with so much to learn and so many firsts like assisting with my first funeral of a guy from our own small group the week I came on staff. There was my first wedding to tie the knot for two dear friends from Alpha, one who had been homeless when Jesus found him sleeping on the park bench the year before. My second wedding was a unique destination wedding for my niece on an island sandbar on the Mississippi River. I even got to preach to our congregation of 1500, a one-time privilege since I was hired to connect people, not to preach.

A few months later I journaled,

> Thank you Lord for fulfilling this forty-year-old desire of my heart. I'd given up on being a pastor and almost forgotten, but You didn't. Who would have thought this possible? I'm a 63-year-old woman. Your mystery is unfathomable and beyond what I can imagine.

I loved the privilege of being in a church where women were allowed to pursue their gifts, even as key leaders. I was grateful to our senior pastors, Happy and Dianne Leman, who embraced women in leadership and gave me this very special privilege enjoyed by few women. Happy's favorite Bible passage expresses it well:

> *Now to him who is able to do immeasurably more than all we ask or imagine, according to his power that is at work within us, to him be glory in the church and in Christ Jesus throughout all generations, for ever and ever! Amen.* (Ephesians 3:20–21 NIV)

Thank you Lord for this wonderful opportunity to passionately make Jesus known to your people and giving me these years in the best job ever. Thank you for the hundreds of people I got to touch in your name. To You be all the glory.

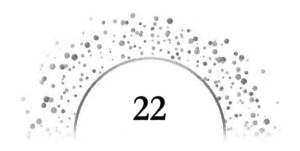

22

God's Lost and Found

Jesus did many other things as well. If every one of them were written down, I suppose that even the whole world would not have room for the books that would be written. (John 21:25 NIV)

W hen I first began writing this book, I was elated that finally I would not have to limit the number of stories I could share when I gave a talk. Surely I could tell every one of our GodStories in a book, but they wouldn't fit. I still had to pick and choose stories that illustrated different aspects of His character.

In this chapter I've gathered a few stories that highlight His passion to find the lost. Of course, Jesus came to restore our lost relationship with the Father as He illustrates in stories/parables in Luke 15 (the lost coin, the prodigal son, the lost sheep). Perhaps my stories are modern day illustrations as I've found that He also enjoys helping us find lost things when we ask for His help.

For the Son of Man came to seek and to save the lost. (Luke 19:10 NIV)

Lost Keys

My pastoring years were packed with people and events so I laid aside the mission of writing a book for that season. I hadn't added one word to the manuscript for over three years although God continually added GodStories.

So at age 66 I decided to take a four-day book writing hiatus all by myself, a rare travel experience to jump start the writing again. The day before making this 4 hour trip I was anxious and stopped by the mall for some morning exercise to relieve some stress. As usual I chose the closest parking space to go inside to exercise. I parked my car and got all prepared to multi-task, tuning in upbeat worship music on my iPhone, plugging in my iBuds, and sorting through my prayer cards.

Ready. Set. Go.

Through the mall I walked at lightning speed. Well maybe it was just a light speed. Thirty minutes later, my body cried, *Enough!* so I gladly set out for my car to check exercise off my *to do list* and get on with the busy day. Reaching for the car keys hanging from my belt clip, I discovered with horror that they were gone. Oh no! They had been hanging there when I got out of my car. I had dropped them somewhere in the mall during one of those 2000 steps. But which one?

I prayed, "Help, Lord. Would you show me where my keys are? I've lost my keys and now I'm losing my confidence. Can I manage this four-day road trip all by myself?"

Back I traipsed into the mall. I began to realize how impossible this search could be. I had been so absorbed in the music that I was oblivious to which stores I'd walked through. But I felt strangely guided and kept walking until I was at the opposite end of the mall. The Macy's shoe display looked familiar, so I went in and began walking down the aisles, zigzagging to the back of the store. I stopped in front of a sales clerk standing there.

Out of the blue, I casually asked, "Have you seen any keys?"

She reached under the counter and replied, "These?" as she held up my car keys.

Unbelievable! I had no clue where my keys had fallen to the floor. But my loving Father did, and He directed me right to the exact location and prompted me to ask the one person who had seen them and put them out of sight.

Why should this surprise me? It did although God has shown me again and again He delights in showing us how He is present to help when we trust Him.

In all your ways acknowledge him, and he shall direct your paths.
(Proverbs 3:6)

I did a little thanksgiving jig for His restoring both my lost keys as well as my confidence that on this trip He would give me the keys to getting the book finished.

Arriving at my retreat, I prayed this passage from Psalm 71:18:

Even when I am old and gray, do not forsake me, O God, until I declare your power to the next generation, your might to all who are to come. (Psalm 71:18 NIV)

During those days, I was aware of God's pleasure as His words tumbled out onto the page, and more of the book took shape. I regained confidence that it would be done well and in His timing.

Lost Hearing

God continued to show up in trouble, telling us to trust Him and it would be okay, especially with our financial needs. As I read Psalm 50:10, "I own the cattle on a thousand hills." I prayed, "Father, could you please send us a cow?" He had many times, not four-legged ones, but just as miraculous.

Don's hearing had been steadily declining. We had checked into hearing aids a few years before and found the hearing aids he needed would cost roughly $4300. Where were we going to get that kind of money? Even if we had it, there were other pressing things higher on our list of needs. As his hearing dropped to 30% in both ears, Don was becoming less able to hear people in social settings and unable to hear what others were saying in the factory setting. We kept asking God for help and believing.

Keep on seeking and you will find. (Matthew 7:7)

A year later the phone rang, and one of our pastors asked, "Does Don need hearing aids? I am holding in my hand a check made out to the church with a note: 'for Don Vincent's hearing aids.' Can you come pick up this $5000?"

We were overjoyed and praised God. He had sent money through an anonymous donor. The amount was also significant. We thought the hearing aids would be $4300 but they cost $4950.

I vividly remember the day Don got his new hearing aids when he was 66 years old. When I called him on his cell phone, I heard him crying as classical music played in his truck, "This music is incredible–all these instruments." Soon we were both in tears as he recounted all the new sounds. Now instead of repeating one in every three comments, he only asked me to repeat one comment in the first three days.

What a week of answered prayer. It was Wednesday when Don got his hearing aids. On Thursday, we ordered new glasses after cataract surgery paid totally by insurance. On Saturday I commented, "I've got a new man." Thank you, Lord for coming through at just the right time just like you promised.

> *So let's not get tired of doing what is good. At just the right time we will reap a harvest of blessing if we don't give up.* (Galatians: 6:9 NLT)

How true. Thanks, Lord, for sending us that cow.

Lost Vitality

Shortly after this I faced a painful wakeup call. My doctor warned me that I was headed for a stroke and diabetes if I didn't take better care of myself. She asked me if I had thought of retiring because I obviously was under way too much stress. I prayed and sensed God speaking as I journaled,

> The next ten years will be powerful or pitiful. They will be ten years of energy and enjoyment or ten years of struggle and fatigue and poor physical health. The choice is yours. It will be a costly decision either way. Either way you pay. One lifestyle brings life; the other brings living death. "Choose this day *whom* you will serve – pleasure or Me.
>
> Choose this day *how* you will serve – in pain and sickness or in health and energy. And know that You do not choose only for you. Many will follow the path you choose, for you are a leader who models Jesus to others. If you model a healthy lifestyle, many will be enriched and set free. Your life matters.

The decision to dedicate my body to God and to follow His directions would waiver, and fully committing to this would take a long time. Still today this word is a powerful reminder that I daily need to choose to make healthy lifestyle choices.

> *Choose today whom you will serve...as for me and my family, we will serve the LORD.* (Joshua 24:15 NIV)

Lost Billfold

I remember the particular month when I realized how losing things is common as we grow older. First, it was my billfold.

On Sunday I was looking through my purse when I discovered that my small billfold was missing. "Oh no," I cringed. "What was in it? Let me see, money... my driver's license... uh, oh, my bank debit card and several credit cards... oh, and those four $50 gift cards for our favorite restaurants and yikes–my one and only spare car key. When did I see that billfold last? Seven days ago. Oh God, I need your help. You know everything, and you know where my billfold is. Show me where to find it."

Then Don and I began recalling where we'd been that week. We ran by a Mexican restaurant where my large purse had tipped over on the floor. We searched and asked if the waiters had seen it. Nothing. Nada. On Sunday night our small group joined in prayer.

On Monday I combed the house and the car several times and called everywhere I'd been, including that restaurant again. I followed up on any fleeting thought, expectant that God would show me where it was. I thanked the Master at finding the lost and asked Him to use this to teach me His ways. I kept on asking and searching.

On Tuesday morning I sat silently to listen. I didn't feel it was necessary to report everything missing and start replacing the cards as there were still no unusual charges. But I had run out of clues. I sensed that the billfold was in a hidden place, a very well-hidden place. That restaurant kept coming to mind, so I went back to search again for myself. I looked under all the booths—no billfold.

As I sat in the booth where we had been, I peered into a narrow crack between the booth and the wall and saw a small dark area. I thought, "maybe that's my billfold" but decided it was just a support post. The crack was too small to check out, so I pushed the bench back until it hit the table behind it. I still couldn't reach that shadowy area, so I gave up. I thanked the manager, apologized for leaving the booth out of place, and left empty-handed.

I ran to my car in the pouring rain and shut the door. Just then the manager came running out with a big smile, waving my billfold in the air. When he had tried to slide the bench back into place, something was holding it away from the wall. That's when he discovered my billfold tightly wedged in the crack. A secret place indeed. It was hidden so well that it might never have been found.

I braved the rain to go back inside to thank the señor profusely and bless him with a little reward as I shared the story with him how I had prayed for God to show me where the billfold was hidden. I was so elated.

Don had looked –no billfold. I had looked—no billfold. But then God had revealed its location and there was the billfold. The lost was found.

When my Father answers a small personal need like this, His love becomes so outrageously intimate that I know how much He cares.

> *Don't worry about anything; instead, pray about everything. Tell God what you need, and thank him for all he has done. Then you will experience God's peace, that exceeds anything we can understand.* (Philippians 4:6,7 NLT)

So often peace arrives even before the answer when I thank Him for what I am confident that He will do and as I wait for Him to do it again!

Lost iPhone

My next big loss was only a week later. I was coming home from getting groceries in town and realized that I had left my phone in a cart in the parking lot. I hate to admit that it wasn't the first time I'd lost my iPhone but when I asked God, I'd always found it.

Not this time. I began tracking it with the "find my iPhone" app and saw it was moving on the tracker screen. Someone had stolen it. I followed the tracker into Walmart and when I got close to the phone, I turned on the remote alarm, hoping to find the thief, with no thought of what I'd do if I caught them.

But no phone miraculously appeared. Two days later I bought a new $840 iPhone. As an afterthought I called to see if our home or auto insurance might cover it. I was shocked to find that it actually did since I was over 64. The following day the check was in the mail, another upgrade by God's grace.

Lost Hitch

That same day God protected us from much greater loss. Don was driving 65 mph down the interstate when his trailer hitch came loose on his portable welder, smashing its radiator as it slammed into the rear of his truck. We praised God that the safety chains held and the trailer did not detach flying into who knows what. Don figured the welder was toast with little chance of finding a replacement on that vintage radiator. But his older radiator repairman had him up and going for $75. I'm so glad the Lord watches out after His high maintenance kids like us.

Loss of Normal

Don's struggle with hearing led to his retiring the July he turned 67, but he planned to keep working and would be his own boss again. Many folks longingly look forward to retiring to simple days of fun, freedom, rest and reward. Most are probably caught off guard like we were by the accompanying grief over the loss of normal: familiar daily routines, work identity and the fulfillment of working with co-workers on common goals and projects. Then there's the loss of the usual paycheck. As Don dealt with this adjustment, he quickly transitioned to focusing on the future and opening a small metal fabrication shop. Now he often worked 8-10 hour days but by choice. He was whistling once again.

Don was thriving. I was not.

At age 68 I was still going strong and loving pastoring with no thought of retiring. But it was a season of swift change in our church, and I was feeling unsettled. Key leaders began going in different directions, and the harmony and collaboration we had been enjoying began to fade. Positions were shifted around, and in a matter of months, four fellow pastors, dear friends of mine, were gone as the church transitioned more leadership to the younger generation.

I felt that the changes were too abrupt and I struggled with the fairness of how it all happened. But life isn't always fair, even in a Christian environment. I realized I wasn't clearly seeing the whole picture either. None of us do.

Then I began struggling with where I now fit with all the changes. As the atmosphere got more tense, so did I. I cried out, "Help, Lord, settle me down. Show me what to do. I really don't want to get old and cynical. My goodness, I don't even want to get old."

In August, my brother treated my sister and I and our husbands to a wonderful vacation in Hawaii. I was sitting on a bench at Pearl Harbor texting a pastor friend asking how things were going at work. She responded by showing me the outline of our church's newly re-organized leadership team. I saw that I was no longer included as a key leader.

Pearl Harbor seemed like a fitting place to hear such news as I was feeling under siege in my own little world. It hit me hard enough that I even struggled to enjoy this tropical paradise as I pondered the past and what might lay ahead.

But too soon we were back at home and back to work. Over the next few months I began adjusting to the changes and was able to focus on doing my job the best that I could and leave the rest to God. Things were actually going smoothly, and I was at peace again.

Then one Monday in September, I was driving down the road and asked God a simple question, "God, I'm not getting any younger. When should I quit pastoring at the Vineyard?"

I heard very clearly, "This week."

"What?" I replied, totally disbelieving.

"I will tell you exactly how and when." I recognized that voice, but it certainly wasn't the answer I had in mind. I had no immediate plans to leave this job I loved. Yet the voice was so real, so out-of-the-blue, and so specific, that I knew it was God. We had just dropped Don's full-time income. Surely the Lord wouldn't want us to drop another one. To be sure, I jotted the message down to pray about later.

Don was out of town that week, and he called me Wednesday morning. Before I could tell him what I'd heard, he said to me, "Honey, I know that this is going to sound strange, but as I was reading my Bible this morning I felt God say you are supposed to quit your job this week."

Wow! God not only had spoken but had told us both the same thing. So without reasoning about it any further, I resigned on Friday, and true to his word, God provided an excellent time and space to resign and share my heart with my senior pastors.

My incredibly fulfilling days as a pastor were now over. It was finished. It was okay because my life with the Lord is what defines me, not my job.

The word spread quickly that I was retiring. At first I bristled when people asked me how I was enjoying retirement. When I resigned, the word *retire* was not my intention nor in my thoughts. I resigned my job because I sensed God was saying that this season in my life was over. Seeing how long it has taken me to finish His book assignment, it probably was time to shift my focus.

A few months before resigning, a team of prophetic people invited me for a night of personal prayer and encouragement. They shared impressions of what was to come: traveling, writing, speaking in other churches with a great deal of godly humor. God also helped me picture what retirement meant for me, "I am re-tiring. I am getting new tires ready to hit the road afresh." Now that made sense. I opted for all-terrain tires for hitting any rough road ahead, confident that no matter where it led, we could handle it together with Jesus.

For in him we live and move and have our being. (Acts 17:28 NIV)

Lost Mobility

A couple years later a new challenge hit us. One beastly hot September day, Don, age 69, came in from the shop and sat down in his easy chair. He said, "I think I'm in trouble. My head feels dizzy, and I don't have any feeling on my left side."

I immediately thought, "Oh no, a stroke." I said, "Let's get in the car and I'll take you to the hospital to check things out. You may be having a stroke."

He replied, "No. I'll just sit here in the chair a while and cool off and see if it goes away."

I told him, "You can sit in the car and see if it goes away. I'll head toward the hospital and turn around if you recover."

After additional protests I said, "Get in the car or I'm calling 911 for an ambulance." So Don headed to the car after he tried to put his billfold into his jeans pocket three times but kept dropping it because he could not feel his hand nor his pocket.

On the way we sped and prayed. We arrived at the ER in a flash, and as they began all the tests, I shot out a quick text to 45 close friends to pray with us. Don began to improve immediately. His blood pressure was stabilizing, and the feeling began to return to his arms and legs.

The doctor came in and confirmed that he was having a stroke. The nurse brought a consent form so that she could administer the shot that reverses symptoms by opening the blood vessels. When I read about the 20% chance of death from the injection, I asked if she could wait ten minutes on the shot.

At first she said no but then reluctantly agreed. Meanwhile Don continued to get better and they agreed he did not need the shot. Within 3 1/2 hours all of the stroke symptoms disappeared. He was healed and released from ER with no treatment at all. Jesus had once again come to defeat the attack of the enemy and called forth life out of death, restoring that which had been destroyed.

We have heard so many stories of stroke patients who faced years of limited mobility or resulting death that we were humbled to be spared this trial. We don't understand but realize that it was a definite upgrade from God for which we were praising Him with fervor.

I cried out, "Oh Lord, our very existence is truly in your hands. We see how things can change in a heartbeat. We know that this could have been the end of life as we have known it. *'Even though I walk through the valley of the shadow of death, you are with me'* (Psalm 23:4 ESV). Thank you for sparing Don's life and restoring his quality of life once again."

God Restores the Lost

I've left out many stories on how God restored what we had lost such as my wedding ring which had mysteriously appeared in my jewelry box after it had been missing over a year.

You get the picture. Our all-powerful Father is interested in every detail of our lives. He wants us to ask.

> *...Yet you don't have what you want because you don't ask God for it.* (James 4:2 NLT)

I remember a time when I wouldn't pray for things which seemed too unimportant to take to God. Then I came to realize He loves helping us also in small ways. It doesn't deplete any of His vast power when we ask for help with the little things like finding something lost. He specializes in restoration. He loves our praise when the lost is found.

He loves it even more when we offer praise as we wait for the answer.

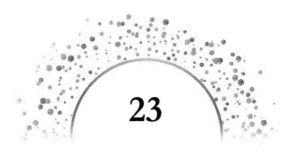

Ever Present in All Seasons

The mind is its own place, and in itself can make a heaven of hell, a hell of heaven. —JOHN MILTON

The Golden Years

When I was young, I enjoyed daydreaming about our golden years way off in the future when our work was done, our dreams had all come true, and we were relaxing and enjoying the good life. As the decade of our 70s fast approached, I asked, "So, where is the gold?"

Comfortable Being Uncomfortable

I used to look forward to slowing down and being truly comfy someday. Comfort – I have pursued her as a companion since I was a little girl curled up in the corner sucking my thumb and twirling the little knots on my blanket during a summer thunderstorm.

Comfort is not a bad companion, but living too comfortably clashes with my ultimate purpose of passionately loving God and others. This lifestyle requires risky action. Experiencing God, not comfort, is what truly brings me joy and fulfillment, so I often ask God, "Make me comfortable being uncomfortable."

> *Consider it a sheer gift, friends, when tests and challenges come at you from all sides. You know that under pressure, your faith-life is forced into the open and shows its true colors. So, don't try to get out of anything prematurely. Let it do its work so you become mature and well-developed, not deficient in any way.* (James 1:2 The Message)

Still this is also a season to simplify life so I can relax and be refreshed. Purposely staying connected with Him is the only way to have a life filled with a busy calling, rest, and simplicity.

Big Red Bites the Dust

Meanwhile GodStories kept coming. Remember the big red truck we found during Alpha? The story continued years later on a wintry 6° day with an unexpected phone call. Don's voice was shaky on the phone.

"I just rolled my truck. Can you come get me?"

I cautiously drove a couple miles down our slippery road until I spied Big Red, our pickup, sitting upright in the field with the front windshield, tools, and contents scattered all around.

I was relieved to see Don slowly walking toward me. He explained how he had hit an ice patch, spinning his pickup 360°and rolling it over through the ditch. Though he was hurting, we both felt strangely calm and confident of God's presence.

Someone had called an ambulance which whisked Don to the ER where x-rays revealed no major damage. He was told to expect some serious pain for a few days from the jostling. We texted family and friends to pray for swift healing and a good outcome from a seemingly bad day. Their encouragements began flooding in on Facebook:

"Wow, what an incredible story of protection...Crazy–life is so fragile...He's a walking miracle AGAIN...So happy he's able to snore tonight!... his typically over-engineered ladder rack may have saved his life!!!...He looks really good for having rolled a truck...Yikes! Angels all around...Oh my. Thank you, Jesus for sparing Don again...There's another chapter for Grandma's book...What a rough way to get a new truck...Don, Don, Don."

All the comments helped make us aware of God's favor as we reflected on how the day could have ended. We snuggled close in bed as we drifted off to a good night's sleep. All the prayers made a difference, and God foiled the enemy's plans once again. Don was back in his welding shop working all the next day. It is hard to keep a good man down.

A Problem-free Life

The following week we were praising God that life was going well, thankful that Don had survived. Then a series of other trials hit, and we were visibly shaken again. Don's back was throbbing, and I wasn't well. Then my youngest sister Pam discovered metastatic breast cancer and shortly after, my beautiful sister Becky died. Trouble seemed to be popping all around and within.

When Don's pain increased, he went to our chiropractor who showed Don the x-rays he had taken, "I can help you with this spine issue, but I can't help you with this as he pointed to a shadow on the x-ray. "It looks like that might be an aortic aneurysm unrelated to the accident. You need to take these x-rays right now to your cardiologist."

No-one in ER had noticed the aneurysm, but it was there. Had it not been for the accident, we might not have known until too late, but now we check it out regularly but don't really worry about it since God is also watching with us.

So don't worry about tomorrow, for tomorrow will bring its own worries. Today's trouble is enough for today. (Matthew 6:34 NIV)

One day I just told God, "I'm tired. I have enough GodStories. Can't I just live a problem-free life now?" But then I realized that as I was requesting "No more stories please" I was saying, "No more miracles needed" in the same breath. So I quickly added, "No, no, God, that is not at all what I desire. I want to experience Your power until I draw my last breath. I realize I grow closest to You during hard times."

Truck Bucks

After Don's accident we needed to find another truck for Don's fabrication business. The appraiser totaled Big Red, sending us an email that the settlement check would be $9730, which was about what we expected. Overwhelmed and knowing it wouldn't be enough for another truck, we cried, "Help, Lord," and waited.

Three weeks later I was relaxing in front of the TV when a thought popped in my head, "Go look at the title." The impression came out of the blue, and I recognized it as a prompting from God. I drug myself out of my comfortable easy chair and searched through the filing cabinet.

I pulled out the truck title and asked, "What now?" as I scanned the title, not really sure what I was looking for. Then I saw it. The title said *Used.* Wait a minute. Our insurance company had noted a *Prior Branded* salvage status that led to a hefty $5000+ deduction from our settlement.

I first thought, "This can't be. Nah, they won't increase our settlement. "

But then I began recalling all those times God had given us an upgrade, and I asked Him once again for His favor. Immediately faith began to rise up within me. Hadn't I seen Him do more than we could imagine over and over again throughout our lifetime?

I emailed an appeal with a picture of title to the appraiser. Within the hour God sent His upgrade with the appraiser's response raising the settlement amount to $15,520. The Lord had just given us an extra $5790. He did it again. Thank you, Lord.

Unbelievable! I held my breath until the next Tuesday when I actually held that check in my hand. As I thought back, I also realized we had only paid $11,500 for Big Red originally, and after driving it for six years we'd made $4000. God provided more than enough to buy a replacement truck. Listening and obeying Him pays, this time in cash.

Big Bertha

I created a wish list of all Don wanted so that I could help him comb the Internet for the ideal truck: Ford F350, 4-wheel drive, 7.3 Diesel engine, extended or crew cab, long bed, 2000 or newer make with <200,000 miles, under $14,000, located nearby. I also added "one that is sharp looking!" We prayed, googled, scouted the newspaper and auto lots and made a two-hour road trip to check out candidates. Too short...not strong enough...too worn out or too classy...not healthy or too gassy...none fit the bill. That ideal truck seemed scarcer to find than hen's teeth.

Then our next-door neighbor mentioned to Don, "I have a truck you might be interested in. Come take a look." So that afternoon we moseyed across the back yard to his shed, expecting yet another reject. There sat Big Bertha.

As the guys talked, I added the check marks to the Don's list, one by one, checking off every single item. Our truck had been sitting fifty yards away at our next-door neighbor's just waiting for us to pick her up. Thank you God for Big Bertha. May she live a healthy, productive, and long life at the Vincent Homestead where life is good, far from perfect, but full of God's provision.

Hold Me Tight

God also brought help in improving our relationships. After no longer being apart with 9-5 jobs, Don and I spent lots more time together which was challenging. Age 68 seemed a good time to hone our marriage skills. So when dear friends invited us to join four couples to study *Hold Me Tight: Seven Conversations for a Lifetime of Love*[10] by Sue Johnson, we eagerly said *Sure*. For eight weeks we read a chapter had a hard conversation and then gathered on Tuesday nights for supper, lively conversations, and prayer.

You'd think we'd be good at communicating by this time, but quality connections require frequent upgrades and ongoing effort. This fun small group helped us learn to have hard conversations and afterwards feel closer, not farther apart. It was fun discussing her statements:

> Love is the central source of joy and suffering...
> True love is about emotional bonds, not bargaining deals for profit and loss...
> It is hard to kiss the lips at night that chew your ass out all day long.

It wasn't as fun having difficult conversations. One morning Don said, "Here is what I think God is saying for you today," and before he could finish his sentence, tears immediately welled up in my eyes.

I was learning when my emotional response was far bigger than the comment deserved, I needed to ask, *"What is up? Why did that comment really trigger me?"*

As we tabled the conversation until I had calmed down, I realized how much I dislike Don pointing out any way I hadn't measured up to his expectations. First I wrote in my journal,

> My feelings are so raw right now. I was afraid Don was going to tell me one more thing I am doing wrong. Sometimes I keep him at arm's length because I'm afraid he's going to point out some failure. Then I hear things that he isn't even saying: 'You're not good enough. You are a screw up .' I was triggered because I am still trying to be perfect. People pleasing, fear of failure, perfectionism—these all seem to spin together. Lord, help me to listen and learn, not to shut him down and to be able to receive helpful input from Don.

In the uncomfortable conversation that followed I shared what was behind my irrationally getting upset, helping Don understand how to avoid triggering me in the future. Bottom line: after sharing our feelings, we felt closer which was now our goal after having difficult conversations.

An Old Mystery Solved

During this marriage refresher I got the answer to a *why* question that had plagued me for years. It began when Don had made an expensive purchase without our talking it over first. It wasn't the first time.

When exploring the *why* of this habit, Don remembered after an incident on the farm. As a teen he decided that if you are convinced your way is right, you should go ahead and do it. You can ask for forgiveness later.

This faulty principle explained a thirty-year old mystery of why Don had set the poles and begun building our river cabin before talking with me. This discussion helped Don change this habit, and we became closer as we made decisions together before acting on them.

While in the past we often just avoided confrontation. Now we tried to communicate when we disagreed. Sometimes those disagreements don't even happen if we think ahead of how our decisions or comments might trigger the other person.

Learning to have emotionally vulnerable conversations was a win-win, especially for Don. Words have always come faster for me, so he would often retreat without attempting to share what he felt, and we would go our separate ways with unresolved differences. Now Don is no longer content to just let things go and the one most likely to say, "We need to process what just happened."

We are also learning how to affirm each other. I remember lying in bed when he said, "I don't know what I'd do without you. I don't think I could live without you. Whenever there is a hard thing or discouragement, we are back to back for support. I look over my shoulder and you are there. You always believe in me, no matter what." I melted in gratitude for being privileged to live with this man. Affirmation for the person we live with is a priceless gift we can give each other.

I could fill another book with stories of how God has taught us to cherish each other over fifty years. We have learned that our marriage thrives as we have emotionally healthy conversations. This never-ending work reaps huge rewards.

"One kind word can warm three winter months." – Japanese Proverb

Celebrate Good Times, Come On

Soon I was celebrating another *Big 0* year with three milestones:

70 years ago I began life on earth.

60 years ago I began life with Jesus.

50 years ago I began life with Don.

This threefold chord, Jesus, Don, and I, has made our life incredibly rich and strong.

A person standing alone can be attacked and defeated, but two can stand back-to-back and conquer. Three are even better, for a triple-braided cord is not easily broken. (Ecclesiastes 4:12 NLT)

How blessed I have been to live over fifty years of life with my best friend Don; yet what an even bigger blessing it has been to have Jesus actively adventuring with us.

I have come to love the story that the Lord is authoring in my sometimes broken, far-from-perfect, everyday life. He amazes me how He can use us even with our shortcomings to reveal His abundant life.

An email from our pastor friend Ben says it well in his weekly leader's lifeline[11]:

At the end of his life story as Jacob is preparing to impart his final blessing on his kids, he is inspired by the Holy Spirit to proclaim, "God has been my shepherd all my life, to this very day." (Genesis 48:15)

Somehow, someway, through everything, Jacob could trust that God was his shepherd . . . leading, guiding, directing, re-directing, redeeming bad choices, sinful behaviors, and things done to him, turning the unhealthy, ill-informed, and disobedient free-will decisions of his entire clan into good.

And you know what? God is still doing the very same thing. This encourages me! You see, he doesn't predestine everything. He's not in "total control." Lots of stuff happens in our lives because there are two opposing teams on the field, there are two kingdoms in conflict.

But because God is infinitely wise and powerful, He is able to take the complicated, painful, confusing, mixed-up mess of our lives - and our leadership at home, in the marketplace, and in church - and "make it good."

Likewise, I have been amazed how God has taken the mixed-up menagerie of my life and made it good as He continues to fill it with His NeverEnding GodStories. He is with me to the end of this life and beyond.

Immanuel, God is With Us

It was Christmastime again. My daughter Christy asked me to speak at their "Moms in the Middle" party for a group of 40-50 moms of school-aged children. As I thought about what to share, I asked, "Lord, what is your special message for this group of moms?"

I heard one word: *Immanuel.*

That was enough. Isn't that what Christmas is all about?

All this took place to fulfill what the Lord had said through the prophet: "The virgin will conceive and give birth to a son, and they will call him Immanuel" (which means "God with us"). (Matthew 1:22, 23 NIV)

I wrote down some thoughts and added a few Christmas stories from my journal that illustrated Jesus as Immanuel. The day came and I headed to Indiana. The party was festive! The goodies were yummy.

Laughter filled the room as I shared some of our family stories witnessing a very present Jesus. Tears flowed as I shared how the doctors said she would be barren, and then He gave Christy the priceless gift of children. I told how angels appeared to little Kelsey on the ledge just like they had in the Christmas story, and then ended with encouraging them to be expecting Jesus, our Immanuel, to show up at any time.

And then He did!

As I began to sit down, a young mom in the audience named Abi raised her hand and asked if she could add a short story. I said, "Sure."

She came up front and began,

My name is Bozena in my country of Poland, but you can call me Abi. I want to tell you about my grandma in Poland. She was a very strong Christian woman who lived well into her 80's. My family had cared well for Grandma but toward the end of her life they could no longer care for her at home, so they took her to one of Poland's facilities for the elderly and dying. It was overcrowded, so the nurses were often cold and impatient.

Grandma kept getting worse and developed painful bedsores. After three weeks she was frail and malnourished. She often cried because she wanted to leave so badly, but they wouldn't release her in such poor condition. She asked God to take her away from this place one way or another because she couldn't stand it anymore."

That next morning a doctor came in, and she asked him, 'Where have you been? I haven't seen you around."

He smiled, "I am always here. You'll now be under my observation."

Every day the doctor came in and sat on her bed and told her wonderful stories. He asked her questions that got her mind off the pain. He kept bringing her nourishing soup and soothed the bedsores with a special oil. Very soon the sores healed, and Grandma was strong again. '

She asked the doctor his name. He replied, "I am Dr. Immanuel."

The next day the head nurse called her family to come and get Grandma as she was no longer dying and did not need their care. On the way out the door, she asked if Dr. Immanuel was in so she could thank Him.

The head nursed replied, "Doctor Who? We have no doctor here with that name. You haven't had a doctor in your room since you came."

My Grandma just smiled because she knew that Dr. Immanuel had healed her. She lived for several more years praising Jesus, her Immanuel.

As Abi took her seat, the room was silent as we sat in awe as Immanuel, God with us, had filled the room with His Presence revealing Himself to all of us who were seeking Him.

In the small group discussions that followed, other moms shared their own encounters of how they had experienced God showing up supernaturally. Many were even telling their stories to others for the first time. But hearts were full of faith, confident that He truly is with us.

Not the End

Jesus, Immanuel, has always been present to give me abundant life. His Presence is my most prized gift. Sharing His Presence with others is my gift back to Him.

Although I decided to wrap up this book with stories around age 70 I have continued to fill new journals since then with many more incredible stories and anticipating many more to come as I partner with Him.

Though I look forward to heaven, I'm not eager to jump on the next bus. I cling to this life like most people do, which makes sense as our Creator designed humans for life eternal. Our desire for living is embedded deep within us. This earthly life is all we have experienced so far. But I am terminal and will pass on, and so will you. When my time here is over, I want to be able to say like Paul,

As for me, my life has already been poured out as an offering to God. The time of my death is near. I have fought the good fight, I have finished the race, and I have remained faithful. (2 Timothy 4:6,7 NLT)

For my life won't really be over when I go to be with Jesus for the rest of eternity. Never-ending GodStories on earth will be followed by never-ending life with Him in Heaven. The story doesn't get any better than that.

May you, too, experience Immanuel, God with us, in your ordinary days, and may you share your stories of His goodness as you unravel His mysteries.

I began to type *The End* when my phone rang, and I heard a voice saying, "Mom, you're not going to believe this…"

And once again God shouted softly, *"Yes, There's More."* For this was not the end of our adventure with Him. His GodStories are never-ending.